LEGENDARY LOCALS

OF

LOS GATOS
CALIFORNIA

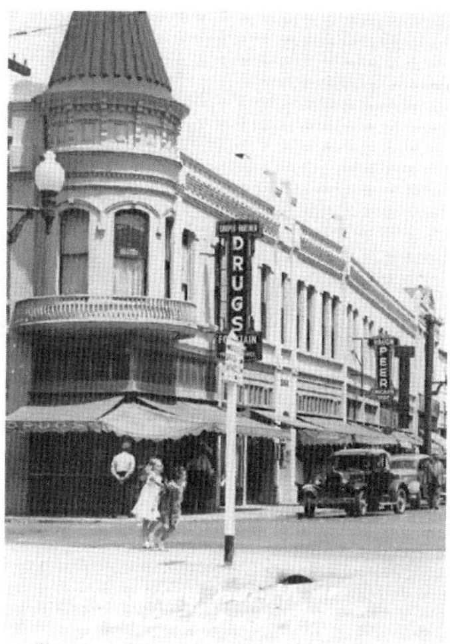

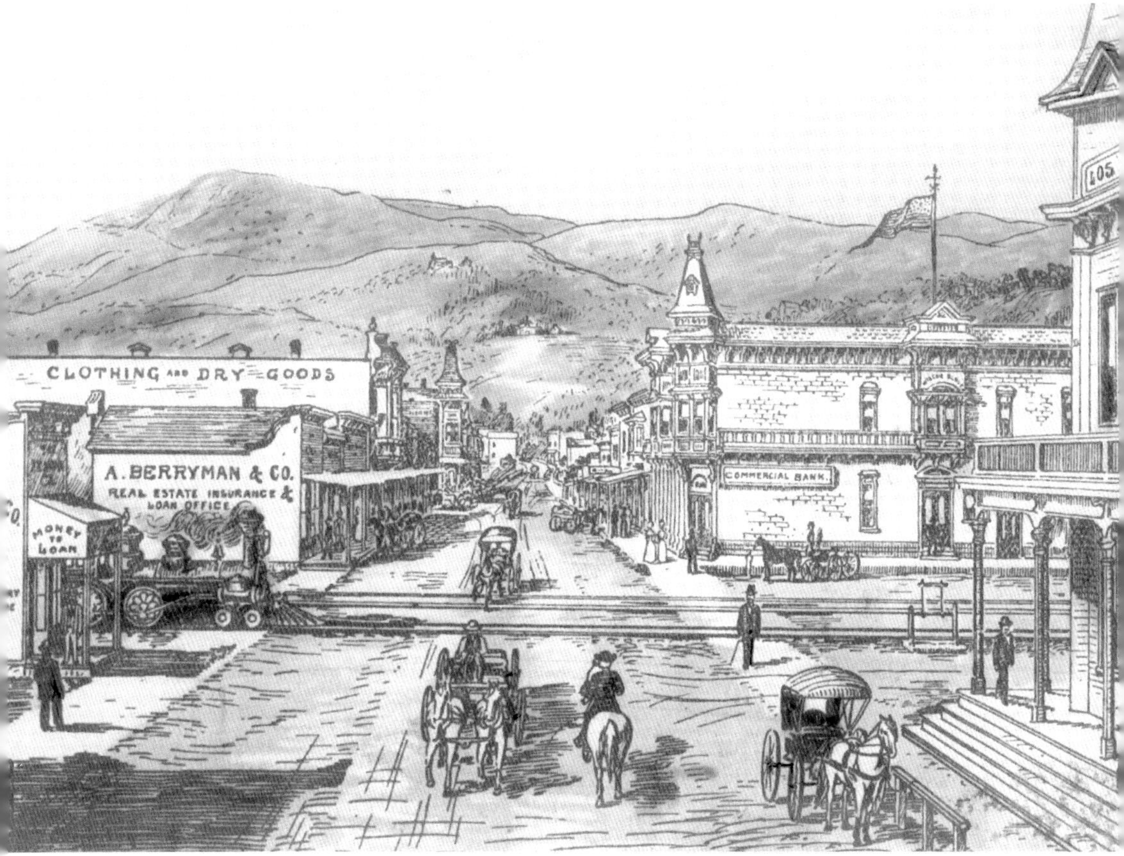

Main Street View

With wooden buildings and sidewalks and a doubtful water supply, East Main Street burned down in 1891 followed by West Main Street in 1901. This view is to the east.

Page 1: The Heart of Los Gatos

The symbolic center of Los Gatos is the La Cañada building, at the corner of Main Street and Santa Cruz Avenue. For many years, it housed a drugstore and soda fountain. The signature turret and cupola lend a Victorian aura, pictured here around 1935.

LEGENDARY LOCALS

OF

LOS GATOS

CALIFORNIA

PEGGY CONAWAY BERGTOLD
AND STEPHANIE ROSS MATHEWS

LEGENDARY LOCALS

ISBN 978-1-4671-0135-6

Legendary Locals is an imprint of Arcadia Publishing
Charleston, South Carolina

Printed in the United States of America

Library of Congress Control Number: 2013949993

For all general information, please contact Arcadia Publishing:
Telephone 843-853-2070
Fax 843-853-0044
E-mail sales@arcadiapublishing.com
For customer service and orders:
Toll-Free 1-888-313-2665

Visit us on the Internet at www.arcadiapublishing.com

Dedication

The Los Gatos Library History Team dedicates this book to Donn Waters, who joined us on our journey and left us way too soon.

On the Front Cover: Clockwise from top left:
Steve Wozniak, built the first personal computer (Courtesy *Los Gatos Weekly-Times*, see page 58); Peggy Fleming, Olympic gold medal in 1968 (Courtesy Peggy Fleming, see page 94); Barbara Berricke Kelly McKiernan, wife of "Mountain Charley" (Courtesy Museums of Los Gatos, see page 15); Charles Erskine Scott Wood, built the Cats Estate (Courtesy Huntington Library, see pages 98, 99); Hal Chase, major-league baseball scandal (Courtesy Chase family and Chris Goode, see page 93); Therese Libante, owner the Gem City French Laundry (Courtesy Janet Libante Goodman, see page 65); Bruce and Diane Ogilvie, sports psychologist and businesswoman (Courtesy *Los Gatos Weekly-Times*, see page 106); Chris Benson and Johnny Hannegan, owners of C.B. Hannegan's (Courtesy *Los Gatos Weekly-Times*, see page 110); Chris von Saltza, three Olympic gold medals in 1960 (Courtesy Los Gatos Public Library, see page 95).

On the Back Cover: From left to right:
Louis O. Sporleder Sr., businessman and volunteer firefighter (Courtesy Steve Sporleder and Patricia Shirley Sporleder, see page 31); Neta Snook Southern, aviatrix who taught Amelia Earhart to fly (Courtesy Museums of Los Gatos, see page 48).

CONTENTS

ACKNOWLEDGMENTS

The authors gratefully acknowledge the many pioneering families who have contributed personal photographs and stories over the past 10 years to "Hooked on Los Gatos: the Library and Museum History Project." Your photographs appear throughout this book. Unless otherwise noted, all images are courtesy of "Hooked on Los Gatos: the Library and Museum Project" or were found in the original collections of the Los Gatos Public Library or the Museums of Los Gatos. We especially thank Dale Bryant and Dick Sparrer of the *Los Gatos Weekly-Times* for allowing use of vintage newspaper photographs, some dating to the 1950s.

Valuable contributions to this effort were made by the following people and organizations: Gay Arnott; Randy Attaway; the Baggerly family; Brian Bergtold; Chuck Bergtold; Ed Burke; Frank Burrell; Betty Balch Chase; the Hal Chase family; the Cilker family; Paul Curtis Jr.; Shirley Davis; Peggy Dallas; Gil and Sandy Decker; Joseph P. Doetsch Jr.; Ken Eklund; the Farwell family; Ron Fink; Peggy Fleming; Bruce Franks; Jack "Jackrabbit" Furlow of E Clampus Vitus; Chris Goode; Janet Libante Goodman; Harvard University Archives; Patty Hannegan; Mima Templeman Hardwicke; Denise Harr; Huntington Library; the Jesuit Center; Les Kishler; Jan LeFevre; Library of Congress; John Lloyd; Melissa Maglio; the Marengo family; Wendy Moreno; Mary Nino; Julie Nino-Newman; Betsy Oka; the Parker Ranch, Hawaii; Peggy Panighetti; Debbie Rapport; Kit Ratcliff; George Sakkestad; Santa Clara City Library and Mary Hanel; Santa Clara University Archives; Elayne Shore Shuman; John H. Simpson; Patricia Shirley Sporleder; Steve Sporleder; Janet Tam; Valerie Archer Wainwright; the Wedemeyer family; Susan Welch; the Yuki family; the Zanardi family; and Jim Zetterquist.

Some photographs proved difficult to find. We appreciate those who went above and beyond to provide these images: Emie Yamate for the Yuki family portrait; Sinoa Picone for the Vedova photographs; Leslie Gardiner and her husband, John, for the photograph of her great-grandfather Dr. Robert Gober; Camden Wall for the photograph of his mother, Marcellite Garner Wall; David Thayer for the photograph of his grandmother Minnie Rowe Crabb; historian John Boessenecker for the image of Rafael Mirabel; Joanne Rogers for the photograph of Betty McClendon; Cynthia Ahman for the photograph of her great-grandmother Mary Coggeshall; and Patty Porter for the image of her ancestor Magnus Tait.

INTRODUCTION

Long before there was Los Gatos, a peaceful valley was home to the Ohlone Indians, who had settled there as early as 8000 BC. Oak trees covered the valley floor, giving way to soaring redwoods that ascended the surrounding mountains. The land teemed with wildlife: grizzly bears, mountain lions, bobcats, deer, coyotes, and foxes. Spanish explorers arrived in 1769, and Franciscan missionary padres followed in 1777. Then came the Californios, Spanish-speaking people who settled on great land-grant ranchos. The age of the dons commenced, a legendary era.

By the late 1830s, Yankee traders, trappers, rough-hewn mountain men, and ambitious settlers from the American republic approached California by land and sea. However, it was the discovery of gold in 1848 at Sutter's Mill in Colma, and the subsequent torrent of 300,000 souls, mostly men, who poured into California in feverish pursuit of wealth, that brought the most dramatic change to the state.

So difficult was the journey that many forty-niners, as they were called, died on the way. If they did arrive in good enough health to go to the mines, they inevitably found backbreaking work, abundant misery, and often scarcely enough gold to live on. Within a year or two, the "easy pickins" in the goldfields were over. Yet many did find their future in California, even if they did not find gold. A "second gold rush" followed the first, with lumber and land being the payoff.

This photographic history of Los Gatos begins in the Mexican era, with the settlement of Rancho Rinconada de los Gatos. It then highlights some of those who came because of gold but stayed to take advantage of other opportunities. One man, James Alexander Forbes, built his flour mill on Los Gatos Creek planning to make a fortune feeding the miners. He did not succeed, but the mill was the genesis of the town. Charles Henry McKiernan, later "Mountain Charley," also saw an opportunity. Merchants were making more money than gold miners, so he devised a scheme to transport supplies into the gold country. When Indians killed his helpers and stole his horses, he traveled to the summit of the Santa Cruz Mountains and claimed more than 3,000 acres of redwood forest as his own.

Thomas Shannon, for whom Shannon Road is named, nearly succumbed to heat and starvation in Death Valley on his journey but survived and mined with some success. Sarah Bayliss Royce, the mother of eminent Harvard philosopher Josiah Royce Jr., traveled overland for six months in 1849 in a prairie schooner drawn by oxen. Between 1884–1886, while living in Los Gatos, she wrote the story of her dangerous trip and her arrival as one of the first women in the gold fields. Her narrative is important as a first-hand account of America's westward migration. Royce Street is named for her family.

The location of Los Gatos has always shaped its destiny. From its earliest days, the town served as a way station between San Jose and Santa Cruz, first for stagecoaches and then for trains. When the ancient redwood forests of the Santa Cruz Mountains were logged and milled, the lumber produced was transported through Los Gatos for distribution to San Jose and San Francisco. When it was discovered that fruit grew profusely in the mountains, a bonanza of prunes, apricots, peaches, apples, and pears traveled by train through Los Gatos and on around the world.

A shanty called the "Ten Mile House" opened in 1860, the first retail store began business in 1863, and the Methodist Episcopal church held services in 1866. A blacksmith shop opened in 1870 and a one-room schoolhouse in 1875, and the railroad arrived in 1877. A newspaper was published in 1881, a cannery opened in 1882, and a new wooden bridge spanned the creek that same year. A bank was incorporated in 1883, and the first real estate office opened in 1884. It was time to think about articles of incorporation for the town.

Los Gatos was officially certified as a municipal corporation of the sixth class on August 10, 1887. During all the years of its existence, the town has been home to a talented population where innovation, invention, the arts, architecture, education, sports, entrepreneurship, author craft, and other worthy pursuits are encouraged and supported. It has also served, for many people, as the ideal small American town—a place to be proud of, a place that engenders loyalty, admired for its beautiful natural setting and its historic homes on tree-lined streets. In current times, residents work hard to maintain the beauty and history of the place they love to call home.

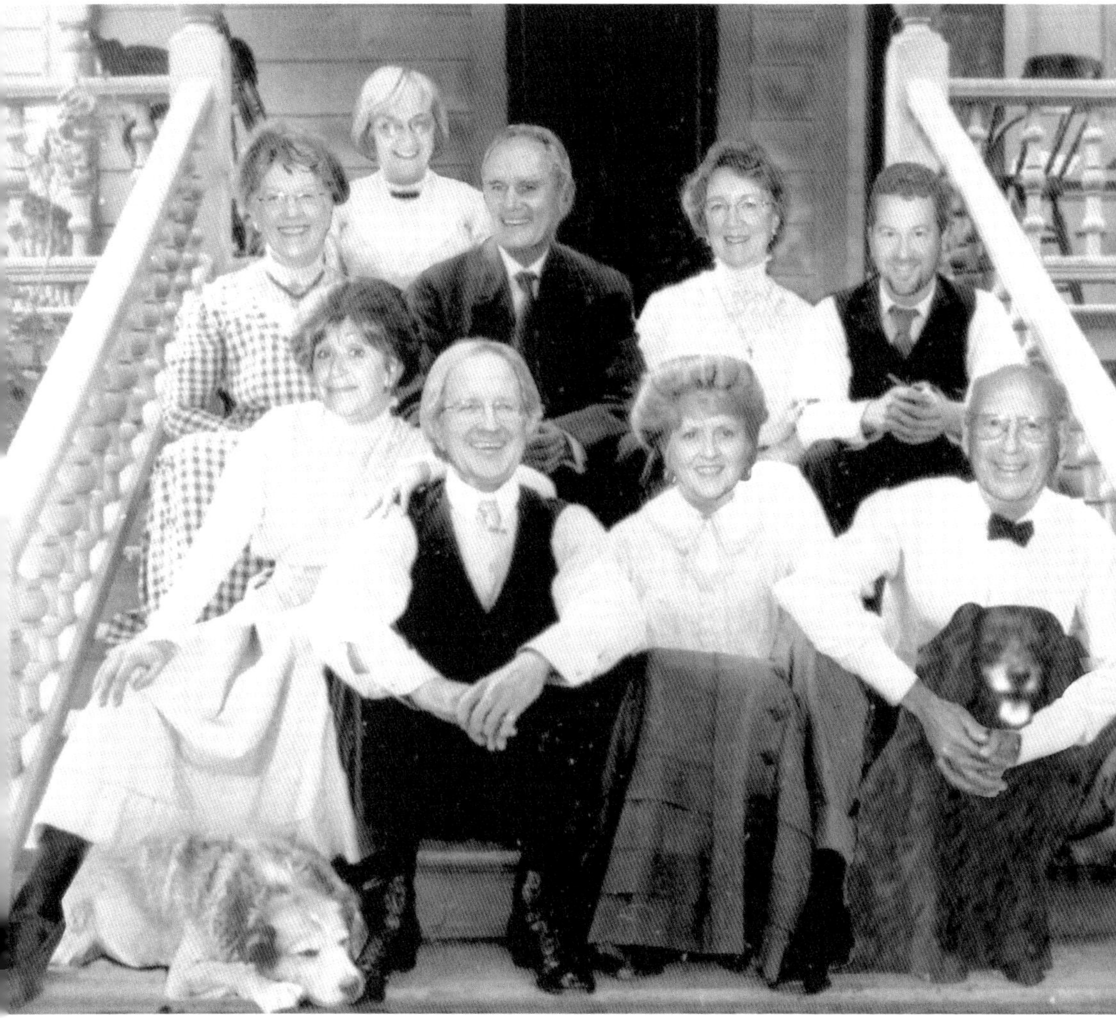

Los Gatos Library History Team

The task of selecting approximately 180 people to appear in this book was not an easy one. The History Team at Los Gatos Library spent two years on an exhilarating journey, making lists, discussing accomplishments, conducting research, and searching for photographs. Members of the team who helped establish the history project and shared authorship of this book are, from left to right, (first row) Stephanie Mathews, Paul Kopach, Peggy Conaway Bergtold, and Bob Hill; (second row) Lyn Dougherty, Donn Waters, Kathy Cusick, and Gordon Cooper; (third row) Betty Balch Chase. Here, the members of the History Team at Los Gatos Library have stepped into an original portrait of the Lyndon family, taken around 1910 on the front steps of James Lyndon's house at No. 1 Broadway.

CHAPTER ONE

The Vanguard

The term "Los Gatos" is Spanish for "the cats." It was an appropriate name for the area, since the hills and plains for miles around were covered not only with trees but often with a dense growth of chaparral frequented by quail, rabbits, and deer, upon which wild cats feasted. Mountain lions made their presence known with their unearthly cries, reminding one of the voices of human beings in mortal agony.

Into this wilderness stepped two men, Jose Maria Hernandez and Sebastian Fabian Peralta, recipients of a Mexican land grant of more than 6,000 acres. They began construction of an adobe house as early as 1835 in what is now Vasona Park, producing their own earth-and-straw bricks. In a 1931 interview, Hannah Worden Hall Gonazlez, granddaughter of Jose Hernandez, recalled that many "portholes" were built into the walls of the adobe so that her grandfather could protect the family from grizzly bears and also fend off Indians who tried to steal the rancho's horses.

Despite the difficulties faced by early settlers, the beauty of the landscape reminded them why they had chosen to settle where they did. The green of the rolling foothills in springtime, the redwood trees of the ages, the clear air, and the pure water gladdened their hearts. David E. Gordon, born in 1834 in New York State and a pioneering newspaperman, first visited Los Gatos in 1855. He recalled Los Gatos Creek as a "magnificent stream, one which impressed the onlooker with something of awe," with crystal-clear water running between bold, bluff banks.

Hernandez and Peralta did not stay on their land for an extended period. Hernandez sold 2,000 acres to James Alexander Forbes in 1852, not long after his wife died in childbirth. In 1853, Peralta sold 2,500 acres to a Frenchman, Claude Simond, for $2,500. Pioneer John Jackson Roberts purchased the original Los Gatos rancho adobe in 1865, along with 114 surrounding acres, and provided lodging for teamsters driving wagons between San Jose and the mountain sawmills. Englishman Jonathan Parr also purchased a portion of the original rancho.

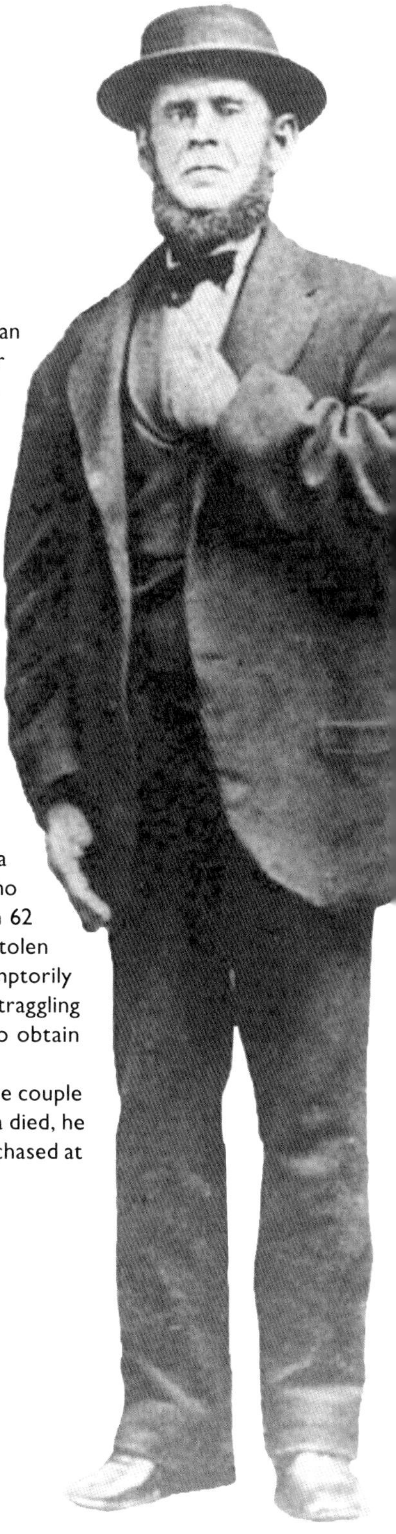

Jose Maria Hernandez (c. 1808–c. 1875) and Sebastian Fabian Peralta (1794–1859)

Jose Maria Hernandez (pictured here) and his brother-in-law Sebastian Peralta were granted 6,631 acres of land in 1840 by Mexican governor Juan Bautista Alvarado; it was called Rancho Rinconada de los Gatos. Hernandez and Peralta constructed an adobe home in what is now Vasona Park as early as 1835. The house was occupied by Hernandez and his wife, Maria Gertrudis Cibrian (1810–1852), and their children along with Peralta and possibly his first wife, Maria Gregoria Cibrian (1806–1837).

Hernandez, born in California, was the son of Juan Maria Hernandez (1776–1849) and the grandson of Justo Lorenzo Hernandez (1731–1792), both born in Mexico. Jose and Gertrudis were married at Mission Santa Clara de Asis in 1830 and were parents to about 11 children.

Peralta, born at Mission Santa Clara, was the nephew of Luis Maria Peralta of Pueblo de San Jose de Guadalupe. He served as a soldier at the San Francisco Presidio and in 1833 headed an expedition of San Jose inhabitants in search of horse thieves, which resulted in the death of 22 Miwok Indians. Peralta again appears in historical accounts when in February 1846 he rode into the Laguna Seco Rancho camp of Bvt. Cap. John C. Fremont (1813–1890), who had come into Mexican California on a "surveying" mission with 62 armed men. Peralta pointed out several horses that he declared stolen from his Los Gatos rancho several months earlier. Fremont peremptorily ordered him from the camp and later wrote that Peralta was a "straggling vagabond" who deserved a severe horse-whipping for trying to obtain horses under false pretenses.

In 1846, Peralta married Maria Paula Sepulveda Pacheco, and the couple built the second house on the rancho, to the north. When Peralta died, he owned less than 300 acres of the original rancho, which were purchased at auction by Jonathan Parr. (Courtesy Santa Clara City Library.)

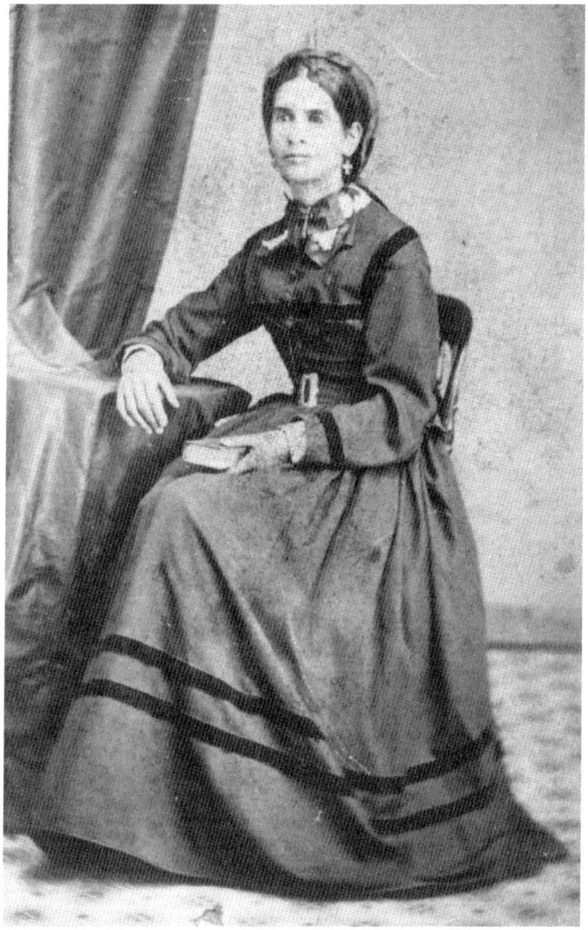

Maria Francisca Hernandez Filson Worden (1831–1910)
Francisca was the oldest child of Jose Maria Hernandez and Maria Gertrudis Cibrian. On December 6, 1847, at age 16, she married Hippolite Filson, a native of France, at Mission Santa Clara. The couple lived on the Los Gatos rancho and had four children.

According to the *Santa Clara Register*, tragedy struck at Rancho Rinconada de los Gatos on the evening of October 20, 1852. A band of "some eight or ten desperadoes, supposed to be Mexicans or Sonorians" attacked the house and killed two men, perhaps including Filson. Some members of the Hernandez and Peralta families were said to be wounded. It is not known if Francisca, pregnant with her fourth child, was among those injured.

The newspaper speculated that the bandits were desperate men who were disappointed in their search for gold and that the Santa Clara Valley was the "highway" between the mines and the Mexican territories. Citizens were organizing for protection against the bandits.

Jose Hernandez lost his wife, Gertrudis, only two months before the murders, when she died in childbirth on August 24. In late 1852, Hernandez sold 2,000 acres of the original rancho to James Alexander Forbes. He married Maria Expectacion Pena (1831–1902) on January 9, 1854, at Mission Santa Clara. The 1860 federal census finds Jose and Expectacion living in San Luis Obispo with their three children; Jose was working as a laborer. By 1870, they had moved to Concord and had five children. Jose died sometime between 1870 and 1875.

Francisca remarried in 1858 to Stephen John Worden (1820–1890), a native of Vermont. The couple moved to Concord in 1861, and they were the parents of seven children. (Courtesy Santa Clara City Library.)

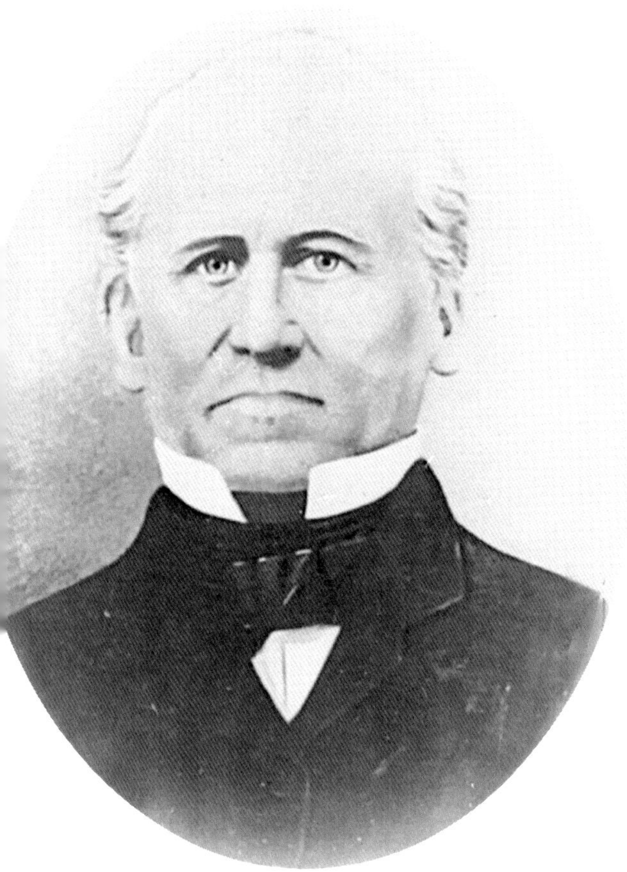

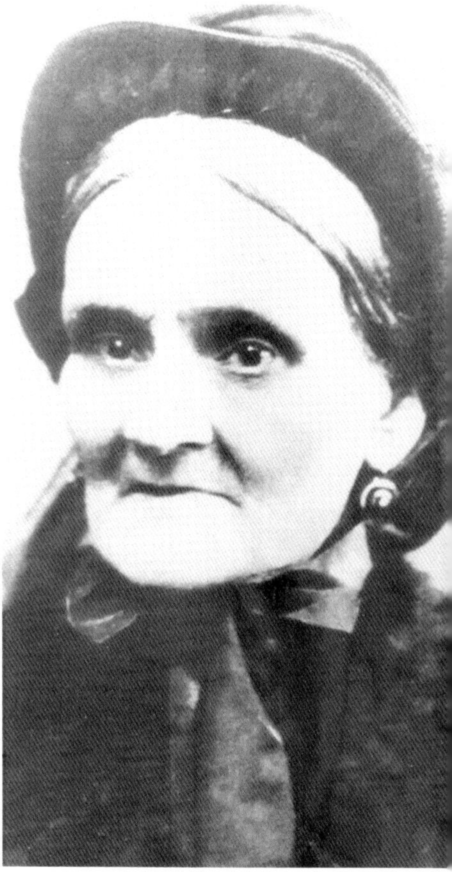

James Alexander (c. 1804–1881) and Maria Ana Galindo (1815–1884) Forbes

James Alexander Forbes was a man who lived his life to the fullest, whether it was leaving his home in Inverness, Scotland, at the age of 12 to live in his mother's native land of Spain, where he attended Salamanca College and served in the military, or traveling with his uncle Francisco Rodriguez to South America, seeking adventure and wealth when he was older. He may have furthered his education under the direction of Jesuit priests in Montevideo, Uruguay, and he may have fought on the side of Argentina during a war with Brazil. It is often hard to separate fact from fiction in the telling of his life's story, and sources frequently differ.

Forbes's uncle was apparently killed in an earthquake in Chile, and the young man set out for the promised land of California. He survived a shipwreck along the way, and according to his 1881 obituary, arrived in Yerba Buena (San Francisco) in 1829. At that time, California was under Mexican rule. Forbes was ambitious, and from his arrival until his death in Oakland in 1881, he participated in many of the possibilities that life in California offered. He was married to a Californio woman, Maria Ana Galindo, at Mission Santa Clara in 1834, which then enabled him to become a Mexican citizen. In 1844, he received a Mexican land grant of 1,939 acres, El Potrero de Santa Clara, granted by Gov. Manuel Micheltorena.

When Forbes married Ana Galindo, his parents' names were recorded as John Alonzo Forbes (1770–1817) and Marta Rodriguez. It may have been his mother's death around 1816 that caused his move to be near her family in Spain. Ana Galindo's parents were Juan Crisostomo Galindo (1783–1841) and his wife, Ana Jacoba Bernal (1789–1835). James and Ana Forbes were themselves the parents of 12 children. Six of their sons attended Santa Clara College (now Santa Clara University), which Forbes helped to establish.

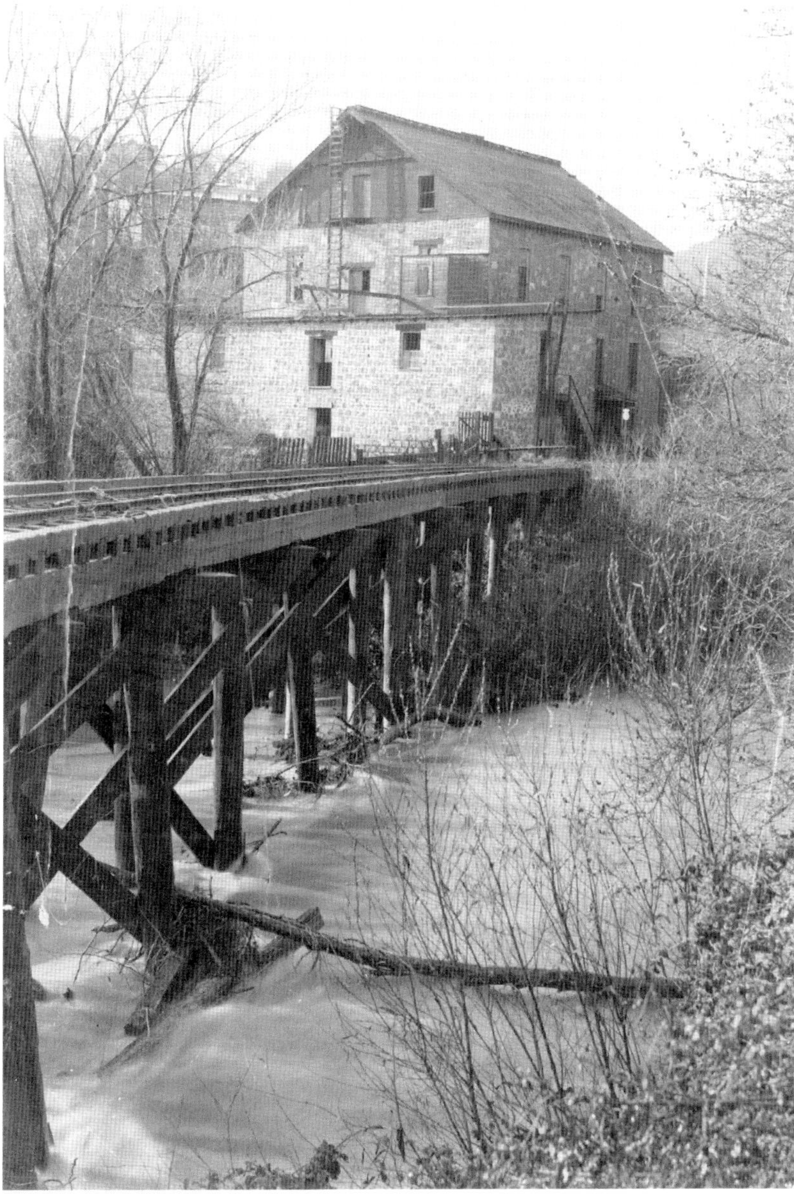

Forbes's Legacy

Among his accomplishments, Forbes served as British vice-consul to Mexican California and in 1848 was appointed as the first British consul to the State of California. He was an agent of Hudson's Bay Company, invested in the Almaden Quicksilver Mines, and wrote the first history of California, titled *California: A History of Upper and Lower California*, published in 1839 in England. Forbes's real legacy, however, is the part he played in the founding of Los Gatos. Hoping to cash in on the need for flour production in the years following the Gold Rush, he purchased about 2,000 acres of land from Jose Maria Hernandez and borrowed money for the construction of a mill (pictured here). He was overwhelmed by technical problems, however, and the project caused him to go bankrupt and lose the property. In later years, the mill was successful under different ownership, but it was Forbes who planted the seed that eventually blossomed into Los Gatos.

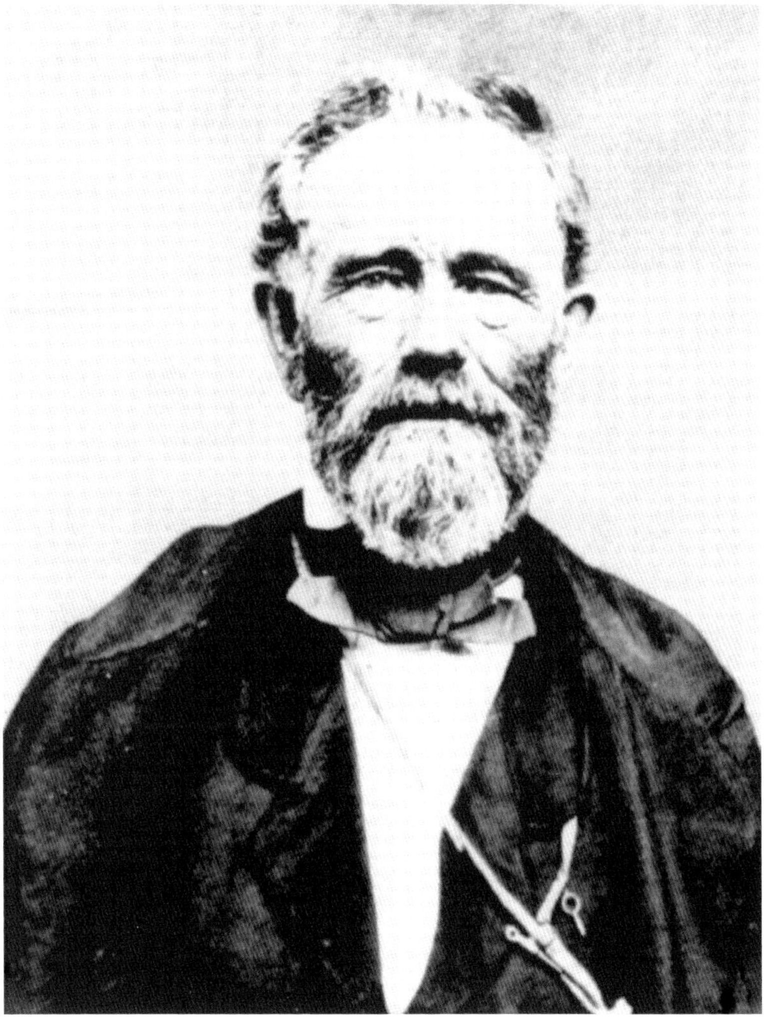

Zachariah Jones (1806–1874)

Zachariah "Buffalo" Jones was a teetotaling, Bible-pounding, militant Methodist firebrand who arrived in the Pueblo Lands of San Jose in 1846. He traveled across the plains with his wife, Mary Erwin Jones (1811–1895), and their children. The couple had married on January 1, 1829, in Ohio, where Jones was working as a blacksmith and had a reputation as a "fighting man" who would take on all comers. In 1847, he opened the first hotel in San Jose, called the Half Moon House. In 1848, he purchased the first sawmill on Los Gatos Creek, erected about a year earlier by Julian Hanks and Isaac Branham. He paid $3,000 for the mill, which was located in the canyon two miles south of the future site of Los Gatos. He laid out his own town, Jones Mill, and named the creek after himself. But he sold the mill and 480 acres in 1860, tired of numerous disagreements concerning a toll road through his property.

Jones was an excitable man who apparently had lungs of extraordinary power. His voice was said to "echo among the hills," and thus he earned the sobriquet of "Buffalo." During his time at the sawmill, he decided to give up his sinful tobacco habit. His Methodist pastor wrote that deprived of his stimulant, Jones would "rush from his cabin, climb along the hillside, run leaping from rock to rock, now and then screaming like a maniac." A native of Tennessee, he was greatly disturbed when the South lost the Civil War. Jones's pastor finally reported that "his storm-tossed soul lost its rudder," and Jones spent his last years at the Insane Asylum of California at Stockton, established in 1853.

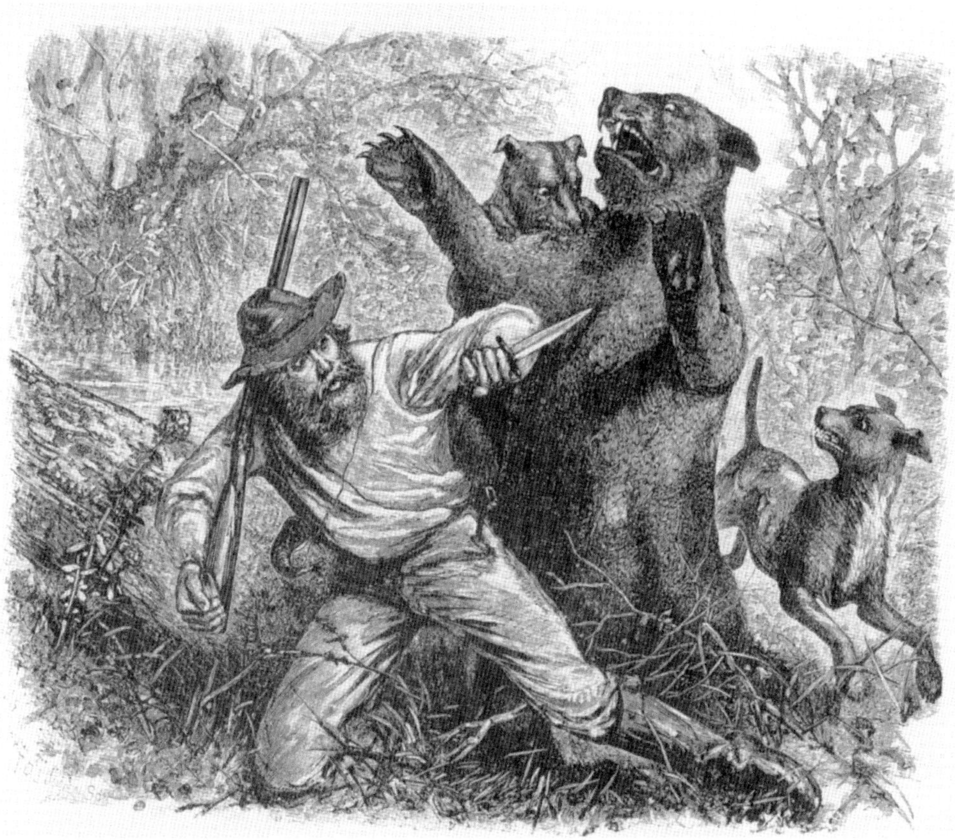

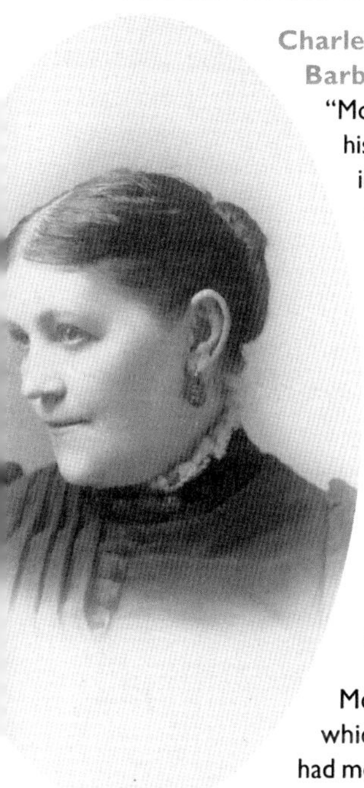

Charles Henry McKiernan (c. 1830–1892) and Barbara Berricke Kelly (1846–1910)

"Mountain Charley" McKiernan was born in Ireland, but little else is known about his early life. He arrived in San Francisco in 1850 determined to make his fortune in gold. He had beginner's luck and decided to invest his earnings in the purchase of mules and horses to transport supplies into gold country. That venture was successful until Indians killed his helpers and stole his livestock. Looking for a more favorable situation, he settled near the summit of the Santa Cruz Mountains, the first permanent white settler to do so. He lived in the burned out trunk of a giant redwood tree until he finished his cabin.

McKiernan raised sheep and planted orchards and vineyards. Mountain lions killed more than 70 of his sheep in one night, so he turned to hunting game. He killed deer and shipped the meat to San Francisco for a profit. With a *V*-shaped wooden scraper and a team of horses, he gouged out a steep and narrow toll road over the summit in order to generate additional income. His most famous exploit occurred on May 8, 1854, when he did bloody battle with a grizzly bear and lost an eye and part of his skull in the process. He managed to recover from his injuries and lived another 38 years.

Barbara Berricke Kelly emigrated from Ireland in 1855 and married McKiernan in 1862. The couple raised seven children on their summit ranch, which included more than 3,000 acres of redwood forest. By 1880, the family had moved to a home on San Augustine Street in San Jose. McKiernan established a lumberyard to meet the needs of the growing valley.

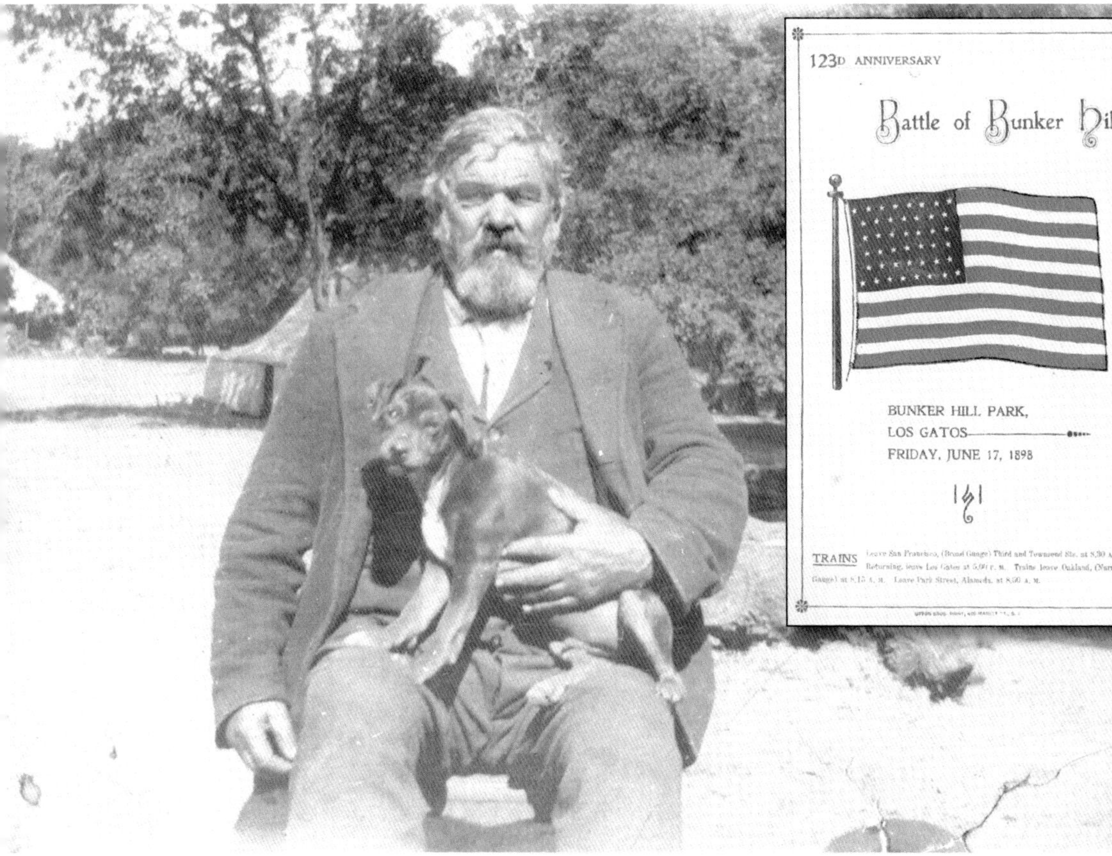

William Cadwell Shore (1830–1905)

W.C. Shore left his home and family in Missouri in 1849 at the age of 19, headed for the goldfields of El Dorado County. He crossed the plains driving oxen, a difficult five-month journey. Such an adventure may have come naturally to a young man who could trace his ancestry to Colonial-era Virginia planters and a Revolutionary War hero, Maj. Richard Goode.

In 1881, Shore and his wife, Mary Ann Adams Shore, moved to Los Gatos with their children, and three years later, he founded the Union Ice Company on the east side of the railroad tracks, south of the depot, about where the post office stands today. Three generations of the Shore family ran the business, which moved to Park Avenue in the 1920s. In the early days, horse-drawn wagons delivered ice to back-porch iceboxes.

Shore had a good eye for prime real estate. His property adjoined Los Gatos Creek, just south of the Main Street Bridge. He later donated a portion of that land, studded with massive oaks and sycamores, to the town for the nucleus of Bunker Hill Park. In about 1901, the Shores moved to Santa Cruz, where they purchased a home and business on Beach Street. In 1924, the Santa Cruz Beach Boardwalk's Giant Dipper roller coaster was constructed nearly across the street from their business, which was a small apartment building. (Courtesy Elayne Shore Shuman.)

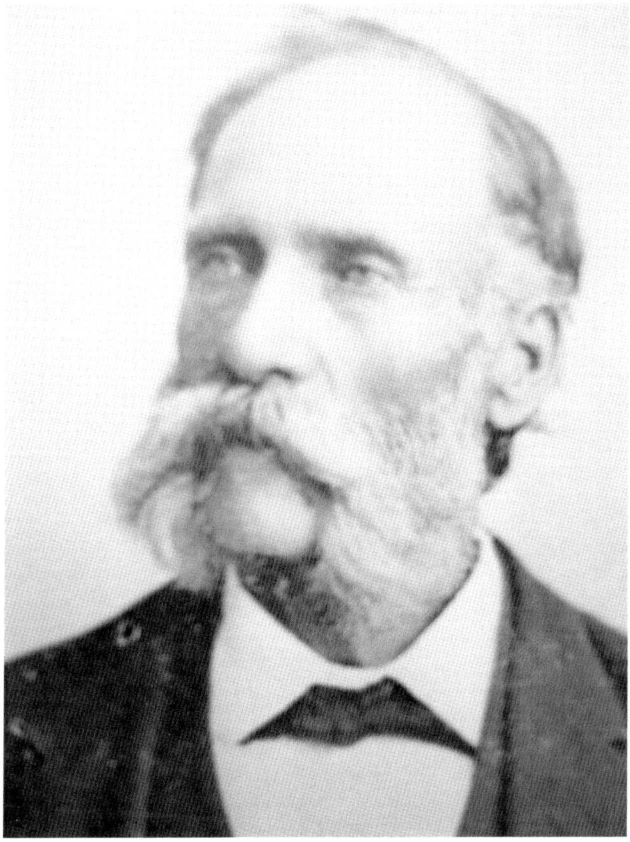

Thomas Shannon (1825–1903)

Shannon Road is named for this Ohio native, who homesteaded 160 acres in that location in 1866. In 1846, at age 21, he enlisted in the 3rd Ohio Volunteers and went off to fight in the Mexican War. After serving for a year, he settled in Illinois but soon joined a group of about 40 young men anxious to go to California for gold. The "Jayhawkers" all swore to stand by their company through any and all perils, even unto death. As each man took the oath, a piece of flesh was yanked from his leg by a pair of iron pincers. If he showed any pain he was considered unworthy of membership.

The Jayhawkers left Galesburg, Illinois, in high spirits on April 5, 1849, and followed the Overland Trail to Salt Lake, the Mormon stronghold. They arrived in late July. Stories were circulating concerning the fate of the Donner Party. They had tried to reach California by the usual northern route but were hopelessly trapped in the snow and cold of the Sierra Nevada. Some had resorted to cannibalism. The Jayhawkers set out on October 2, heading south for Los Angeles.

Unfortunately, the group soon decided to take a "shortcut" to California and struck out due west, determined to cut straight through to the coast. The mountains presented nearly impassable barriers, and when they entered the "Great American Desert," later named Death Valley, the journey took on horrific dimensions. Their water and food ran out, their oxen were half-starved, and they suffered terribly from the heat. "Every member of the party had desperate experiences," Shannon wrote in later years. "It was a miracle that my bones were not left there to whiten in the sun."

Shannon made it to the goldfields and mined on the Yuba River for six years with some success. Some accounts claim that he carried $6,000 in gold coins on his trip to California but buried it somewhere in Death Valley when the Jayhawkers had to abandon their wagons and set out on foot. He married Amanda Blackford (1832–1918) in 1852, and the couple had 10 children. In 1864, those responsibilities did not stop him from enlisting in the 7th California Infantry to serve in the Civil War.

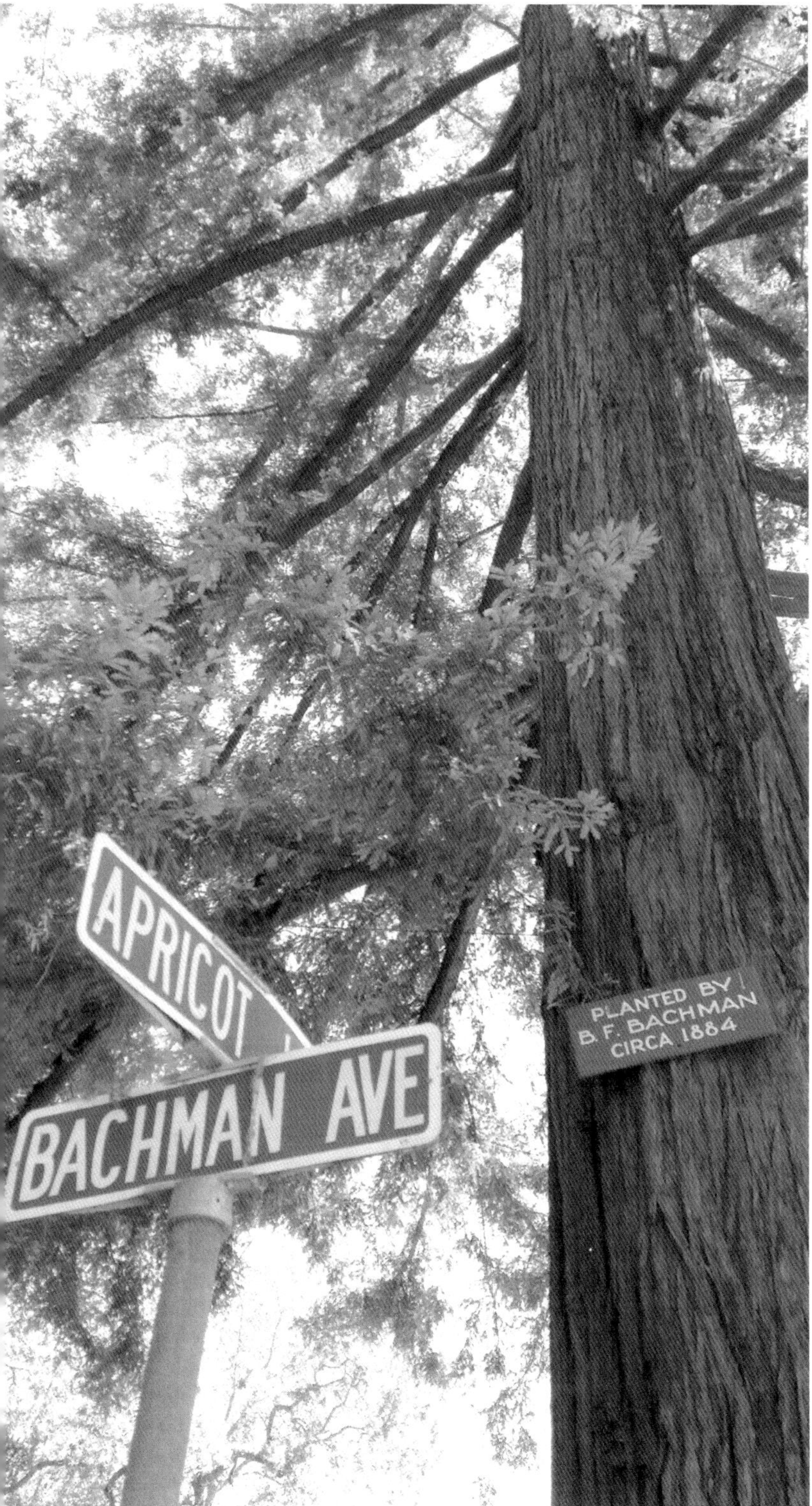

Bachman's Redwood
Benjamin Franklin Bachman moved to Los Gatos in 1880 and purchased 50 acres of choice land. A lofty redwood tree, planted by Bachman in 1884, still stands on the land he once owned, now Bachman Park. (Courtesy Brian Bergtold.)

Benjamin Franklin Bachman (1829–1895) (OPPOSITE PAGE)
Born in Lancaster County, Pennsylvania, Bachman booked passage on the brig *Emma Prescott* in 1849, bound for California via the Horn, to collect his share of gold. Upon arrival in Monterey in May 1850, he joined a party of other young men headed to the mines in Mariposa, where he lived for the next 30 years. In February 1851, because the Indians in Mariposa County had become "very troublesome" to the miners and settlers, he joined a militia group known as the Mariposa Battalion of Mounted Volunteers, whose assignment it was to subdue the Native Americans. The last to surrender were the Yosemites, and when a portion of the battalion, including Bachman, pursued them to their home, they became the first white men to enter Yosemite Valley, on March 27, 1851.

For three years, Bachman worked in the mines, and afterwards he ran Bachman's Saloon and Arcade on Charles Street in Mariposa. From 1862 to 1865, he served as postmaster and was active in the local Republican party. In 1862, he shot and killed a man who assaulted him in his saloon, an action that was ruled self-defense. His saloon, valued at $5,000, burned down in 1866, along with the rest of the business district of Mariposa. In the 1870s, he engaged in the cattle business.

Once settled in Los Gatos, Bachman raised prunes, peaches, apricots, and almonds and lived a quiet life. A lifelong bachelor, he is remembered as a brusque man but an entertaining conversationalist who loved to read. He wore carefully washed overalls when he walked down to the Hotel Lyndon every afternoon at 4:00 p.m. for a card game, carrying a lantern to light his way home. Bachman is buried in Los Gatos Memorial Park.

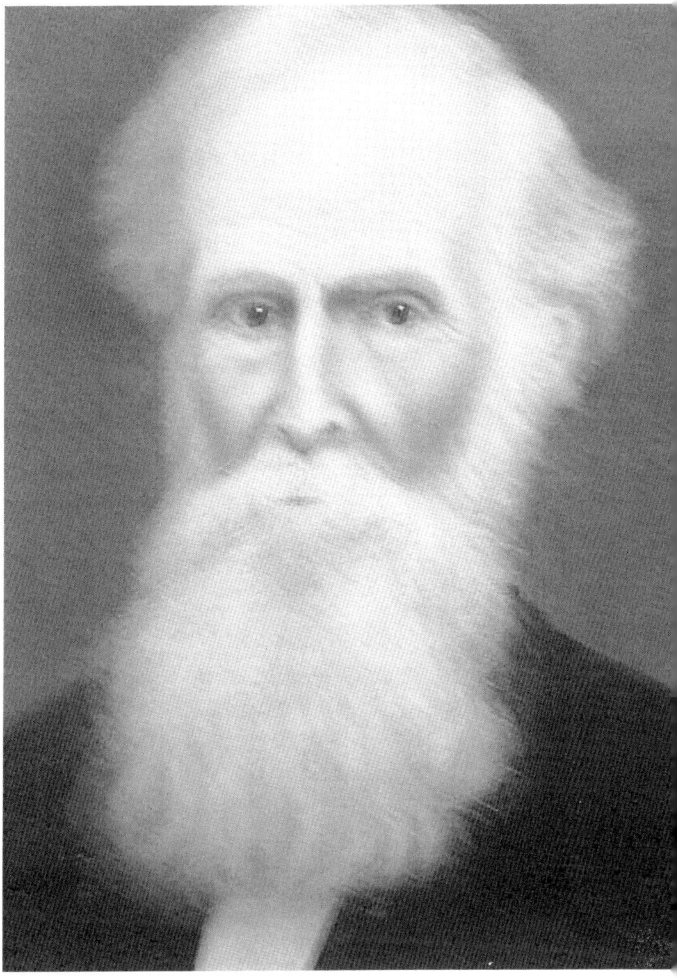

Lyman J. Burrell (1801–1884)
Born in Sheffield, Massachusetts, Burrell was a married farmer in Ohio when, in 1849, he set out on his own for California. He had some success in the goldfields and by 1853 was living in the Santa Cruz Mountains with his wife, Clarissa, and three children. In 1854, he planted some of the first commercial wine grapes in the area. Burrell eventually controlled more than 1,000 acres. He survived encounters with grizzly bears and mountain lions and outlived three of his four wives before his death at age 82. (Courtesy Frank Burrell.)

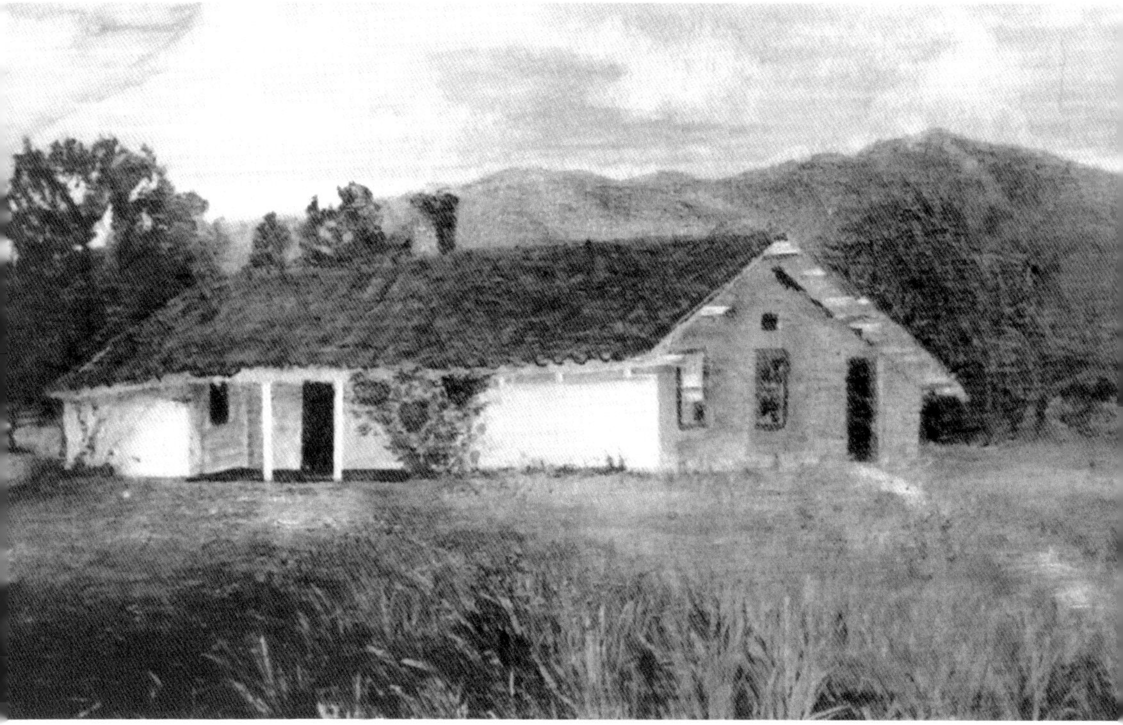

John Jackson Roberts (1824–1889)

Born in Missouri, Roberts left home at age 17 to engage in trading along the Mississippi River. In 1846, at the outbreak of the Mexican War, he volunteered with the 1st Illinois Regiment. The discovery of gold in California prompted him to cross the plains in 1849, and he arrived at the Feather River in Butte County on September 13. Within a year, he had moved on to Plumas County, where he built one of the first homes in the area. Roberts married Martha A. Colter (b. 1834), the daughter of Judge Hugh R. Colter, of Wisconsin, on December 22, 1852, in Santa Clara. The couple farmed in San Mateo County for 12 years before returning to the Los Gatos area. In 1865, they purchased the original Los Gatos rancho adobe home, pictured here, and 114 surrounding acres. The adobe was sometimes called "the roadhouse on Roberts ranch," as it hosted teamsters and their ox-driven freight wagons traveling between Lexington and San Jose. Roberts eventually tore down the dilapidated building to make way for a frame dwelling. John and Martha were the parents of 10 children.

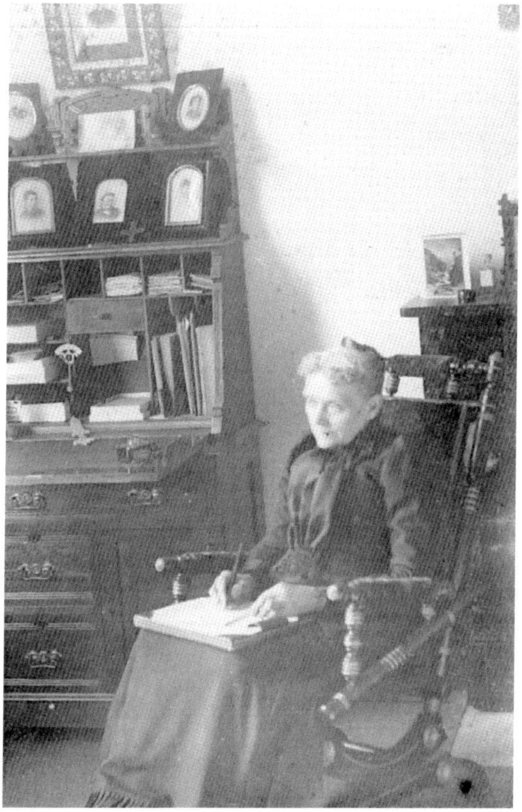

Sarah Eleanor Bayliss Royce (1819–1891)

Sarah Royce was a genteel and refined Victorian woman born in Stratford-on-Avon, England. She loved learning, libraries, and the privilege of living in an enlightened society. When she set out from Iowa for California on April 30, 1849, with her husband, Josiah (1812–1888), and small daughter Mary, traveling in a covered wagon, she forfeited much of what was important to her.

After nearly six harrowing months on the trail west, the Royce family was assisted over the highest mountains by two men from a military relief party sent to gather late-arriving immigrants. Sarah was thankful that Indians had not killed them and that they had escaped starvation in the snow. During the trip, she kept a journal she called her "Pilgrimage Diary." When she first saw the Sacramento Valley she wrote "California, land of sunny skies—that was my first look into your smiling face. I loved you from that moment." And she never looked back.

The primitive life in California mining camps tested all of the perseverance and strength that Sarah possessed. Josiah Royce was not a successful gold miner, nor was he very successful in his other business endeavors. The family moved often and had three more children. Sarah educated her own children and taught school. She credited her ability to carry on in large part to her faith in God.

Sarah's youngest child, Josiah Royce Jr., is recognized as perhaps the most distinguished intellectual that frontier California produced. He was a young lecturer in philosophy at Harvard when he asked his mother to write down the story of her journey to California, based on the diary she kept. Her plain-spoken narrative was published by Yale University Press in 1932 as *A Frontier Lady*.

Sarah and her husband moved to Los Gatos around 1882. He was employed as a mail agent, and they lived on Santa Cruz Avenue. Sarah wrote her story between 1884 and 1886, while she was a resident of the town. When Josiah Royce Sr. died in 1888, Sarah moved to San Jose to live with her daughter Ruth, the first librarian at San Jose Normal School (now San Jose State University). Royce Street in Los Gatos is named for the family. (Courtesy Harvard University Archives, HUG 1755 Box 144.)

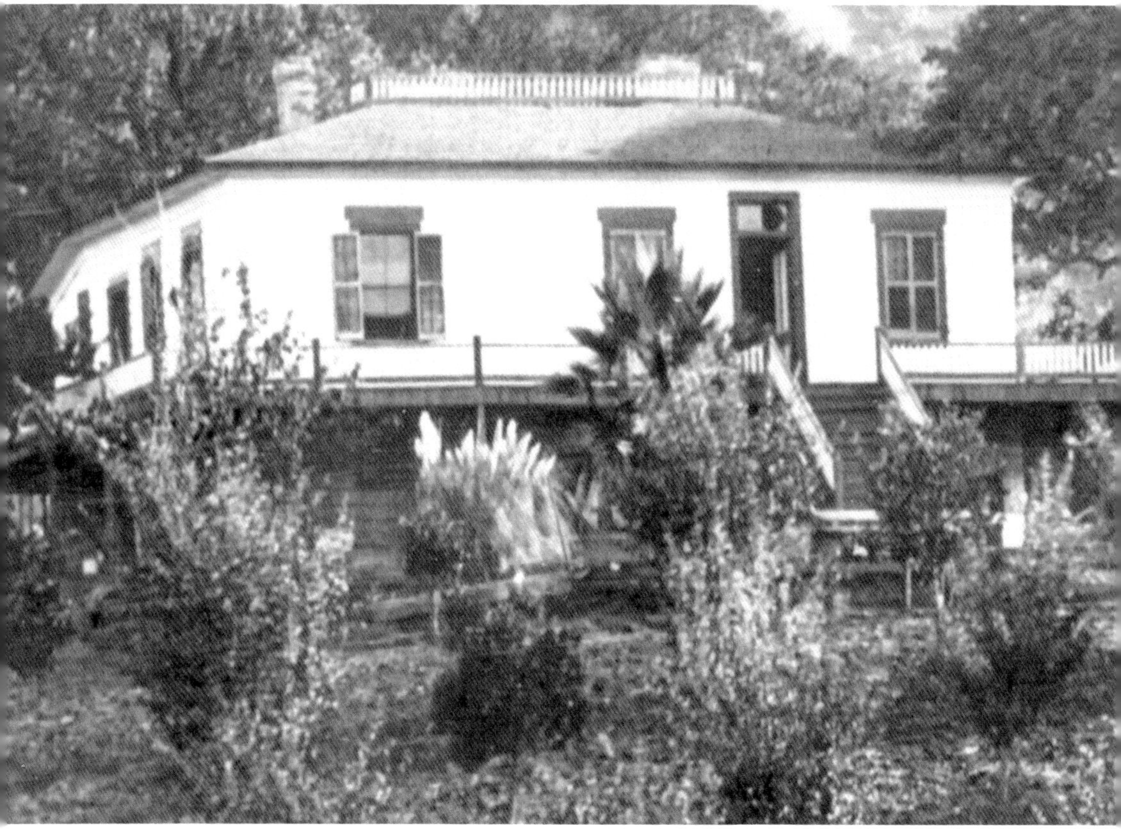

Harvey Wilcox (1822–1890)

Born in New York in 1822, Harvey Wilcox left home at the age of 17. He was entrepreneurial from the start and by age 22 was in Iowa engaged in the manufacture of steel ploughs, which were transported to New Orleans in flat-bottomed boats. He married Harriet S. Demmond (1826–1891) in 1844. In 1849, he traveled by way of the Isthmus of Panama to California, arriving in San Francisco in February 1850. He proceeded at once to the gold country near Downieville and labored for a year with moderate success.

In the following decades in California, he engaged in a number of pursuits, including sheep ranching. Harvey and Harriet settled on their 40 acres of land in the hills just south of Los Gatos in 1881. They built the home pictured here of native redwood and pine and planted 1,600 orange trees. The Jesuits purchased the Wilcox ranch and orchards in 1886.

When Pres. Benjamin Harrison visited Los Gatos in 1891, Charles F. Wilcox (1852–1897), oldest of Harvey and Harriet's children, presented him with "a luscious basket of Los Gatos oranges," presumably from his father's old orchard.

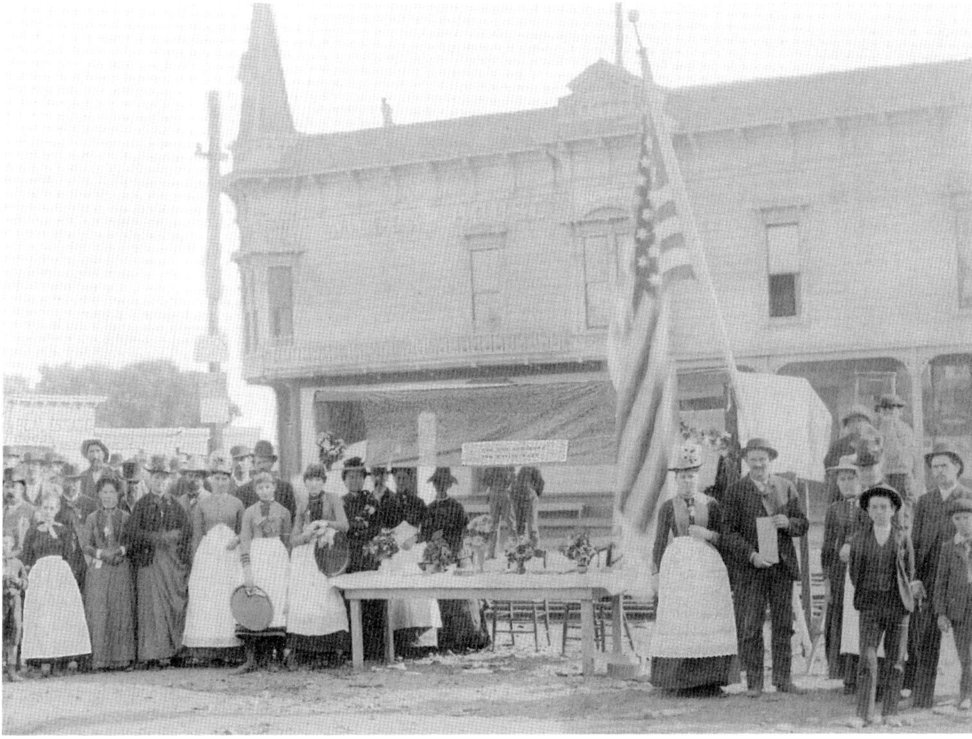

Wilcox House (1887–1901)
On August 22, 1887, the 35-room Wilcox House opened across from the railroad depot. Two days later, Harvey Wilcox traveled to San Francisco to complete arrangements for an excursion train which would travel from San Francisco to Los Gatos, filled with prospective buyers for 170 lots in the Almond Grove Addition. A rally in favor of Prohibition is shown in front of the new hotel. (Courtesy Chuck Bergtold.)

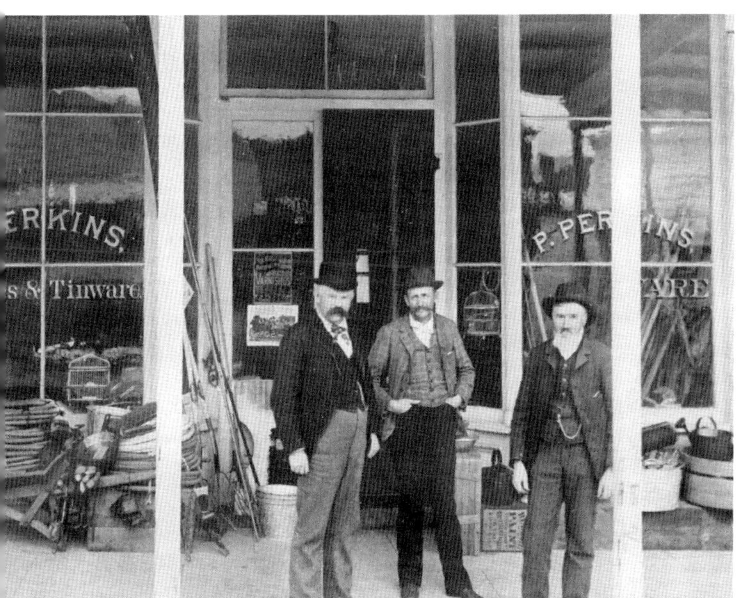

Palmer Perkins (1822–1892)
Palmer Perkins was a native New Yorker who answered the call of gold in California. After some years in Placerville, he moved to Michigan, only to return to Los Gatos, where he helped to fix the boundaries of the town before the 1887 incorporation. Subsequently, he was elected chairman of the board of trustees, the first "mayor." He is pictured at left in front of his business at 23 East Main Street.

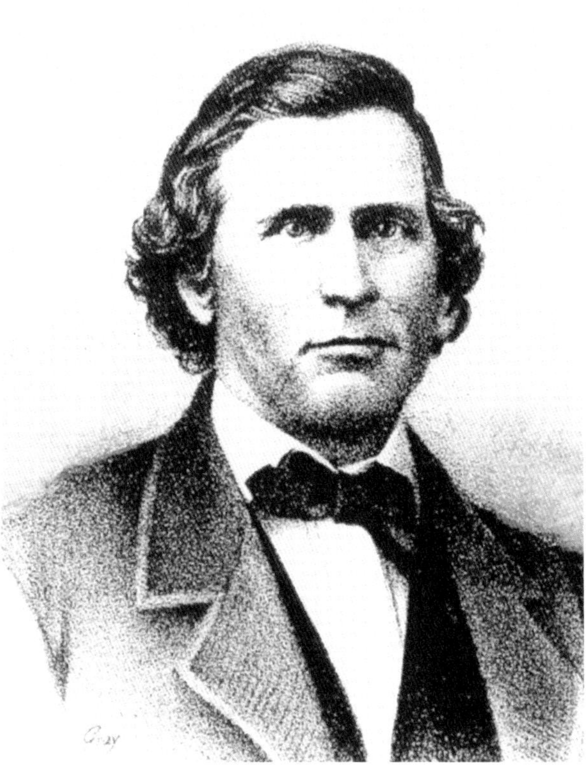

Jonathan Parr (c. 1816–1867)

A native of Staffordshire, England, Jonathan Parr immigrated to America with his family in 1842, settling in Iowa. In 1846, they set out for California, traveling in a caravan of 41 covered wagons. They arrived safely in November, but their arduous journey included instances of stampeding cattle, the killing of a man by Pawnee Indians, and one terrifying day when the wagon train was surrounded by hundreds of hostile natives. By 1856, the Parrs had purchased land in the area that would become Los Gatos. Eliza Jane Lowe Parr and her husband had six children, raised stock, farmed, and purchased more land. Called "the fine old English gentleman," Parr now has a street named in his honor.

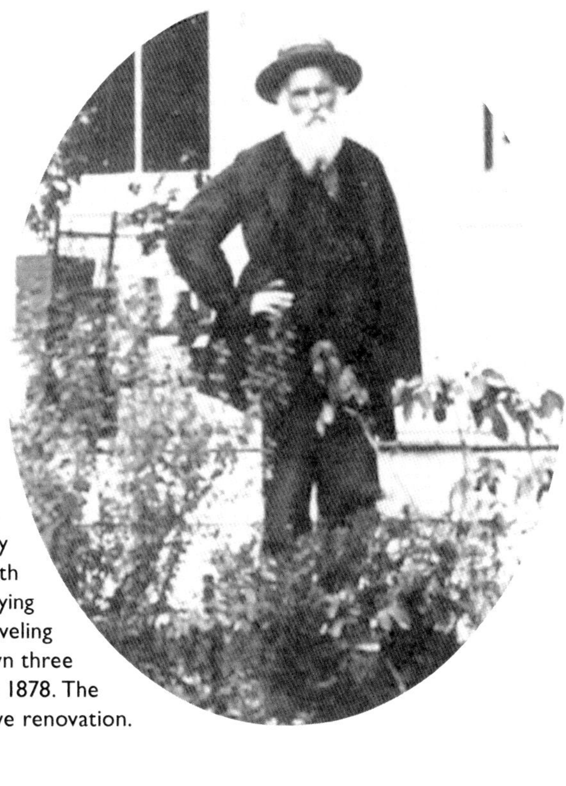

James Kennedy (b. 1805)

In 1859, the Santa Cruz Turnpike Joint Stock Company was incorporated to construct a road from Forbes Mill in Los Gatos through the gap in the mountains to Santa Cruz. In 1867, Scotsman James Kennedy was put in charge of the tollgate at the south end of town, where he also built his house. Paying tolls was not popular with the teamsters traveling back and forth, and they tore the gate down three times before the road was declared public in 1878. The house remains but has undergone extensive renovation.

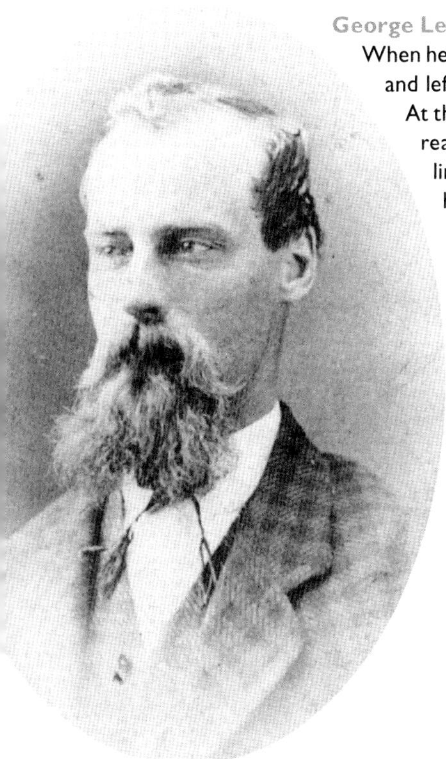

George Lewis Colegrove (1843–1936)
When he was a lad of seven, George Colegrove's father got gold fever and left for California, leaving his wife and five children in Illinois. At the onset of the Civil War, George joined the Illinois Infantry, ready to serve as a wagoner for the Union army. A broken leg limited his service to less than one year, and in 1863, he too headed for California, driving the lead wagon in an immigrant wagon train. On July 15, 1869, as a driver for the Santa Cruz and San Jose Stage Line, he first drove a stagecoach over the Santa Cruz Mountains.

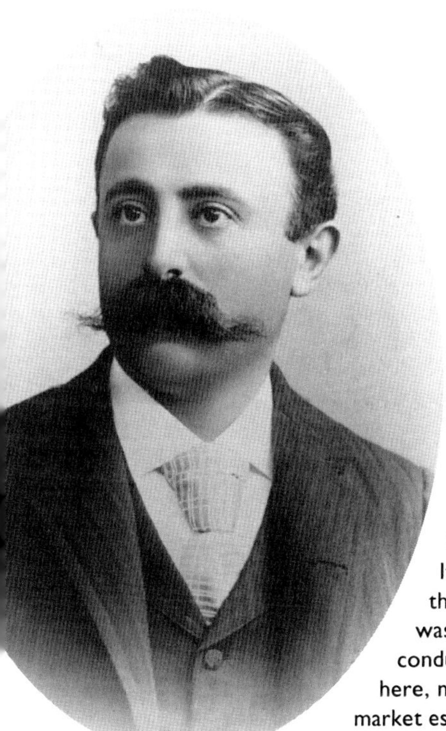

Edward C. Yocco (1857–1901)
Italian immigrant Gioachino Yocco (1822–1889) came around the Horn to California seeking gold in 1849. He found mining was cold, hard work and settled in San Jose in 1850, where he conducted a grocery business. His son Edward C. Yocco, pictured here, moved in 1883 to Los Gatos, where he managed the meat market established by the Goldsworthy brothers in 1870. He died of typhoid fever three days before his 44th birthday.

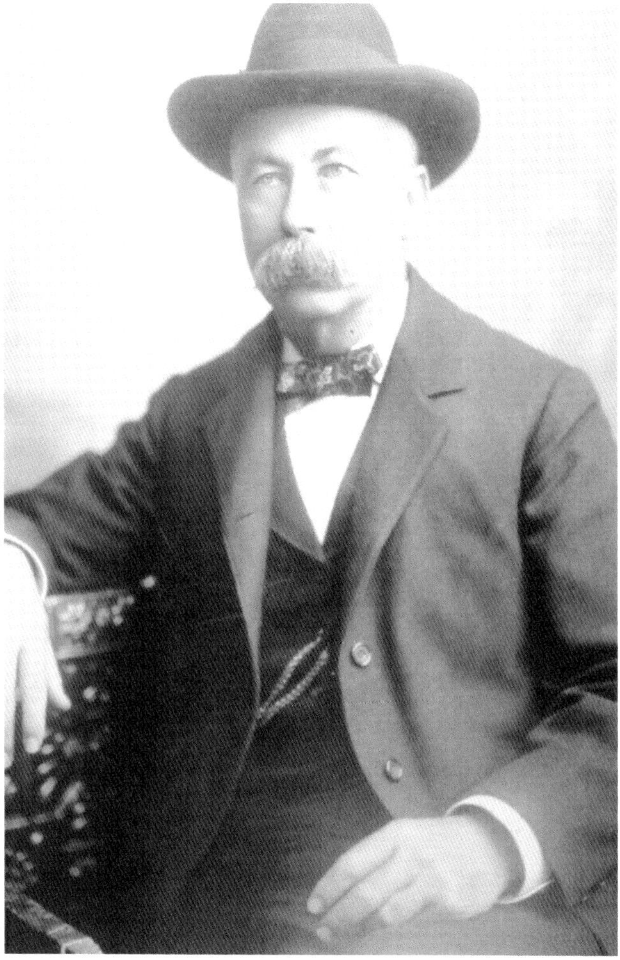

John Weldon Lyndon (c. 1836–1912)

The Lyndon family appears in the 1851 Canadian census under the surname "Linden," living in St. Georges de Clarenceville, Quebec. Samuel Linden, an Irish immigrant, was born around 1797, and his wife, Polly Caroline, was born in the United States around 1814. The parents and six of their children were living in a one-story log house at that time. Samuel was working as a shoemaker, and they were members of the Episcopal church.

For unknown reasons, sometime between 1851 and 1856, the family moved to Alburgh, Grand Isle, Vermont, and changed the spelling of their name to "Lyndon." In the 1860 US census, Samuel Lyndon is listed as a "day laborer." John Lyndon, who told of leaving the family home at age 10 "to earn his own living," worked on neighboring farms for his board and room and then set out for California in October 1859. He traveled by way of Panama and arrived in San Francisco with 65¢ in his pocket. He quickly found a job in Lexington working for H.M. Hervey, who operated a boardinghouse. Two months later, he took a job in Bernard Joseph's grocery store.

Lyndon worked hard, invested in real estate, and became successful. He bought the Ten Mile House, which eventually evolved into the Hotel Lyndon, built the Theresa Block and the Vermont Block, and subdivided his land and sold lots. His gracious 24-room home, called Lyndon Heights, was constructed in 1886 on land overlooking the town on the site now occupied by Los Gatos Meadows.

In 1872, Lyndon married Theresa Rector (1843–1888) of Oregon. They had two children, Ora Everett and Irma Lyle, who became Mrs. J.D. Farwell. Lyndon married Marian Carson in 1892. He was one of five trustees when the town was incorporated in 1887. Very little happened in early Los Gatos without his involvement.

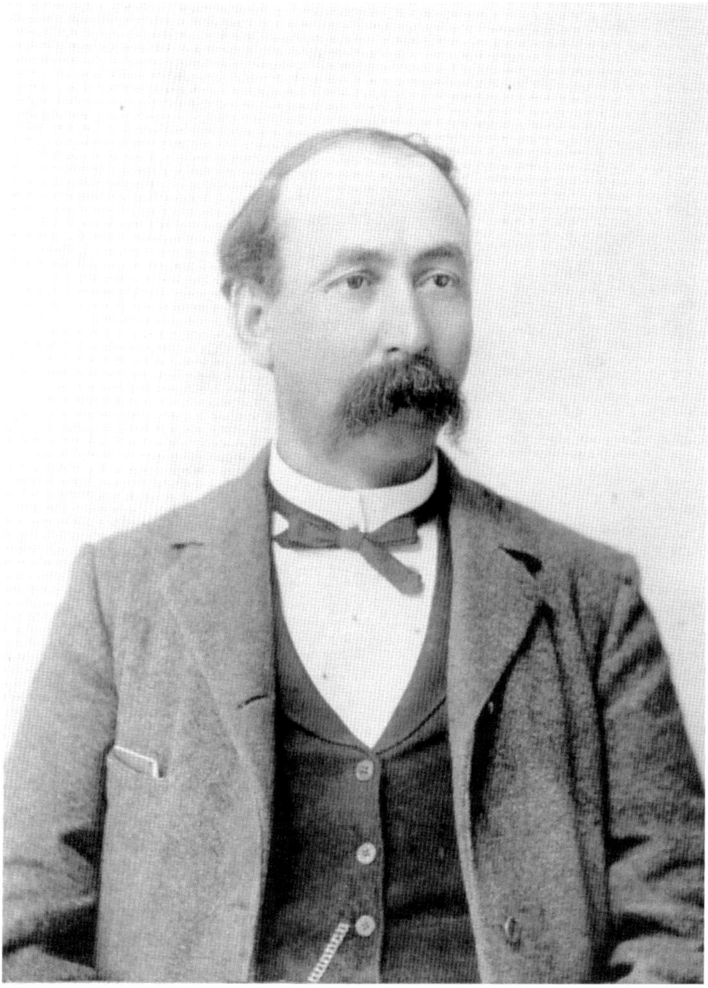

James Hardy Lyndon (1847–1912)

Like his older brother John, James H. Lyndon was an adventurous man. In 1863, apparently anxious to serve in the Civil War, he traveled to Burlington, Vermont, and attempted to volunteer with the 5th Vermont Infantry. He was rejected because he was only 16 years old. On February 26, 1864, still several months short of his 17th birthday, he managed to enlist as a private in the 21st Massachusetts Infantry. Noted for his personal bravery, he fought in and survived the Battle of the Wilderness and the hostilities at Spotsylvania and Cold Harbor, where his regiment suffered heavy losses. He mustered out of the service in August 1865. Born in Quebec, Lyndon became a naturalized American citizen in 1867.

In December 1868, he followed his brother John to California. He managed the Ten Mile House and in 1883 set up a lumber business near the train depot, among other pursuits. In November 1894, he was elected sheriff of Santa Clara County and served for four years. He organized a 100-man posse in 1896 to go after James C. Dunham, the man responsible for the horrific McGlincy family murders in Campbell, but Dunham was never found. Lyndon served as both mayor and postmaster of Los Gatos and was commander of E.O.C. Ord Post No. 82 of the Grand Army of the Republic.

Lyndon married Anna Jane Murdock (1855–1925) in 1873, and they were the parents of six children. He built his home at No. 1 Broadway, where the family often gathered. In 1975, this large house, which had been moved less than one mile away to a vacant lot on East Main Street, burned to the ground during remodeling. James and John Lyndon died within months of each other in 1912.

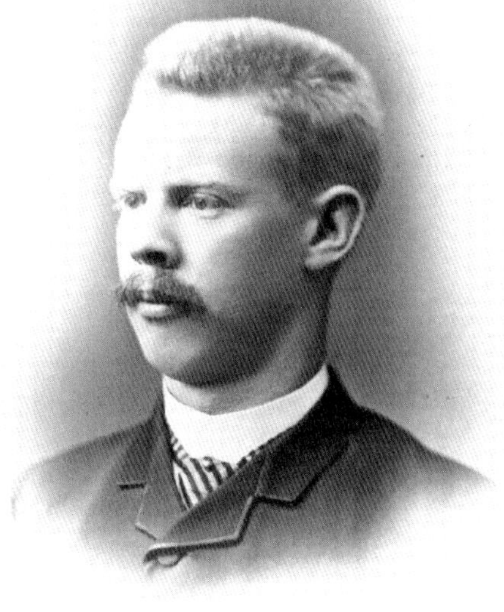

George S. McMurtry (1865–1950) (ABOVE)
George McMurtry was a civic leader and businessman who served as town treasurer for more than 40 years, from 1887 to 1894 and 1914 to 1948. He took time out in 1898 to prospect for gold in Alaska. George's father, Dr. William S. McMurtry (1818–1904), and his mother, Olivia McMillan McMurtry (1837–1916), moved their family from Lexington to Los Gatos in 1868 and into the town's first residence, the old mill house built in 1860 near Forbes Mill. Dr. McMurtry and J.Y. McMillan built the first retail store in town, at 27–35 East Main Street, which was destroyed by fire in 1891. They also partnered with three other men in 1870 to purchase Forbes Mill. Dr. McMurtry came to California for gold in 1849 and was elected state senator in 1863.

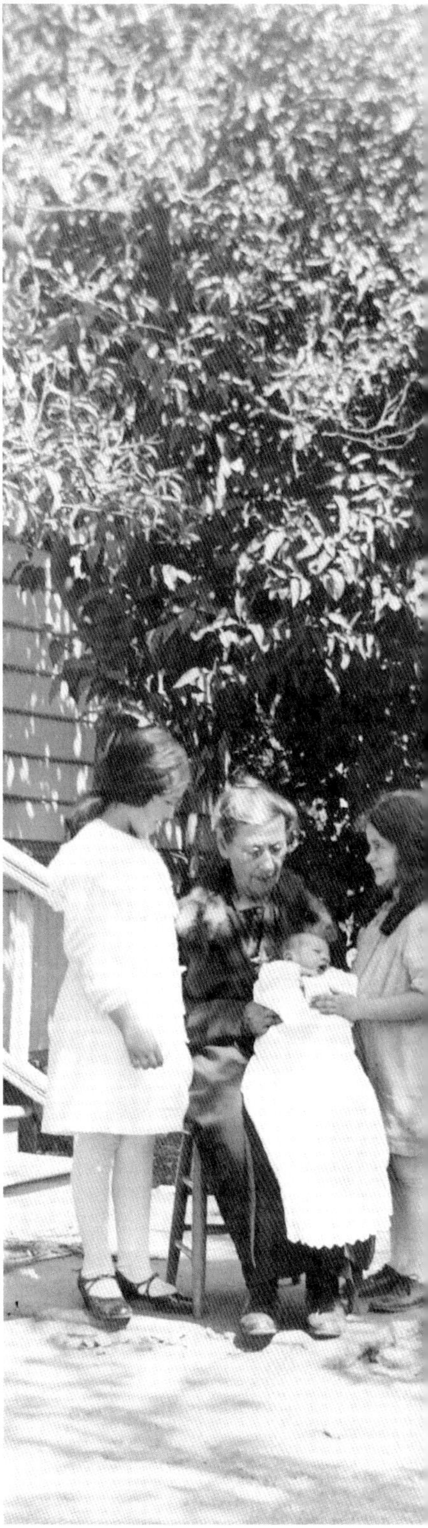

Graziano Nino (1846–1903) and Sophia Antonini (1855–1944) (RIGHT)
Graziano Nino emigrated from Italy in 1867 and started work on the ranch of John J. Roberts. His bride, Sophia Antonini, arrived from Italy in 1882, and by 1886 the Ninos owned 46 acres adjacent to the Roberts ranch on Los Gatos Creek. The couple's six children helped in the fruit orchards and vineyards, and the Nino boys starred on early Los Gatos baseball teams. Both Fisher and Van Meter schools now occupy original Nino land. In this 1931 photograph, Sophia holds her grandson Edward D. Nino, who is dressed in the baptismal gown she sewed as a young woman. It has now been worn by five generations of Ninos. Admiring the baby are two first cousins, Mary (left) and Jean McCarthy. (Courtesy Nino family.)

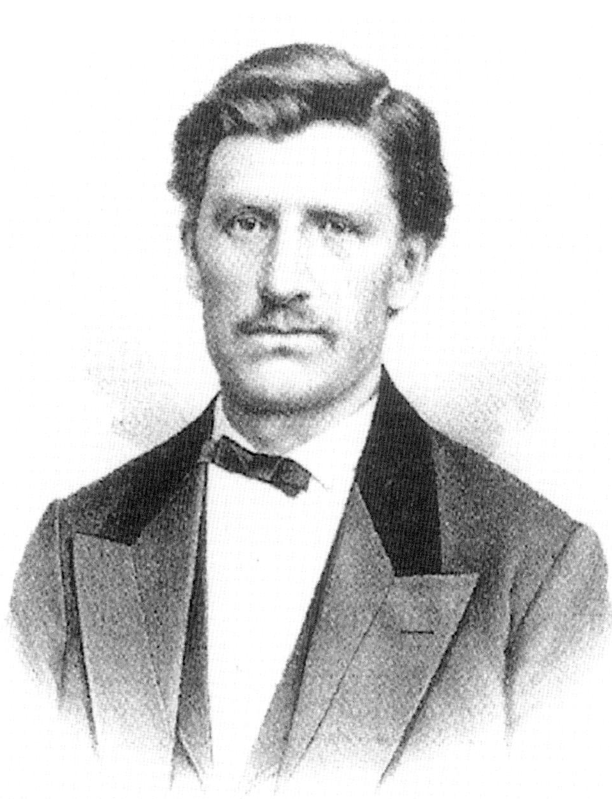

Peter Johnson (1842–1897)
Peter Johnson was a native of Denmark who immigrated to the United States in 1859 at age 17. In 1863, he located in Los Gatos, and for many years, he worked as a teamster, hauling lumber from the Santa Cruz Mountains. He was successful both as a lumber dealer and as a farmer. In August 1889, he was able to ship 700 boxes of Hungarian and German prunes to Chicago.

In about 1874, Johnson purchased 131 acres on El Monte Hill overlooking East Main Street. He created Market Street, perhaps hoping it would become the retail center of town. That never happened, and in 1921, the street was renamed Loma Alta. During a boom time in the fall of 1887, he cut 36 acres into town lots, called the Johnson Addition, and sold them over the next few years. His home at 49 San Jose Road (Los Gatos Boulevard) still stands. His barn and blacksmith shop, later converted to homes, were located across the dirt road.

Johnson married Annie Hays (1852–1917) in 1869, and the couple had eight children. Stacia Street is named for their youngest daughter, Anastacia Johnson Heney (1882–1964). He served as a town trustee from 1888 to 1894 and as mayor his last two years in office. In 1884, he founded the *Los Gatos Weekly Mail*.

The Johnson Opera House Association was incorporated on May 26, 1892, with Peter Johnson as president. Located on East Main Street near Church Street, the building featured a large stage, two private boxes, and seating for 550 people. Seven dressing rooms were located under the stage. Local newspapers called the columned structure "the Pride of Los Gatos." However, financial problems plagued the investors during the building's construction and after it opened on March 5, 1894. The chairs arrived in San Jose but couldn't be delivered for want of funds to pay the freight. Suits were filed for nonpayment of bills.

Johnson apparently borrowed money to meet the obligations of the Opera House Association. But after about five months of operation, the building burned to the ground on August 24, 1894. The cause of the fire was never determined. Johnson was 55 years old when he went to bed on the evening of September 14, 1897, with the gas turned on, and he never woke up.

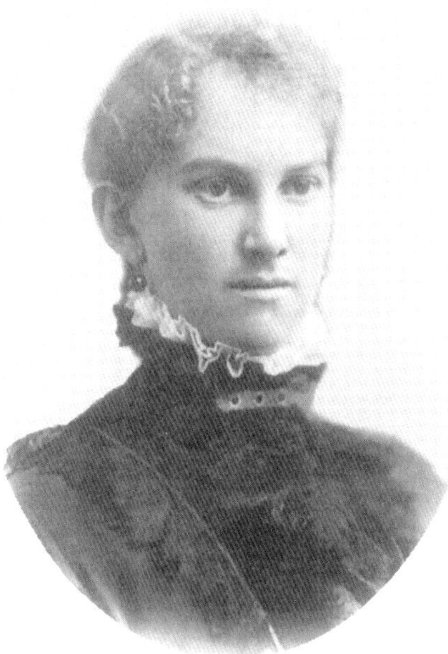

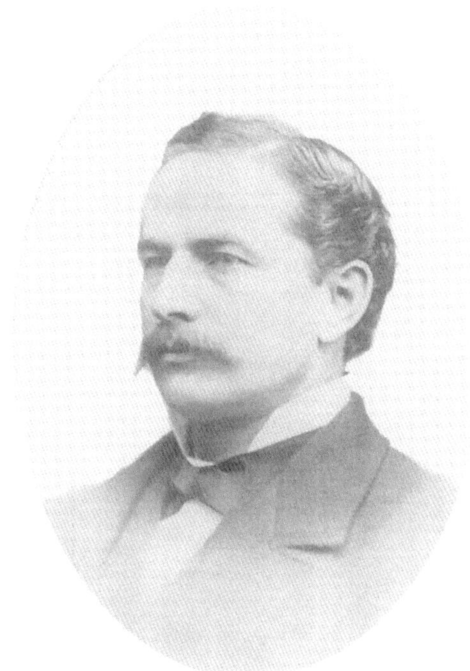

Frank Jackson (1847–1917) and Fannie Fern Ringo (1857–1932)
Fannie Fern Ringo left her Missouri home at age seven, departing with her family on a wagon train headed to California. Their destination was San Jose, where her aunt and uncle, Col. Coleman and Augusta Younger, resided. Colonel Younger was also an uncle to the outlaw Younger brothers, who rode with Jesse and Frank James. Fannie's brother John Ringo was a notorious outlaw from Tombstone, Arizona. He apparently committed suicide by shooting himself in the head while sitting under a tree on a hot July day in 1882.

Frank Jackson, born in New Hampshire, married Fannie in San Jose in 1880. They came to Los Gatos in 1883 and purchased a fruit ranch of 13 acres "in the town." By 1884, Frank was the proprietor of a book, stationery, and jewelry store on Main Street, and in 1885, he became the Los Gatos postmaster. Jackson Street in Los Gatos is named in their honor. (Courtesy Les Kishler.)

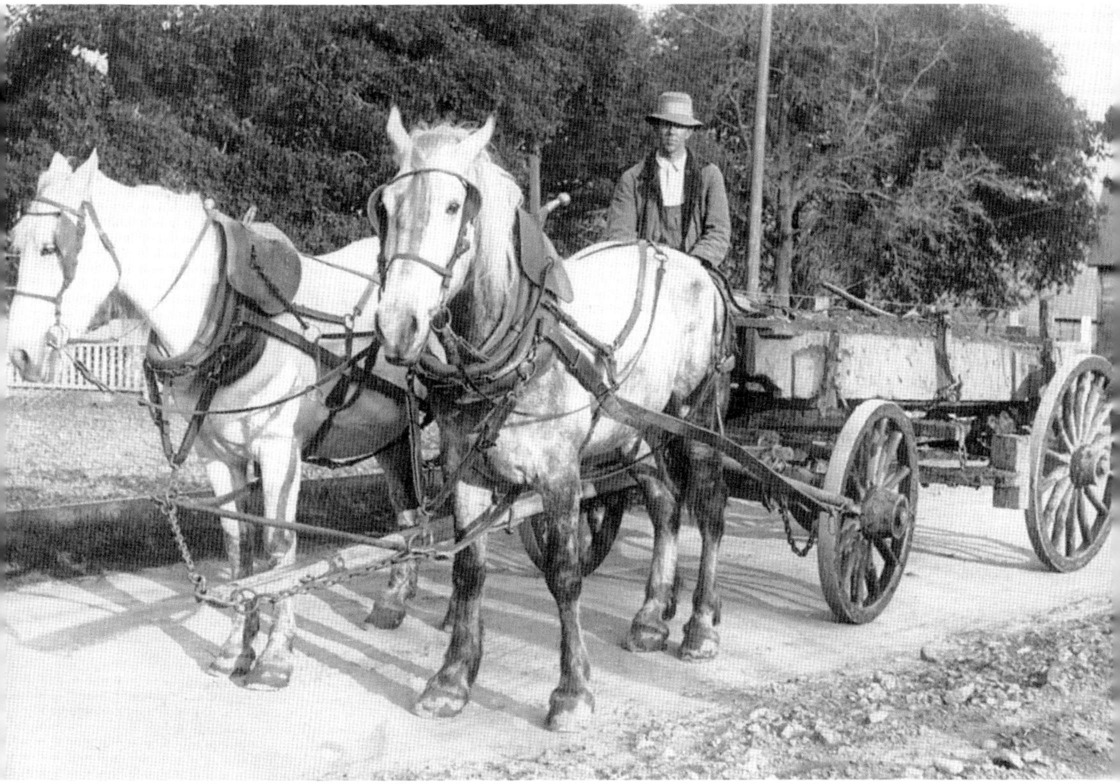

Louis Omar Sporleder Sr. (1885–1954)
Lou Sporleder is shown at work hauling a load for the Los Gatos Transfer Company, an enterprise founded by his father, Wilhelm (William) Friedrich Sporleder (1857–1943). By 1925, the horses had been replaced by a fleet of three Republic trucks.

The Sporleder family emigrated from Iowa and settled in Los Gatos around 1888. Lou was one of eight children of William and Sarah Arminta Blank Sporleder (1857–1946). He began a family tradition when he joined the Los Gatos Volunteer Fire Department in 1902, later becoming assistant chief. In the next generation, Louis O. Sporleder Jr. (1914–1965) followed in his father's footsteps by joining the volunteers in 1938 and being appointed assistant chief in 1957. Louis Jr. was also one of California's top Shell Oil dealers, taking over the town's first service station at the corner of North Santa Cruz and Saratoga Avenues. Both father and son served on school boards, and Louis Sr. served as a town trustee from 1904 to 1916.

The Sporleder firefighting legacy continued into a third generation. All three of Virginia and Louis Sporleder Jr.'s sons have served in that capacity. Douglas Sporleder was appointed fire chief of the Santa Clara County Central Fire Protection District in 1982. His brother Steve is a retired captain with the Saratoga Fire District, and another brother, Bert, served as a volunteer firefighter. (Courtesy Steve Sporleder and Patricia Shirley Sporleder.)

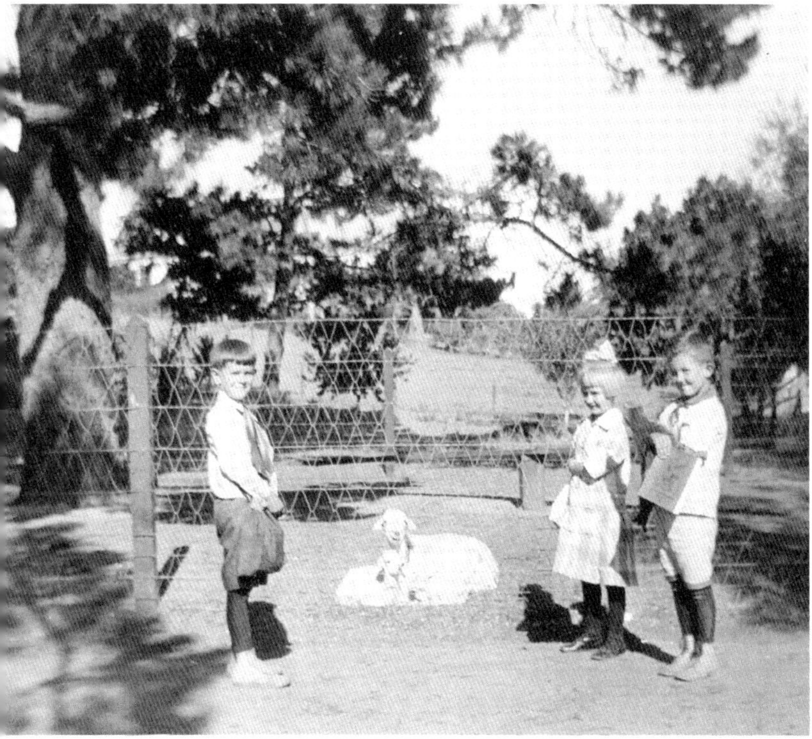

A Family Compound

Don Case, Mary Balch, and Bill Balch (from left to right) enjoyed a nursery school, an orchard, a vegetable garden, tennis courts, a tree house, a footbridge across a creek, a grape arbor, a playhouse, and accommodations for chickens, horses, cows, and goats, all conveniently at home. (Courtesy Balch family.)

Stevens Delos Balch (1877–1953)

"Dean" Balch arrived in Los Gatos from Iowa in 1904 with his wife, Lucy Cosgrave Balch (1879–1954), son Carl (1903–1998), and brother-in-law James Case (1870–1954). Balch and Case purchased controlling interest in the Bank of Los Gatos, which remained a locally owned bank until 1926. The Balch family was instrumental in Los Gatos banking circles for more than 50 years.

Soon after their arrival, Balch and Case acquired three acres of land from Francis McCullagh, bordered by Bachman and Massol Avenues and Los Gatos–Saratoga Road. The families built a compound that included three houses, gardens, and shelters for farm animals.

Both Dean and Carl Balch served terms as mayor. Lucy Balch participated in the town pageants and packed Christmas boxes for the poor. Dean and Lucy had two more children. Bill (1910–2005) was a banker, a member of the library board for 30 years, and a trustee of Good Samaritan Hospital. Mary (1909–2012) was the third woman to graduate in geology from Stanford University. She married Los Gatan Richard Kennedy, lived in Palo Alto, and died at age 102.

When James Case lost his wife, the former Margaret Balch (1872–1921), he married Dorothy Harwood, daughter of Estelle Harwood McMurtry. In addition to his banking career, Case was a founder of the Los Gatos Telephone Company and La Rinconada Country Club. Dean Balch is pictured here holding his pet monkey, Morocco. (Courtesy Balch family.)

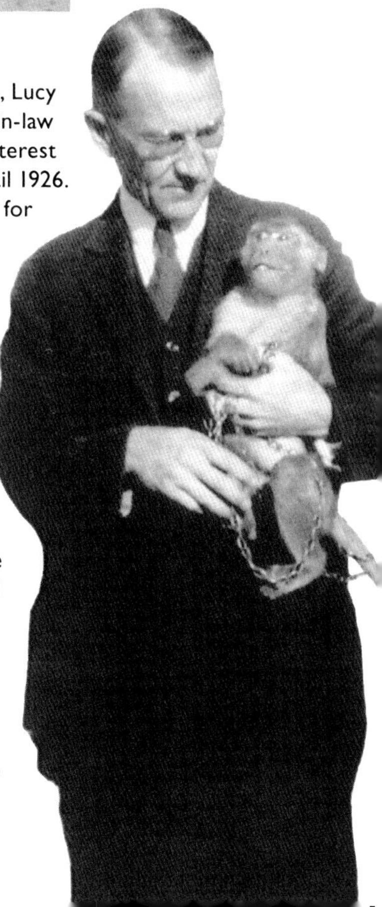

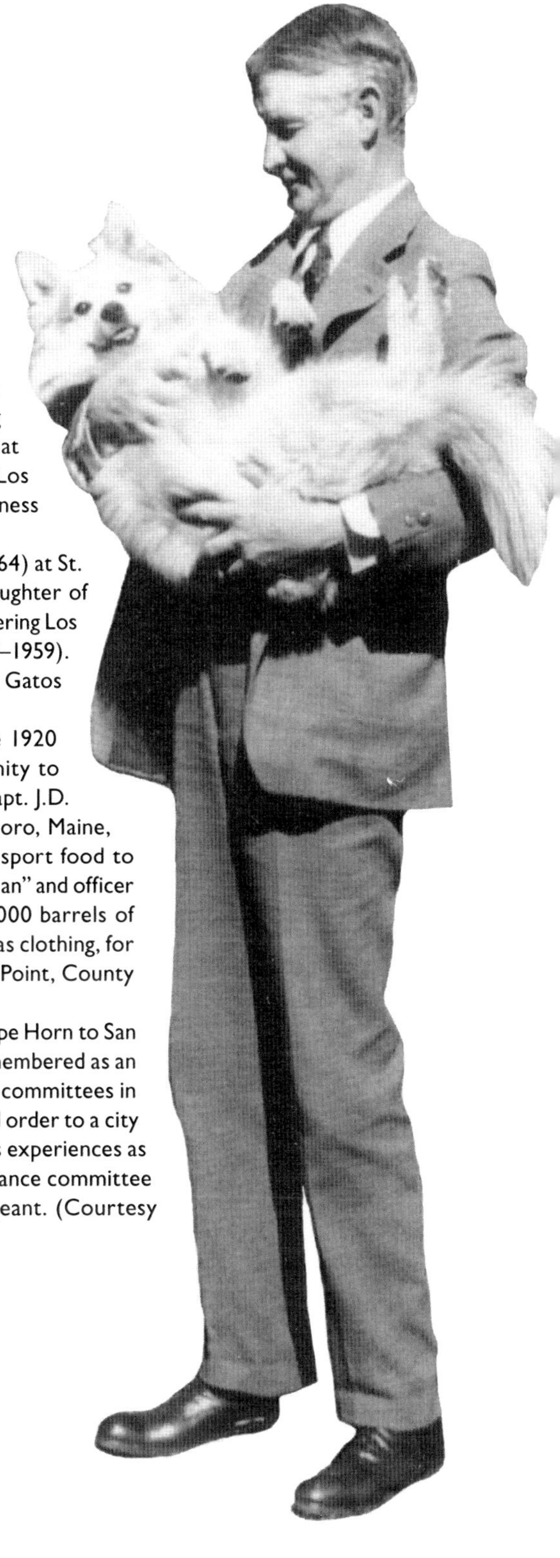

James D. Farwell (1872–1943)
J.D. Farwell, a native of San Francisco, moved to Los Gatos in 1894. His accomplishments included organization of the Glen Una Electric Company at the Hume Ranch, where he was the manager for 25 years. When the first streetlights were turned on in Los Gatos on the evening of June 24, 1896, the electricity was generated from that plant. In 1903, he was one of the originators of the Los Gatos Gas & Electric Company and managed that business until it was sold to PG&E in 1913.

In 1902, Farwell married Irma Lyle Lyndon (1880–1964) at St. Luke's Episcopal Church in Los Gatos. She was the daughter of John and Theresa Rector Lyndon, thus uniting two pioneering Los Gatos families. They had one son, Lyndon Farwell (1907–1959). Farwell was hired as vice president of the Bank of Los Gatos in 1920 and is pictured here at about that time.

When Farwell was recruited to play a part in the 1920 pageant *The Californian*, he had the unusual opportunity to play a character based on the life of his own father, Capt. J.D. Farwell (1815–1887). Captain Farwell, born in Vasselboro, Maine, was a seafaring man who in 1847 volunteered to transport food to famine-stricken Ireland. He sailed as a "volunteer gentleman" and officer on the USS *Jamestown*, a sloop-of-war loaded with 8,000 barrels of corn, beef, peas, potatoes, rice, wheat, and fish, as well as clothing, for the desperate Irish people. The ship arrived at Roches Point, County Cork, in 15 days.

In 1850, Captain Farwell sailed his own ship around Cape Horn to San Francisco, where he worked as a ship chandler. He is remembered as an outspoken member of both the 1851 and 1856 vigilance committees in San Francisco, a citizen's group bent on restoring law and order to a city racked with violence and crime. It was Captain Farwell's experiences as a member of the executive committee of the 1856 vigilance committee that J.D. Farwell, his son, recreated for the 1920 pageant. (Courtesy Farwell family.)

The Yuki Family

In 1898, Tsurumatsu and Hatsuyo Yuki left Japan for America in search of greater opportunities. They arrived in Honolulu, Hawaii, on January 6, 1899, not sure what their future would bring. After their son Takeo (1905–1967) was born, the young family boarded a ship and left for Salinas, California. Tragically, in 1907, Hatsuyo and her newborn died during childbirth. Tsurumatsu sadly continued to work in the fields, with Takeo strapped to his back. In 1911, his relatives sent Ryo Kato, a young woman from their village, to become his second wife. She is seated third from right in this c. 1938 photograph. Tsurumatsu and Ryo became the parents of Masao (far left) and Toshiye (second from left).

Takeo (third from left) grew up to be a smart, intuitive, and hardworking farmer and businessman. He bought land and entered into a partnership with another enterprising young man, Tom Bunn, to establish the Salinas Valley Vegetable Exchange. They shipped lettuce to many parts of the United States, and the two men became known as the "Lettuce Kings." In 1931, Takeo married Miyoko Abe (1913–2009), who is seated far right. They had four children, including Emie (Yamate) and Tom, the two small children in the photograph. Penny (Morimoto) and Herbert were born after this photograph was taken.

Life changed dramatically for the Yuki family on December 7, 1941, when the United States entered World War II. In February 1942, Pres. Franklin Delano Roosevelt signed Executive Order 9066, which mandated the forced relocation of Americans of Japanese ancestry into internment camps. With thousands of others who were sent to desolate, inhospitable parts of America, the Yukis were placed in the lower Sonoran desert camp called Poston II, in Arizona. They remained there for the duration of the war.

Fortunately, with an honest Caucasian partner, the Yukis retained all of their business and land holdings. After the war ended in 1945, they settled in Los Gatos. In 2012, the children of Takeo and Miyoko Yuki honored their departed parents with a generous donation to the new town library. The lobby of the new building is now dedicated in their honor. (Courtesy Yuki family.)

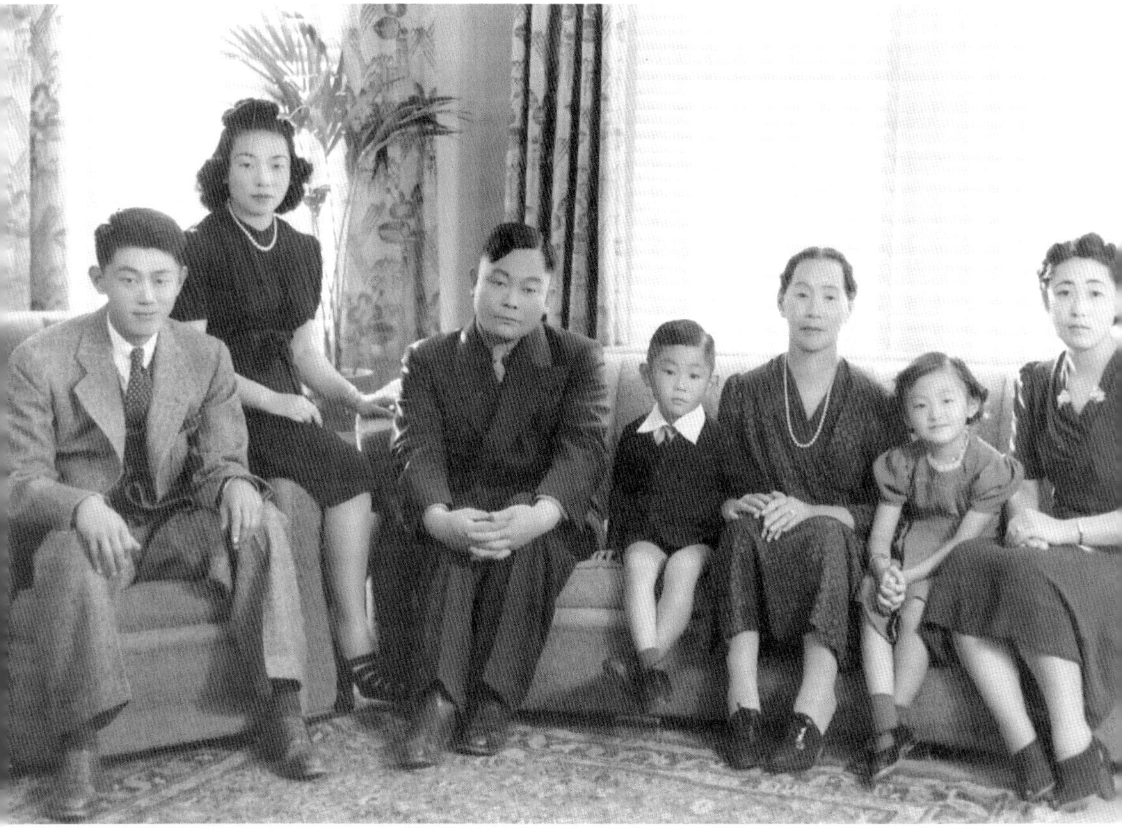

CHAPTER TWO

The Achievers

Ferreting out information on early settlers can be challenging. Only a few left diaries or other manuscripts describing their daily lives and the formidable obstacles they faced. Census records are usually but not always accurate. Newspapers are an excellent resource, especially for establishing dates, but reporting, then as now, can be of varying quality. Gaining credible insight into legends can be especially problematical, since favorite stories are repeated again and again, taking on a life of their own. And family stories, passed on for generations and held dear, may have been embellished over the years and prove less than exact.

In Los Gatos lore, Mary Coggeshall has always been a mystery woman. It is known that she hired J.J. Hill to build the gracious Coggeshall Mansion at 115 North Santa Cruz Avenue in 1891. Her home was one of many stately houses that lined the west side of the street for half a century. She is usually referred to as "a rich widow from Australia," but her story is more complex than that.

Mary's parents were Dennis Barry and Catherine Ryan, natives of Ireland. They were transported to an Australian penal colony by the British courts, along with thousands of other Irish Catholics, usually for minor infractions. Their marriage was recorded in 1839 in New South Wales, and they apparently left Australia not long afterwards, headed around treacherous Cape Horn and up the west coast of South America. The circumstances of their departure are not known. In the 1880 census, Mary's birth on November 10, 1840, is reported to have taken place in Valparaiso, Chile, an important seaport that faces the Pacific Ocean.

Mary Barry arrived in California nine years later, in 1849, at the height of the Gold Rush, and is found in the 1860 census working as a servant in El Dorado County. In 1871, she married Benjamin S. Coggeshall, a prosperous eighth-generation American from Rhode Island. The couple apparently separated in the 1880s, and Mary went on alone to become a successful fruit farmer in Sacramento County. Her life is compelling in its details, as are the lives of many people in this chapter.

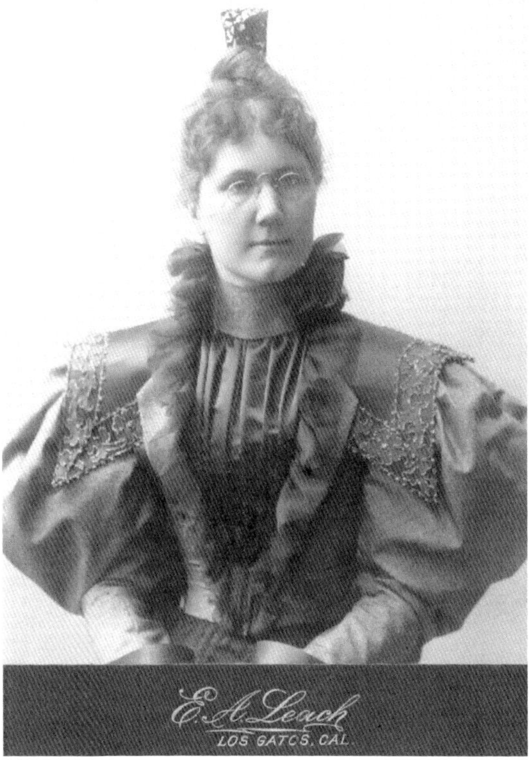

Martha Elizabeth Cilker (1868–1950)

Martha Cilker was the oldest child of pioneers John Cilker, born in Germany in 1833, and Ann Jane Lipsett Cilker, born in Ireland in 1847. Her parents homesteaded 174 acres northeast of Los Gatos in 1867. Martha spent her life as a dedicated teacher, beginning her career as one of the first instructors in the high school studies program at Los Gatos in the 1890s. She later taught in Los Angeles high schools.

Dora Mae Rankin (1887–1979)

Dora Rankin came to Los Gatos in 1900 when her father was appointed presiding elder of the Methodist church. She remembered arriving in Los Gatos on the narrow-gauge train, accompanied by her pet chicken in a paper bag and her big black cat on a red leash. After graduation from Los Gatos High School in 1906, Dora took the teacher training course at San Jose Normal School and taught elementary grades for more than 30 years. During the 1960s, she wrote an engaging local history column titled *As It Was*. She fondly recalled vineyards, apricot and cherry orchards, and picnics in Memorial Park, along the Los Gatos Creek. She never married but lived out her life on Peralta Avenue.

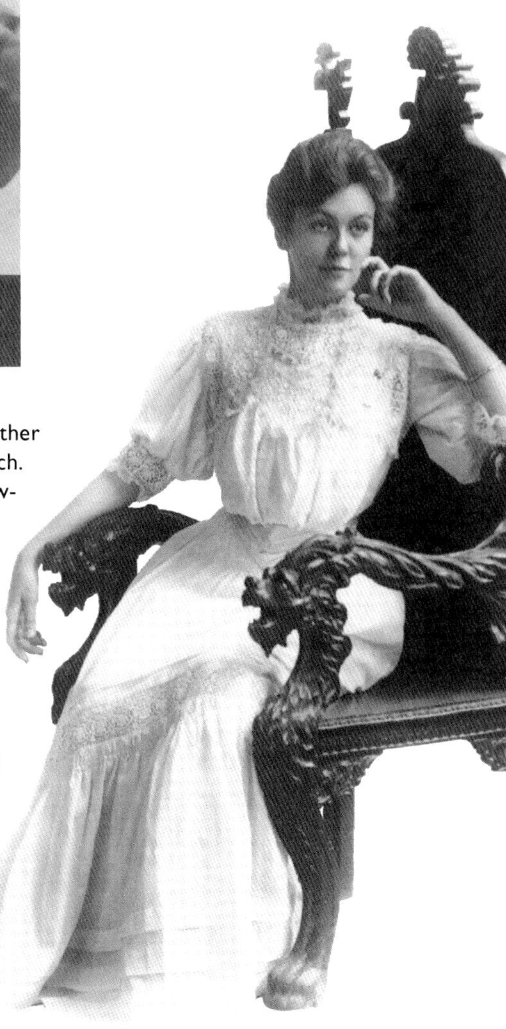

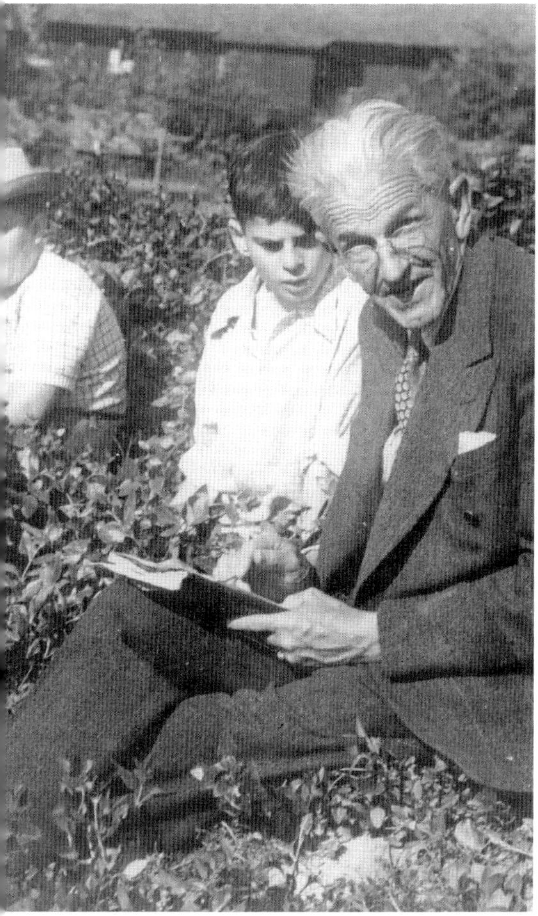

Ernest Andrew Rogers (1881–1957)

At the age of 28, Minnesota high school teacher Ernest Rogers moved to California to pursue his dream of building a school for boys. A year later, he was joined by his family, and his father, Charles Butters Rogers, purchased a small ranch above Los Gatos. Over the next few months, several small buildings from the neighboring Tevis estate were moved to the ranch and located close to the existing ranch house. In January 1911, the first classes of the Montezuma Mountain Ranch School for Boys were held. "Professor" Rogers wanted his boys to develop good character along with their academics, so mornings in the classroom were followed by afternoons of hiking, swimming, and horseback riding. During this time, Rogers founded the Junior Statesmen of America program to further his goal of educating students in good citizenship. Eventually, chapters were established all over the United States. Summer seminars were held at the Montezuma School.

In 1953, a major fire destroyed a number of the school buildings, shown here, and because Rogers was in poor health, he was unable to overcome the loss. The school was closed in 1955, and the property was sold to the Sisters of the Presentation. (Courtesy John Lloyd.)

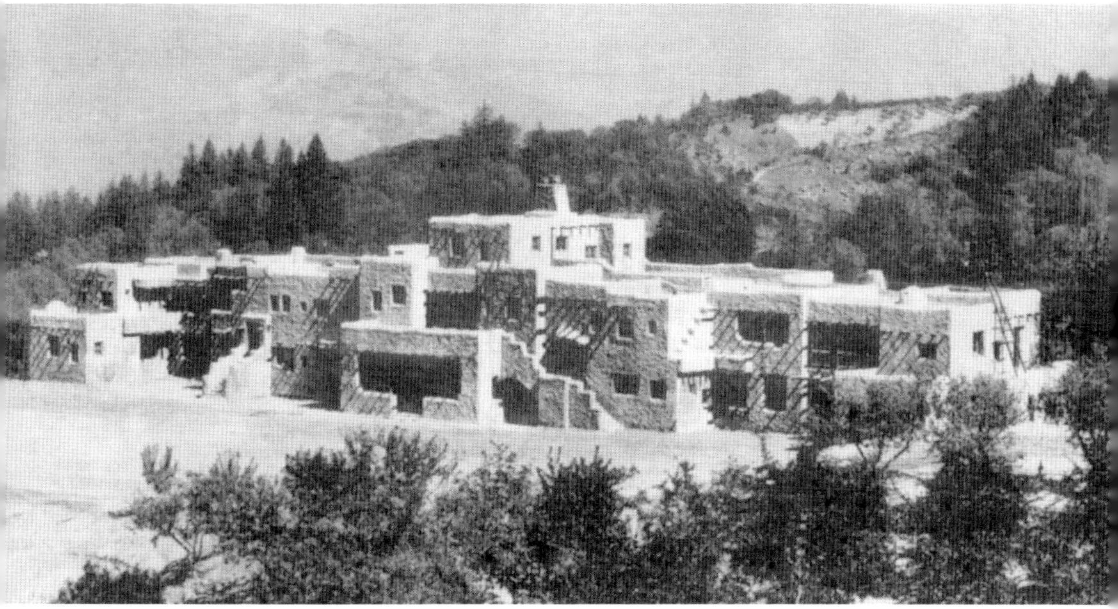

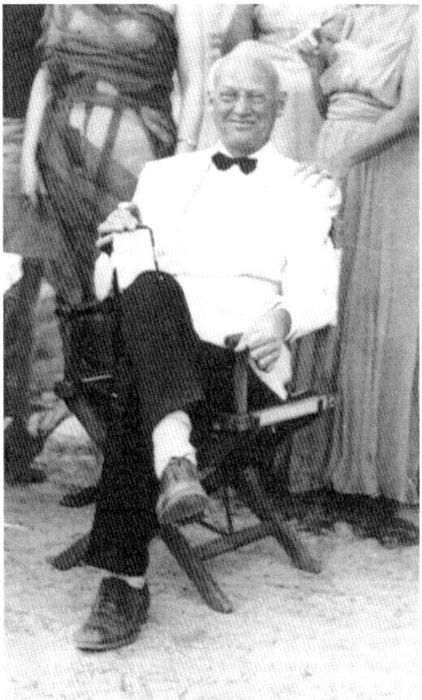

Charles Sherman Hayward (1894–1975)

Charles Hayward was a distant relative of Gen. William Tecumseh Sherman. He was born in Vinton, Iowa, and his early schooling took place in Omaha, Nebraska. He moved to California to attend Stanford University.

Hayward was the musical director for both the University Avenue Grammar School and Los Gatos High School when Prentiss Brown was principal. Any high school student could learn to play the instrument of his choice. Hayward's service to the schools spanned 30 years, from 1920 to 1950. He also led the Haywire Orchestra, an ensemble of local musicians who played at various events and entertained on the Commuter Christmas Special trains in December. (Courtesy Gay Arnott.)

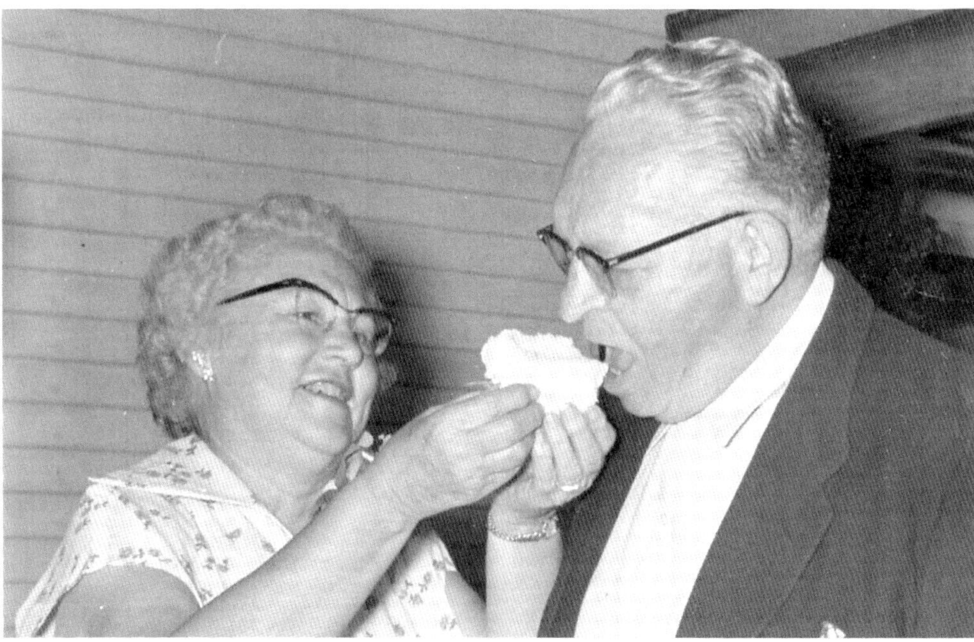

John Prentiss Brown (1893–1964)

Principal of Los Gatos High School from 1931 to 1956, Prentiss Brown served longer than anyone before him in that position, and the high school auditorium bears his name. He played the gatekeeper in the 1940 *Trail Days* celebration to mark the completion of the Los Gatos Santa Cruz highway into town. Brown and his wife, Ida May, pictured here on their 50th wedding anniversary, lived for many years on Magneson Loop. (Courtesy John H. Simpson.)

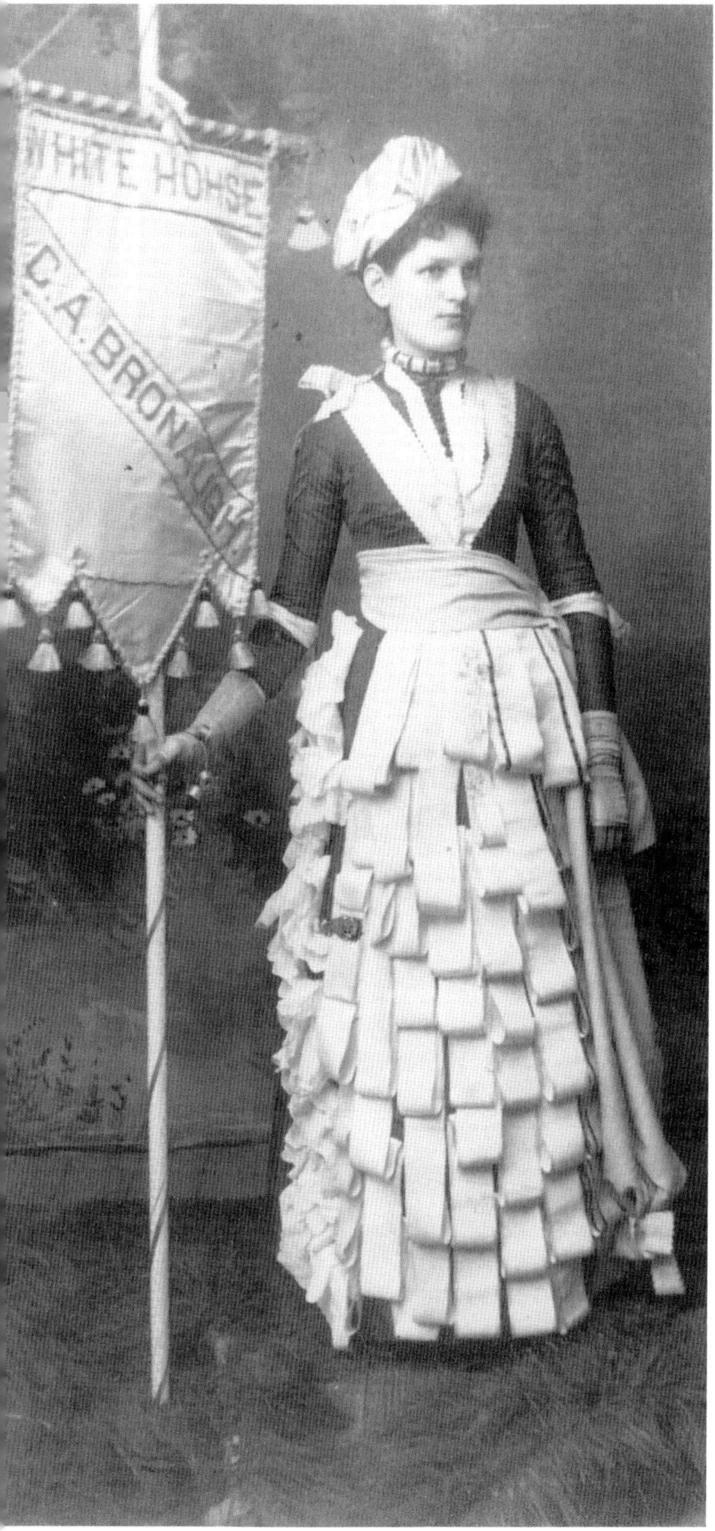

Louise Van Meter (1868–1948)

Louise Van Meter was born in Healdsburg, California, and came to Los Gatos at the age of 12. In 1893, she accepted the position as first-grade teacher at University Avenue Grammar School.

Her teaching methods were unconventional for her time. In her classroom, Van Meter introduced living history, art, and nature. She also advocated for a kindergarten class that would introduce younger children to learning and social skills. Although warm and gracious, Van Meter was also known for her insistence on discipline, and many naughty children felt her ire.

Van Meter taught first grade in Los Gatos for 35 years. She lived with her mother in a small Victorian cottage on East Main Street and could be seen driving around town in a sporty Model A coupe. She retired in 1928. The decision to name the new elementary school in her honor came just before her death in 1948.

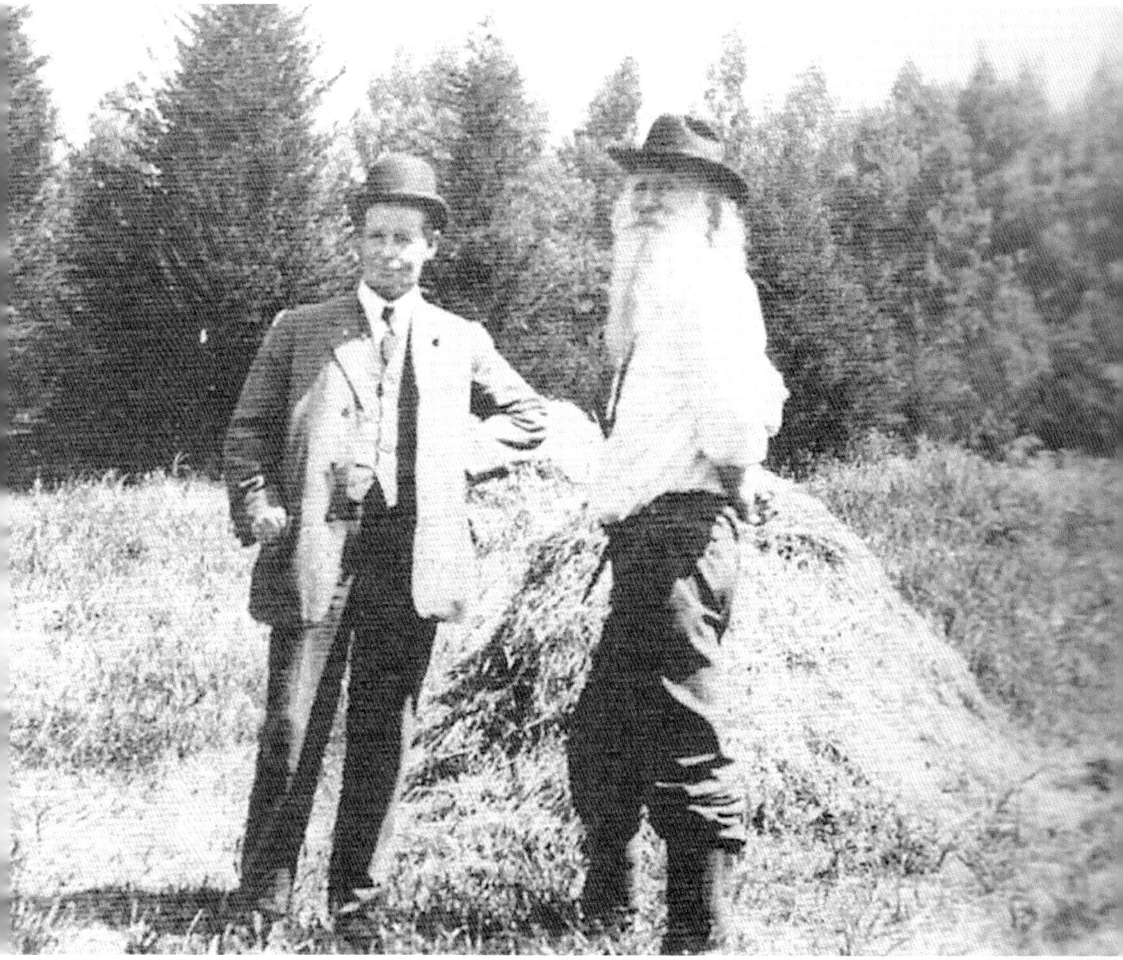

Henry Meade Bland (1863–1931)

Henry Meade Bland (left) was responsible for the establishment of a public high school for Los Gatos. He was born in Suisun, Solano County, the son of a circuit-riding itinerant Methodist minister. After graduation from the University of the Pacific in 1887, Bland was hired to institute a post-graduate course of study at the Los Gatos grammar school to prepare students for college entrance examinations. These classes were the beginning of high school education in town, and Bland served in this position for two years. Subsequently, he worked as an English professor at San Jose State College for more than 30 years. He was a friend of Joaquin Miller (right), the "Poet of the Sierras," as well as Jack London, John Muir, Edwin Markham, and other prominent Californians. Bland succeeded Ina Coolbrith as California's poet laureate in 1929. (Courtesy Santa Clara City Library.)

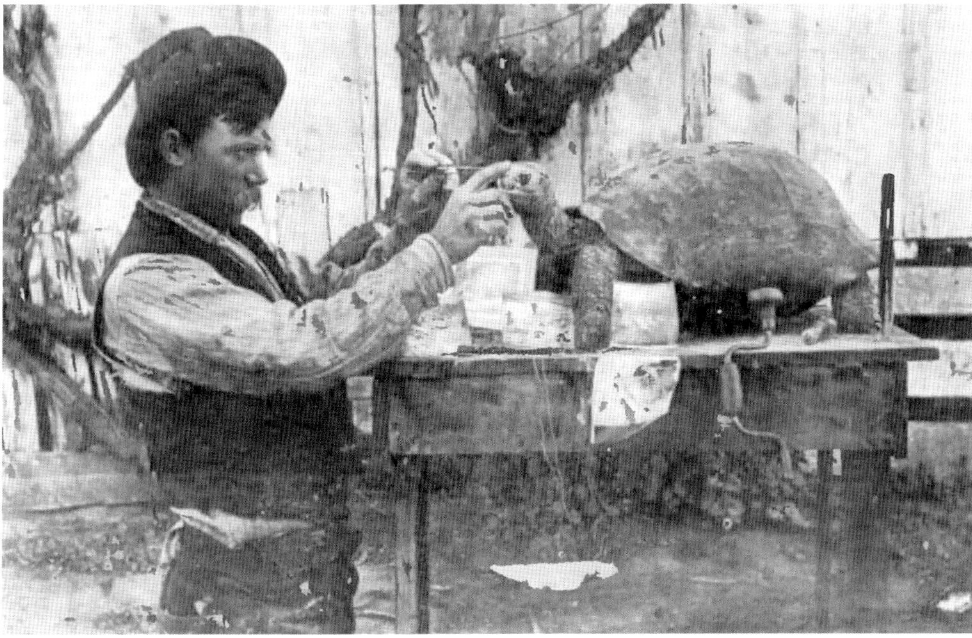

Rollo Howard Beck (1870–1950)
Rollo Beck was born in Los Gatos and, as a child, worked in the area fruit orchards. With only an eighth-grade education but a keen interest in natural history and an introduction to biologist Charles Augustus Keeler, Beck learned about birds. He prepared ornithological specimens for museum collections. He joined the American Ornithologists' Union in 1894 and participated in expeditions in California and to the South Pacific and the Galapagos Islands, where he studied and collected giant tortoises. Beck and his wife, Ida, retired to Northern California and continued their study of natural history. Many of the specimens they collected are housed at the California Academy of Sciences in San Francisco.

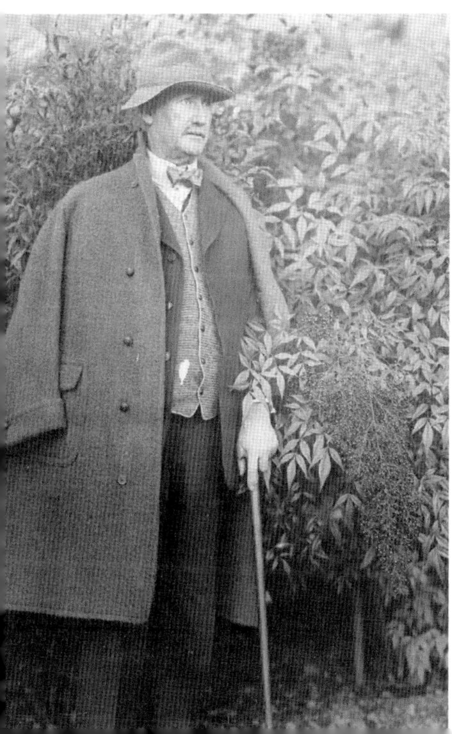

Harry L. Tevis, MD (1856–1931)
In early 1906, Harry Tevis purchased 800 acres of land four miles south of Los Gatos from James L. Flood. Shortly thereafter, the 40-room Flood mansion was "utterly wrecked" by the April 18 earthquake, according to the May 1, 1906, *Santa Cruz Sentinel.* Although he was a medical doctor, his avocation was the study of botany. The Jesuits purchased the estate in 1934 and opened Alma College. (Courtesy Jesuit Center.)

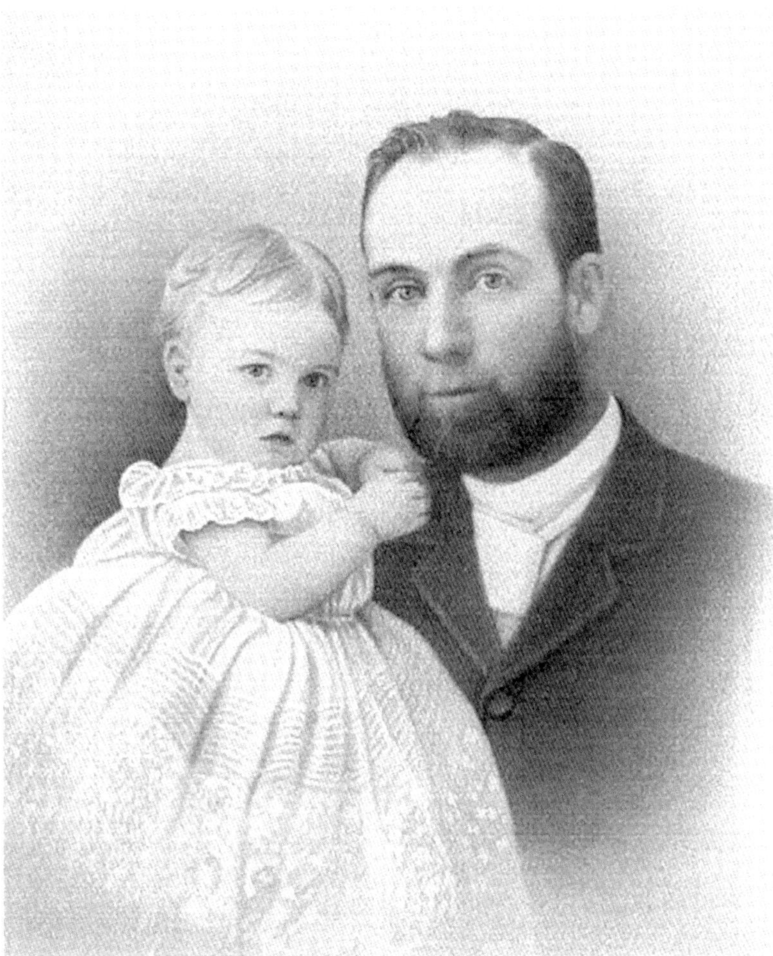

Robert Pearis Gober, MD (1858–1943)

Doc Gober was the son of a Methodist minister, William R. Gober (1824–1908), and his wife, Nancy Porter Beasley (1832–1908), both from proud, old Southern families. She was a distant cousin of Confederate general Robert E. Lee. Reverend Gober and his bride came to San Francisco in 1851 via Panama and then settled in Sacramento for a number of years. In 1864, the family moved to Santa Clara.

In a 1932 interview, Dr. Gober said he could not remember a time when he didn't think of being a doctor. He graduated from the University of the Pacific in 1882 and worked for the railroad to earn money to further his education. When he paid his first year's tuition at Bellevue Hospital in New York City in 1883 with California gold coins, he caused considerable excitement. He received his medical degree in 1884 and came to Los Gatos to set up his practice.

When Dr. Gober arrived in Los Gatos, the town had seven saloons and unofficial horse races between the original cemetery and the Lyndon Hotel. Hard drinking, fights, and horrific accidents involving horses and buggies and trains kept the young physician busy. Scarlet fever, diphtheria, and tuberculosis were not uncommon.

Dr. Gober was married in Los Gatos on June 17, 1886, to Annette May Bean (1868–1921), a daughter of inventor John Bean. In 1889, Dr. Gober and John Bean built a large house on the northwest corner of North Santa Cruz Avenue and Bean Avenue which had identical accommodations for the two families. Dr. Gober had a speaking tube installed beside his bed so that he could talk to patients who knocked on his door at night. The Gobers had two daughters, Helen Porter Gober Coleman (1891–1922), shown here with her father in 1892, and Nancy Cornelia Gober Schmidt (1892–1981). (Courtesy Leslie Gardiner.)

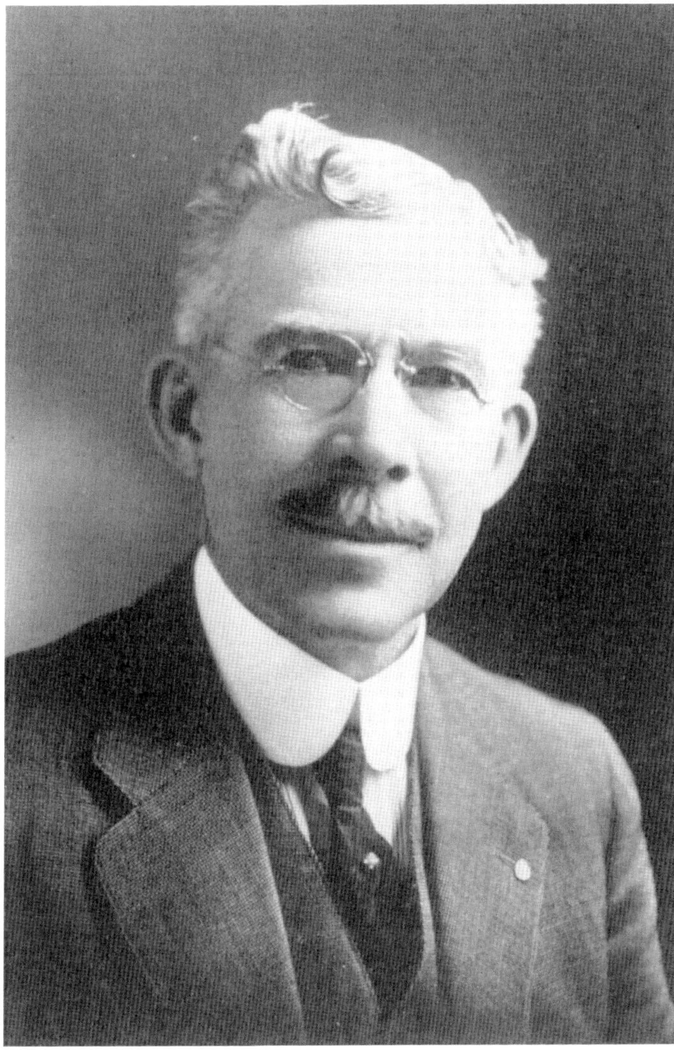

Frank W. Knowles, MD (1858–1936)
Frank Knowles was born in Rock Island County, Illinois, to Smith S. and Mary C. Knowles and grew up on a farm. Following his graduation from Chicago's Rush Medical College in 1883, he headed to Los Gatos to set up his practice. A year later, Dr. Robert P. Gober arrived in town, and the two physicians became friends and often worked together. In 1896, Knowles married Sabra Ann Roberts, the daughter of pioneers John J. and Martha Roberts. Following Sabra's death in 1913, he married Olive Warren, and they had one child, Frank Wesley Knowles Jr.

On the morning of August 19, 1890, Knowles awoke early to go hunting and discovered that George Seanor's 600-seat opera house on East Main Street was on fire. He ran to the nearby Presbyterian church, rang out the alarm, and managed to save his own house by covering it with blankets that were kept wet by a bucket brigade. In 1908, he was a member of the town's first board of health, which was established to deal with the generally unsanitary conditions existing in Los Gatos at the time.

Knowles was a rancher with a 45-acre spread and an original stockholder in the First National Bank of Los Gatos, where he served as director and vice president. Although he had suffered with heart ailments for some time, his passing came as a shock. A lifelong Republican, Knowles was on his way to the polls on November 3, 1936, when he collapsed and died.

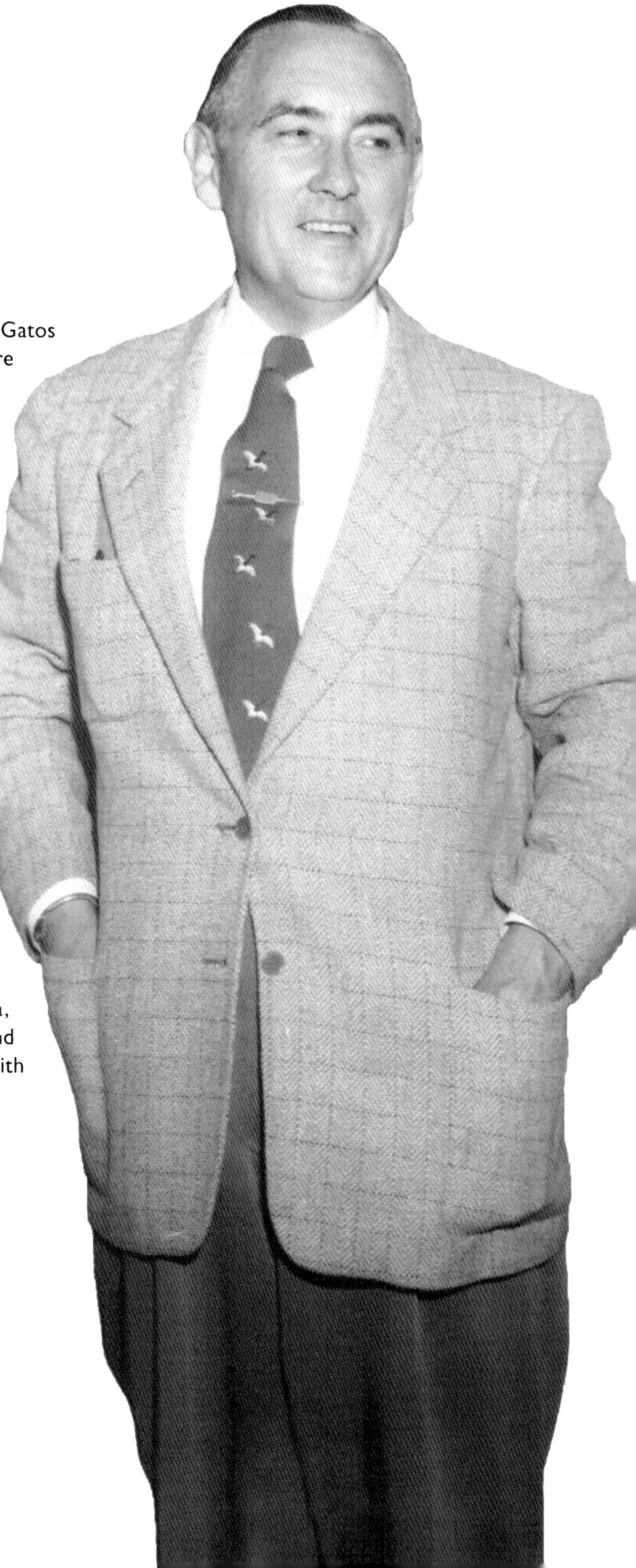

Horace Jones, MD (1901–1984)

In 1925, Horace Jones arrived in Los Gatos to serve a six-month internship before fulfilling his dream of opening his own practice in San Francisco, but he fell in love with the small town of 2,200 residents and decided to stay. Around 1928, he and his wife, Beatrice Kilburn Jones, built a Spanish Eclectic–style home at 18537 Eucalyptus Drive. In 1939, Jones purchased the La Estancia estate at 18000 Overlook Road from Frank McCullagh. The Jones family, which included four children, lived there until 1961, when they sold the 13-acre property to a developer. The main house, redesigned by Willis Polk in 1901, was eventually saved for its historical significance and is now in the National Register of Historic Places. During his 56 years in practice, Jones delivered more than 1,600 babies. His famous patients included Yehudi Menuhin's mother Marutha, Col. Charles Erskine Scott Wood, and John Steinbeck, who credited Jones with effective treatment of his sciatica.

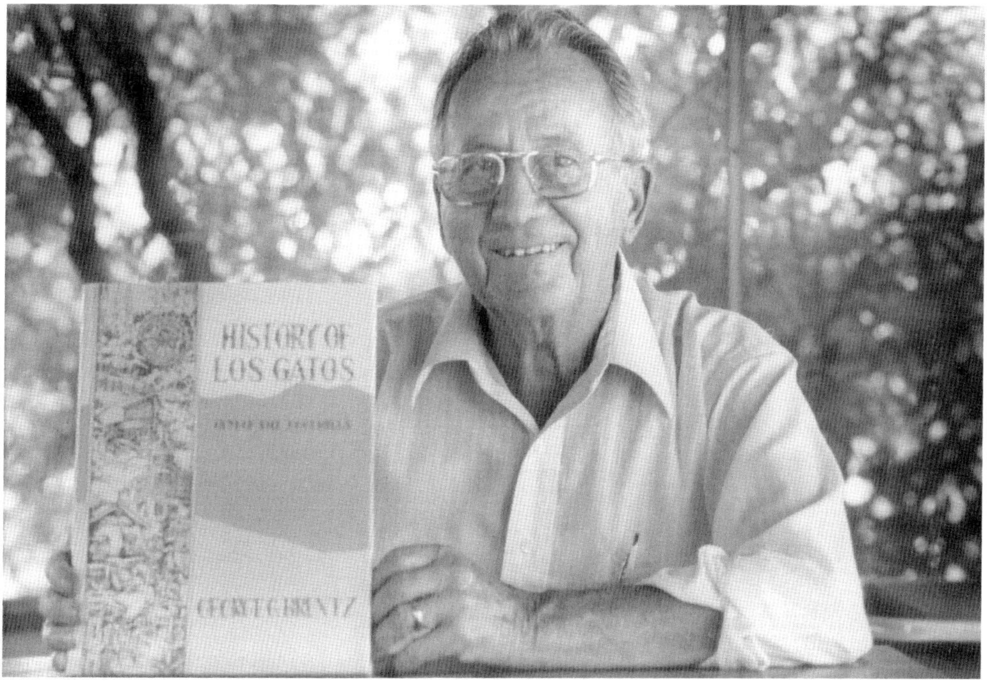

George G. Bruntz (1901–1991)

Dr. George G. Bruntz moved to Los Gatos in 1930. For 16 years, he was a history teacher and director of adult education at Los Gatos Union High School District. For 19 years, he taught at San Jose State College, where he organized and directed the secondary school social science teacher training program until he retired in 1965. He was the author of a number of books, including *History of Los Gatos—Gem of the Foothills*, the first comprehensive history of the town, published in 1971.

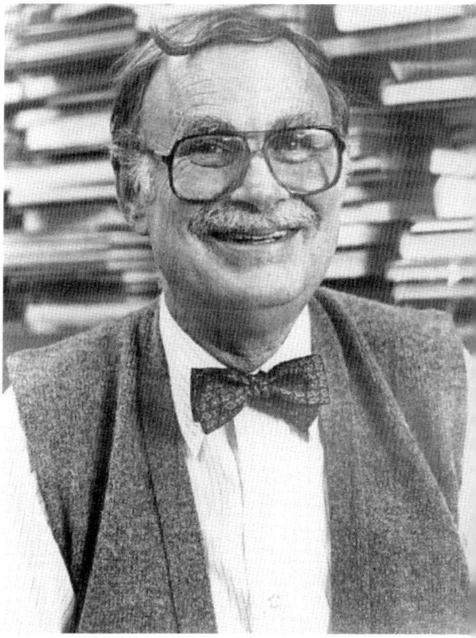

John Schmuck

Appointed town librarian in 1953, John Schmuck served in that position for 34 years, one of the longest tenures of any Los Gatos town employee. A veteran of World War II, he began service in the Los Gatos Carnegie Library on University Avenue. When that building was condemned in 1954, he oversaw the move of library services to the former American Legion War Memorial building on East Main Street. In 1965, he once again supervised a move, this time to the new civic center across the street, continuing the proud tradition of the independent town library, founded in 1898.

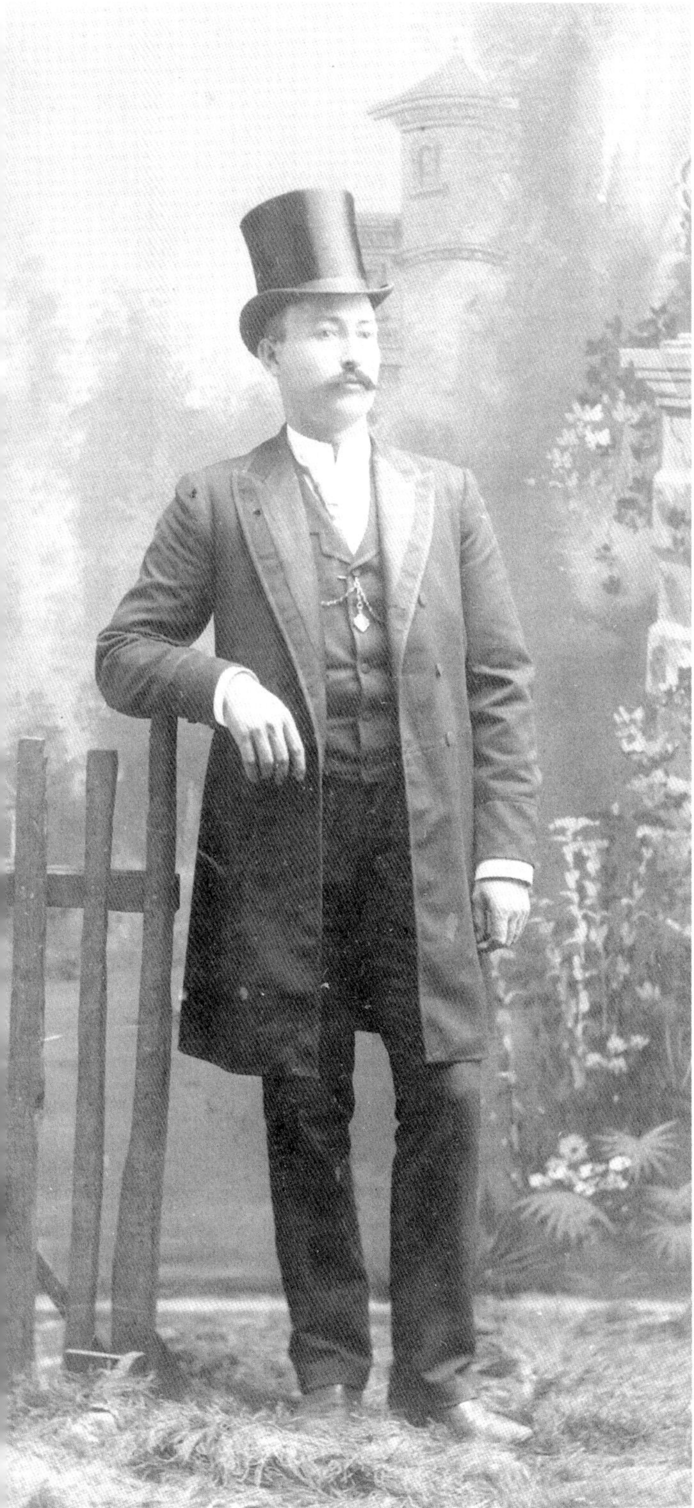

Zephyr A. Macabee (1857–1940)

Zephyr Macabee was one of eight children born to Edward and Matilda Macabee, who came to Los Gatos in 1883 and purchased the Coleman Saloon and Boarding House. Zephyr went to work as a barber in the early 1890s and soon set up his own shop on East Main Street. In 1900, he patented the gopher trap he had invented in the basement of his newly completed home at 110 Market Street (now Loma Alta Avenue). The trap was a success and reduced a severe gopher problem in local orchards.

Zephyr and his wife, Elizabeth Gansburger Macabee (1862–1936), were the parents of three children, Lucile, Roma, and Raymond (1895–1984), all of whom worked in the family business. Raymond learned to make traps as a youngster and continued to do so until age 80. In 1924, the family moved out of their home, where the traps had always been made, so that increased production could take place. In May 2008, manufacturing shifted to China.

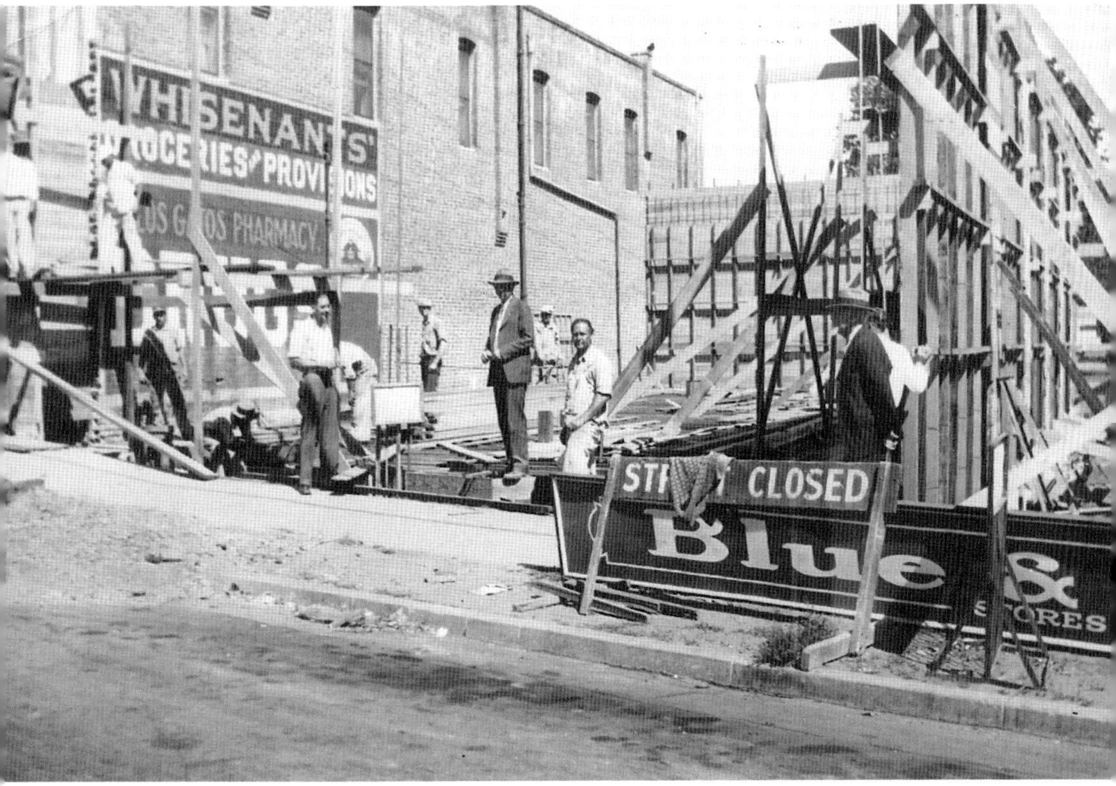

William John Whisenant (1897–1971)
Born and raised in Medford, Oregon, John Whisenant was a graduate of the University of California School of Pharmacy. He settled in Los Gatos in the early 1920s and established a full-service market on East Main Street. Whisenant's Groceries and Provisions baked and sold more than 1,000 loaves of bread per weekend at 10¢ each. To promote business, the store's soda fountain occasionally offered customers 15¢ milk shakes and Eat More ice cream sundaes for 5¢. He invested heavily in Los Gatos property and became a real estate broker in 1933.

During World War I, Whisenant served in the field artillery. In 1942, he was appointed Los Gatos postmaster and served for two years. He also served on the selective service board for 35 years. With the advent of World War II, he opposed drafting Yehudi Menuhin, feeling he was more important as a violinist than a soldier. His view overcame the prevailing attitude of other board members who took a "draft everyone" stance. Whisenant is standing at the center of this 1929 photograph. (Courtesy Chuck Bergtold.)

Neta Snook Southern (1896–1991)

Fascinated from an early age with machines of all kinds, Neta Snook defied traditional female roles by becoming an early "aeroplane" pilot. She attended flying schools and rebuilt a wrecked Canadian "Canuck" plane in the backyard of her parents' Iowa home. After World War I ended, she barnstormed around the Midwest, taking passengers for flights and doing aerial advertising. But the winters made flying tough. With no concrete runways available, she often landed in cow pastures. In the fall of 1920, she moved to Los Angeles.

In California, Neta made a deal to test-fly airplanes in return for commercial use of Kinner Airfield. She resumed her flight instruction business, with Amelia Earhart as her most famous student. Her life changed dramatically in December 1921 when she married William I. Southern (1891–1970). Their son Curtiss was born 11 months later. As much as she loved aviation, Neta's awareness of the danger of flying was heightened given her new circumstances. Her instrument panel consisted of only an altimeter and a dollar watch hanging on a hook. In August 1922, she stepped out of her plane for the last time and retired.

The Southern family purchased prune and apricot acreage at 15891 Shannon Road in 1926. They called their ranch Southern Slopes. Neta raised miniature horses, and in the early 1930s, she signed on as a piece-worker, making coils for the Macabee Gopher Trap Company. In 1976, at age 81, she was still employed at the same task. She died at age 95.

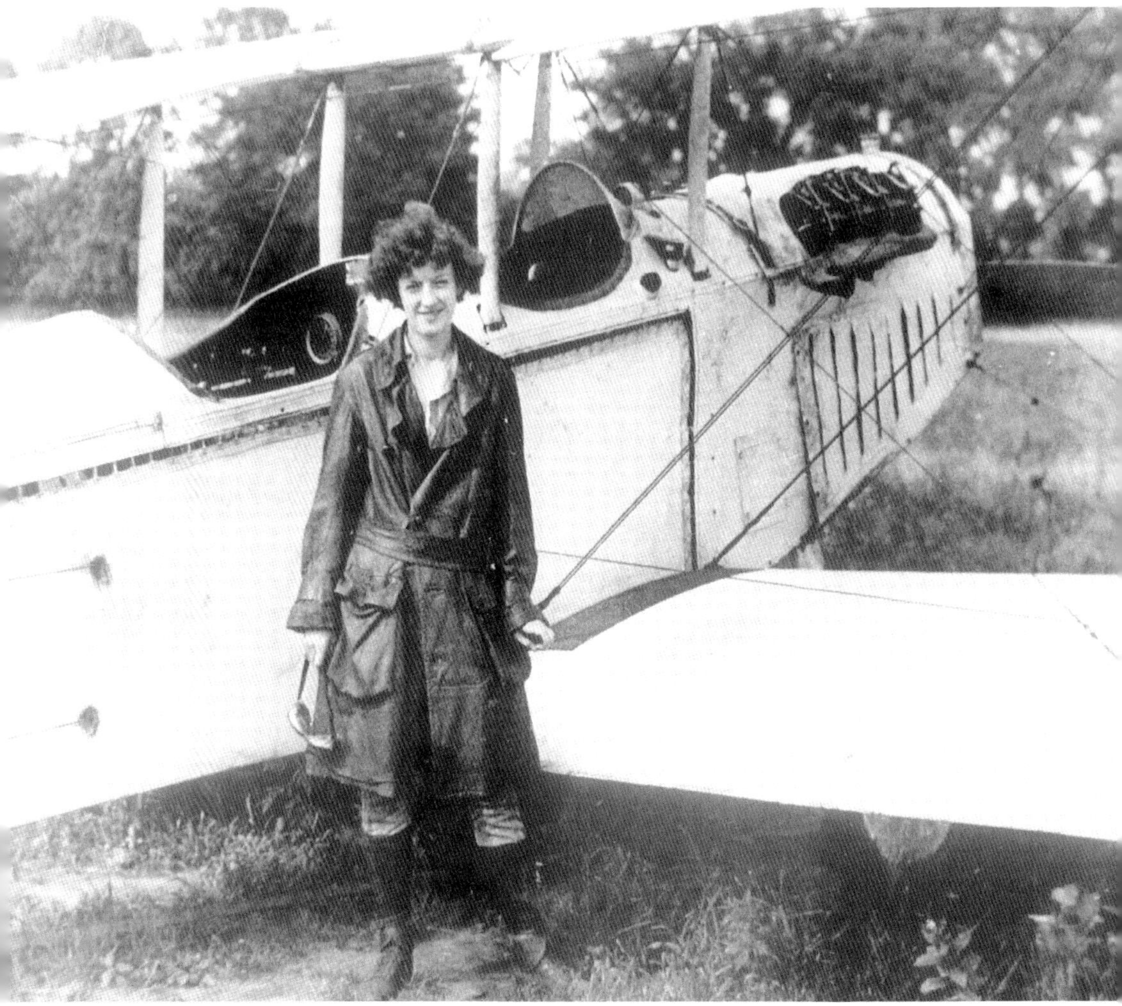

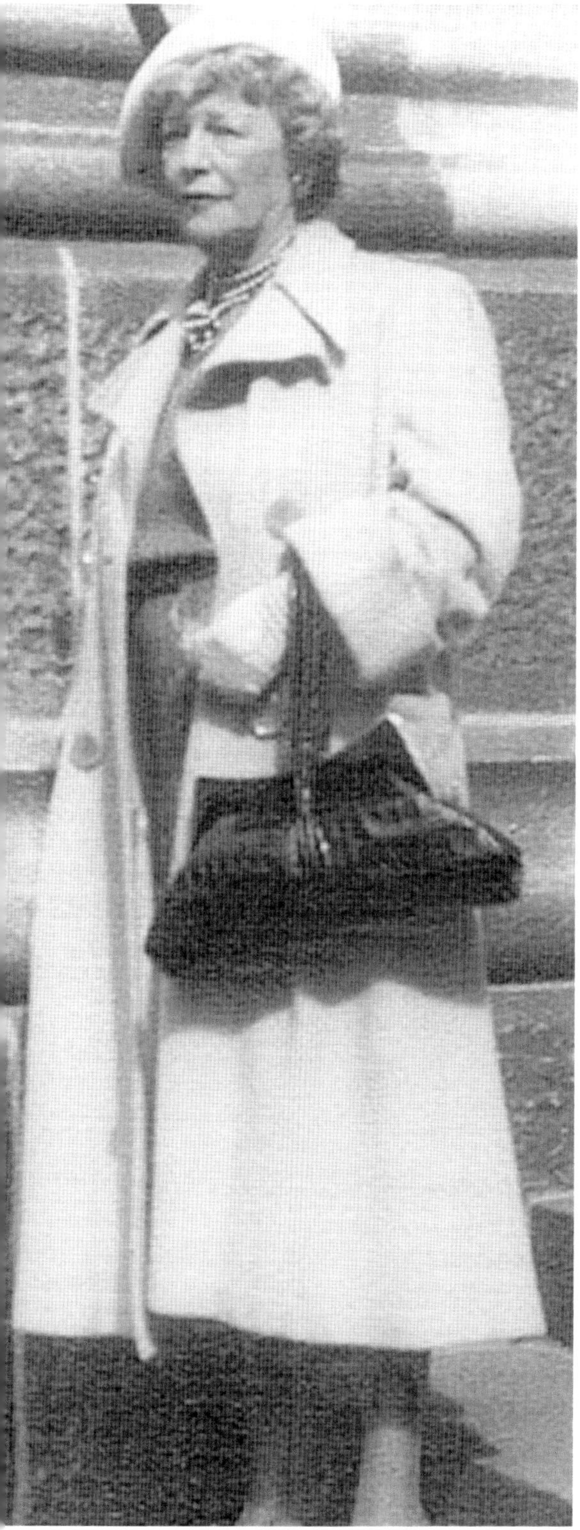

Nell Berryman (1879–1955)
Nell was an expert seamstress, a craft she learned from her mother, Mary Jane Rogers Berryman, born in 1849 in New Jersey. Nell's father was Charles Berryman, born into a mining and farming family in Cornwall, England, about 1843. Charles and Mary immigrated to California and in 1880 were living in the old mining town of Rough and Ready. Charles went to work at the New Almaden quicksilver mines in 1882 and was apparently killed in an accident there in 1893. Their son, Fred Berryman Sr. (1876–1963), was the founder of Berryman Plumbing in Los Gatos.

Nell and her mother lived for many years at 222 West Main Street, designing and sewing dresses for the women of Los Gatos. So successful was their business that by 1924 Nell was proprietress of the Nell-Clare Dress Shoppe, in partnership with Clare Rowell. The shop was located at 53 North Santa Cruz Avenue, and the women conducted business there for almost 30 years. Occasionally, Nell traveled to New York City to purchase dresses and order custom-made corsets for her Los Gatos customers. She played the part of a water nymph in the town's first pageant in 1919, and in 1921, she oversaw the production of the elaborate Chinese costumes for *Keang Foo, the Exile*. Nell was a director and founding member of the Los Gatos Business and Professional Women's Club, organized in 1930. (Courtesy Susan Welch.)

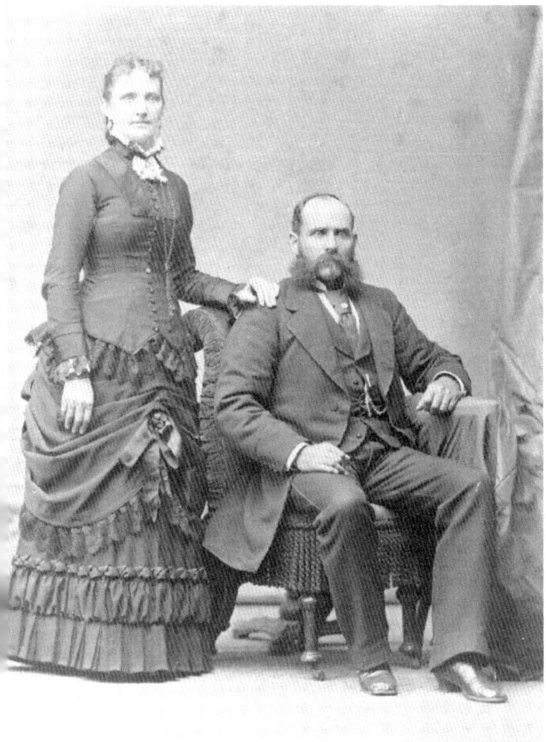

Mary Geneva Barry Coggeshall (1840–1909)

Mary Coggeshall was the daughter of Dennis Barry and Catherine Ryan, natives of Ireland who were living in Australia in the late 1830s, almost certainly "sent to the colonies" by the British government. Thousands of Irish were transported, often for minor crimes. Mary was born in Chile but lived most of her life in California, arriving at the time of the Gold Rush. She appears to have taken positions as a servant before she was married in 1871 to Benjamin S. Coggeshall, a direct descendent of John Coggeshall (1601–1647), the first president of the colony of Rhode Island. Mary and Benjamin are pictured here around the time of their wedding. They were the parents of two children, but later census records show each claimed to be widowed while the other was still living. The Coggeshall Mansion on North Santa Cruz Avenue was built for Mary in 1891. (Courtesy Cynthia Coggeshall Ahmann.)

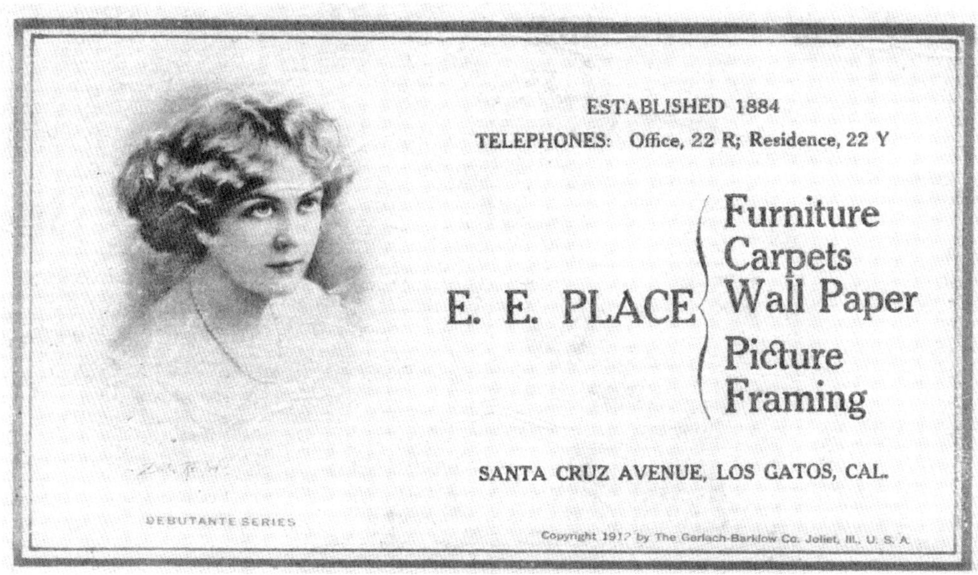

Elvert Ernest Place (1863–1937)

E.E. Place paired his undertaking business with his father's furniture store and opened Place Furniture and Undertaking on East Main Street in 1884. He oversaw the removal of bodies from the old 1850s town cemetery to the new location on Los Gatos–Almaden Road, and in 1917, he also purchased the Coggeshall Mansion on North Santa Cruz Avenue, which served as the Place Funeral Home for more than 50 years. George Place (1888–1972) was the last to run the family business.

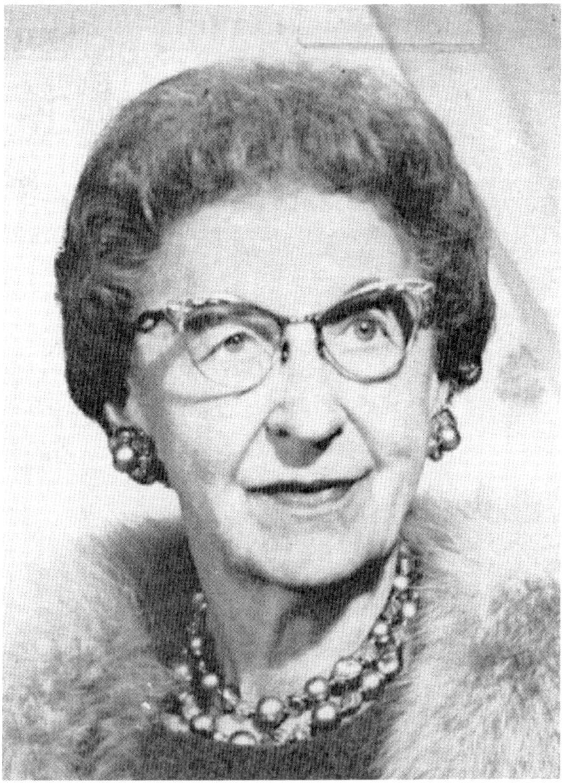

Effie Viola Stapp Walton (1884–1969)

Realtor Effie Walton was the first woman to serve as president of the Los Gatos Chamber of Commerce, and she served two terms. The lands of Aldercroft Heights were part of a large ranch owned by the Stewart family on the outskirts of Los Gatos. In the early 1900s, Effie and her husband, Arthur Walton, bought most of the land below the Stewart ranch house and farmed the existing prune and apricot orchards. Just before the 1920s, the Waltons subdivided a portion of their property into small lots. The first summer cottage was built on a lot purchased for $90, and it still stands on Locust Drive. In the 1950s, Effie and Art developed a shopping area in downtown Los Gatos known as "Little Village," built on the site of the original town cemetery.

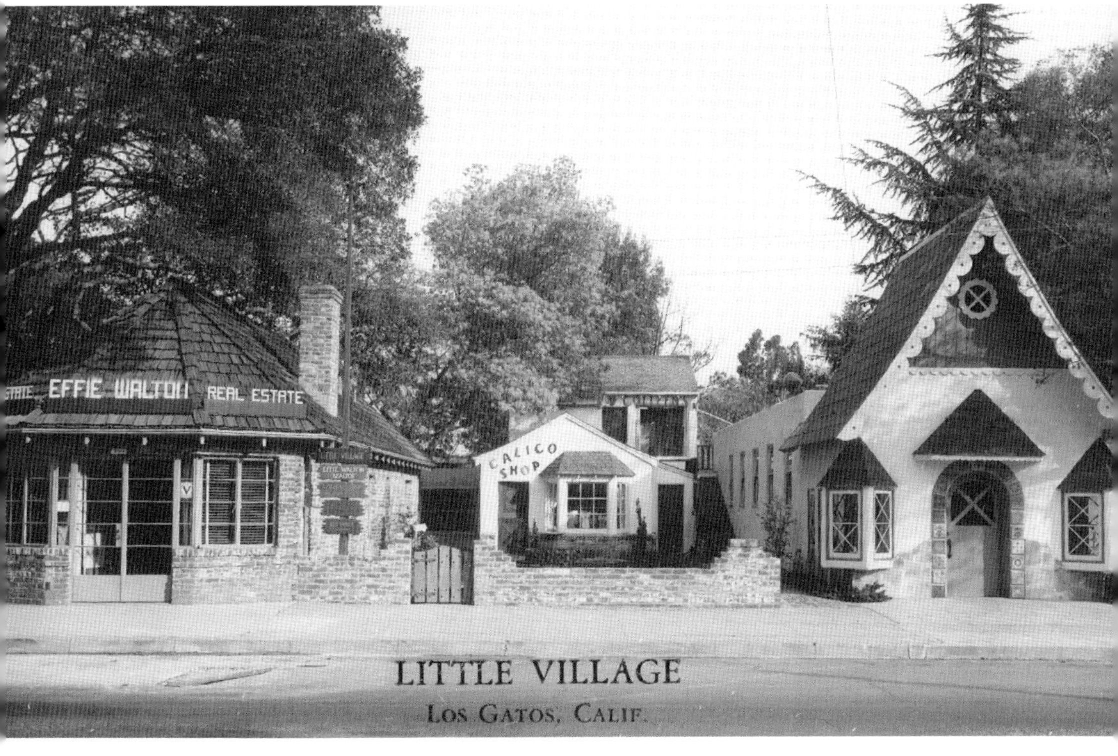

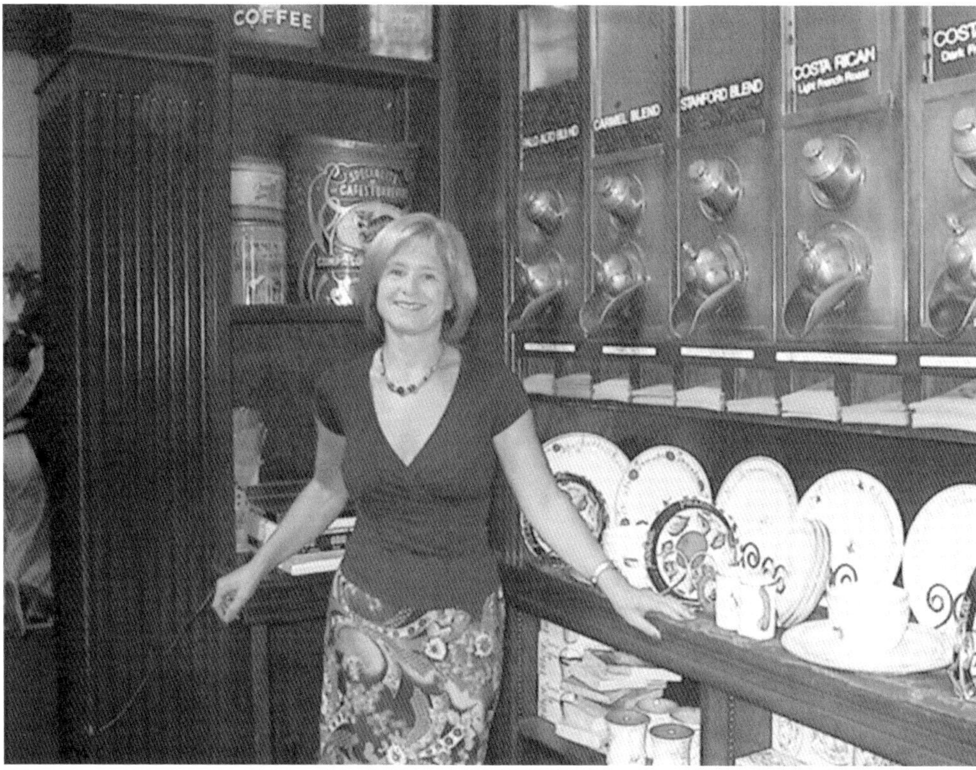

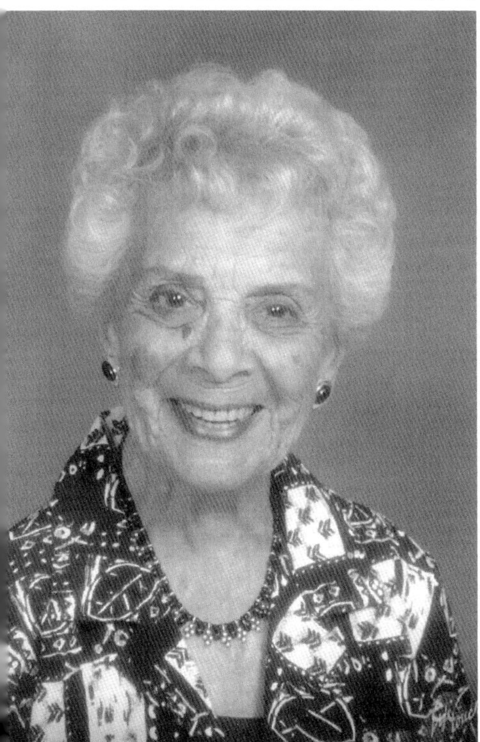

Teri Hope

Thirty years ago, Teri Hope was a single mom working in a women's health clinic and traveling from Los Gatos to San Francisco to purchase freshly roasted coffee. While making that 100-mile round-trip, she wished there was a place in town that could satisfy her craving. In April 1982, she opened her popular Los Gatos Coffee Roasting Company. But Teri is more than a successful entrepreneur. One of her major accomplishments is the establishment, in 2002, of a series of free weekly summer jazz concerts known as Jazz in the Plazz. (Courtesy Ronee Nassi.)

Dolores Juarez Cairns

Dolores Cairns, born in 1908, spent her early years on a 175-acre land grant in Morgan Hill acquired by her grandparents. When she was seven years old, her family moved to Los Gatos, and they eventually built a home at 86 Broadway. As a young woman, Dolores took a job as a typist. She remembers returning home to find that her sister Mercedes and friend Olivia de Havilland had been trying on her clothes, leaving them scattered about the room. In 1936, she married Lewis V. Cairns, manager of the Richfield service station on Santa Cruz Avenue. Now aged 105, Dolores has been a Los Gatos resident and member of St. Mary's Church for 98 years.

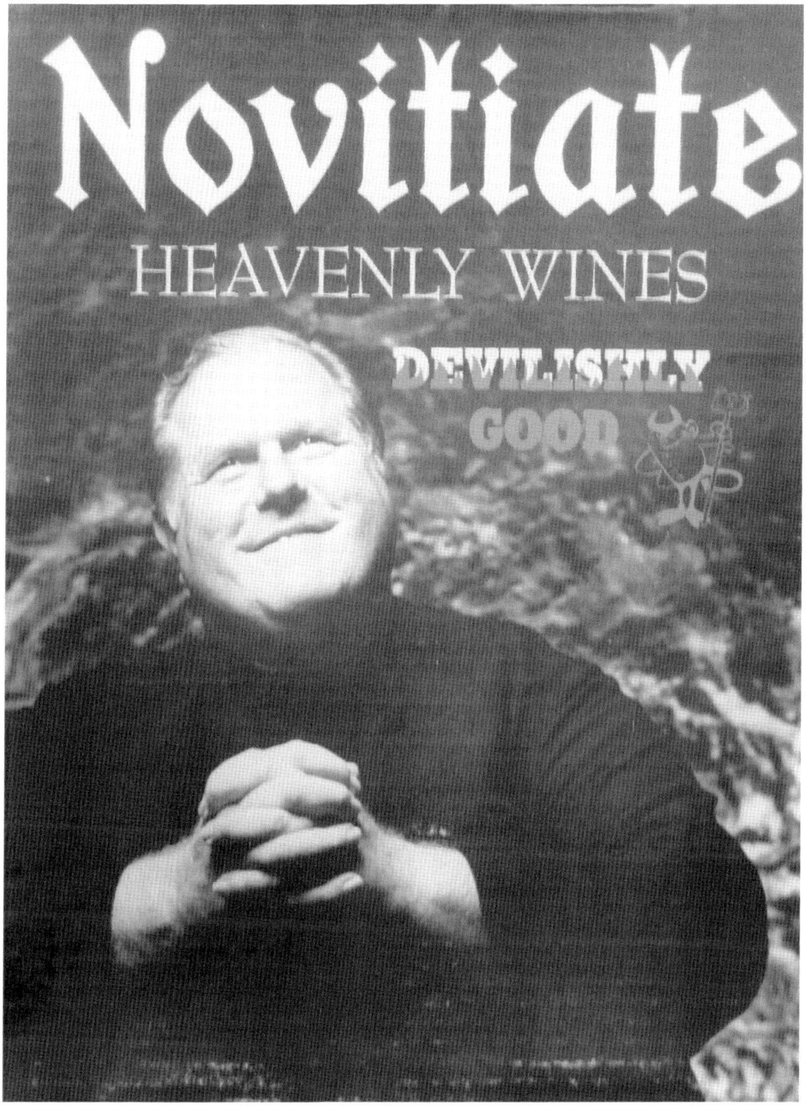

Norbert J. Korte (1929–2010)
Brother Norbert "Biz" Korte was born in San Francisco and raised in Oakland, California. He was a graduate of St. Ignatius High School and attended Santa Clara University from 1948 to 1951. In August 1951, he entered Sacred Heart Novitiate in Los Gatos.

A physically imposing man, Brother Korte was friendly and outgoing. People he met often knew exactly where he stood on any given subject. "Biz" served as chaplain of the Los Gatos Lion's Club and supported the San Jose Blind Center and its educational activities. He was a member of the chamber of commerce and portrayed Santa Claus in the Los Gatos Christmas parades for almost two decades.

In 1969, Brother Korte became the public face of the Novitiate Winery. During this time, he was also a founding member of both the Friends of the Winemakers and the Monterey Chapter of the Knights of the Vines. He began by selling altar wine to other parishes and, as the winery became more oriented towards commercial products, he promoted wine tastings and other related events. When the winery closed in January 1986, Brother Korte helped to finalize the inventory and lock the door. He remained at the Sacred Heart Jesuit Center for the remainder of his life. (Courtesy Santa Clara University Library Archives.)

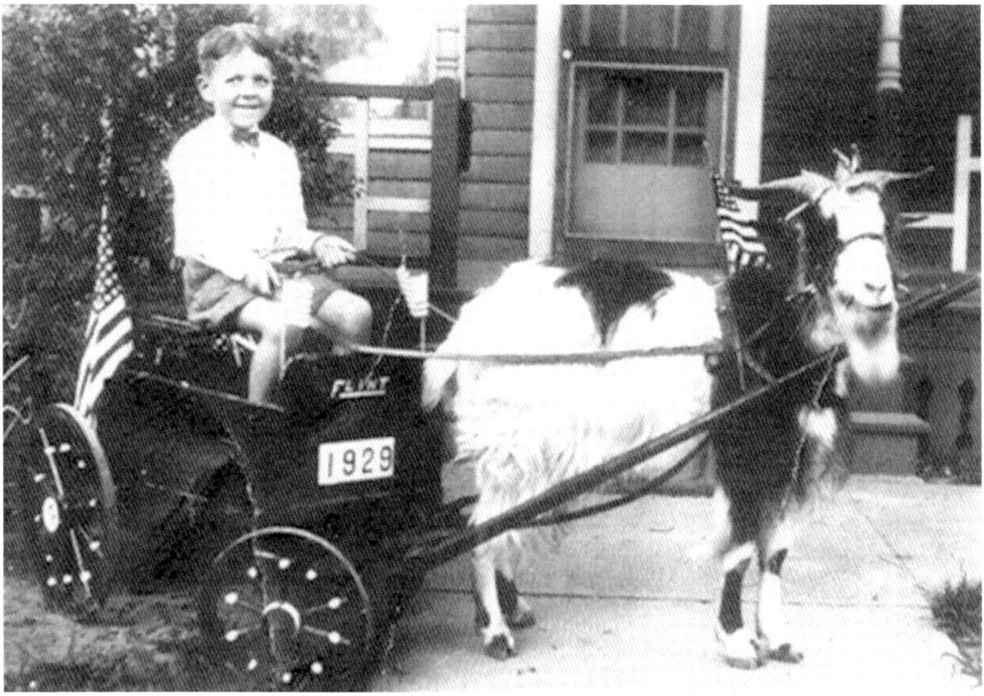

Max Wayne Walden (1924–2007)

Max Walden was born in Missouri and raised in Michigan. In 1964, he purchased the old grammar school on University Avenue in Los Gatos for $180,000 and began to fashion a unique shopping and cultural center. He was influenced by the Tivoli Gardens in Denmark and wanted to provide an environment where artists could imagine, create, and market their talents.

Walden worked with local architect Frank Laulainen to pursue his vision. Once work commenced, the project became known as "Walden's White Elephant." Officially named Old Town, the center opened in 1966 and was an overnight success. (Courtesy Shirley Davis.)

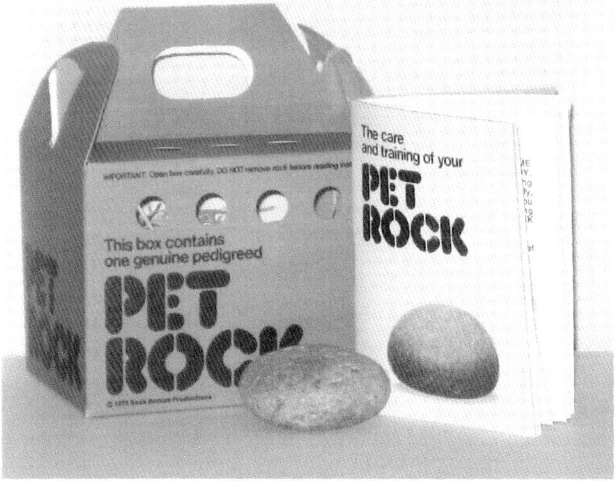

Gary Dahl

In 1975, Gary Dahl was hanging out in a bar with some friends who were complaining about their pets. So was born the idea of a "pet rock," which would require no feeding, no walking, no grooming, and no picking up after. The instruction manual was a work of art. It explained, for example, that it was easy to command your rock to "sit" or "stay" but more difficult to require it to "roll over" and "shake hands." Priced at $3.98 retail, complete with a cardboard carrier with a straw bed and breathing holes, the fad made Dahl a millionaire in a matter of months.

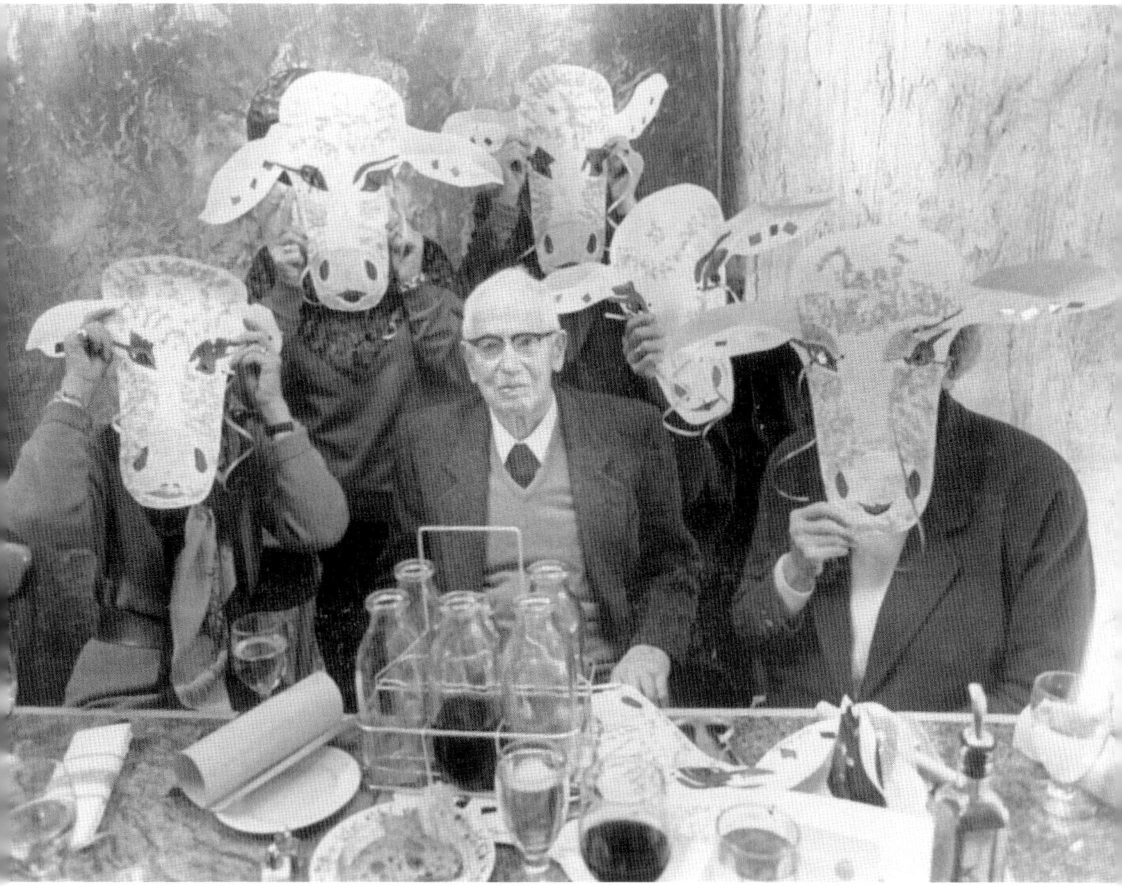

Kenneth Peake (1907–1999)

A gentle man who loved his cows, Kenneth Peake provided unpasteurized milk to the families of Los Gatos and the surrounding area for more than 67 years. Everyone in town knew the Claravale Dairy Farm's green 1969 Chevy delivery truck. During the height of Peake's operation, he had 92 cows on his 11.78 acres in unincorporated Los Gatos. Children from local schools were treated to trips to the farm to learn where their milk came from. Peake originally moved to his property in 1931 and ran the dairy there until financial difficulties and encroaching housing made it impossible to continue. He sold his herd in 1983 to an operation in the Central Valley. When he went to visit his cows and they heard his voice, they ran to him. He was heartbroken and proceeded to buy back six of them and reopen the dairy on a limited basis until 1997. A cow he named Heather was happily grazing outside his bedroom window on the day he died.

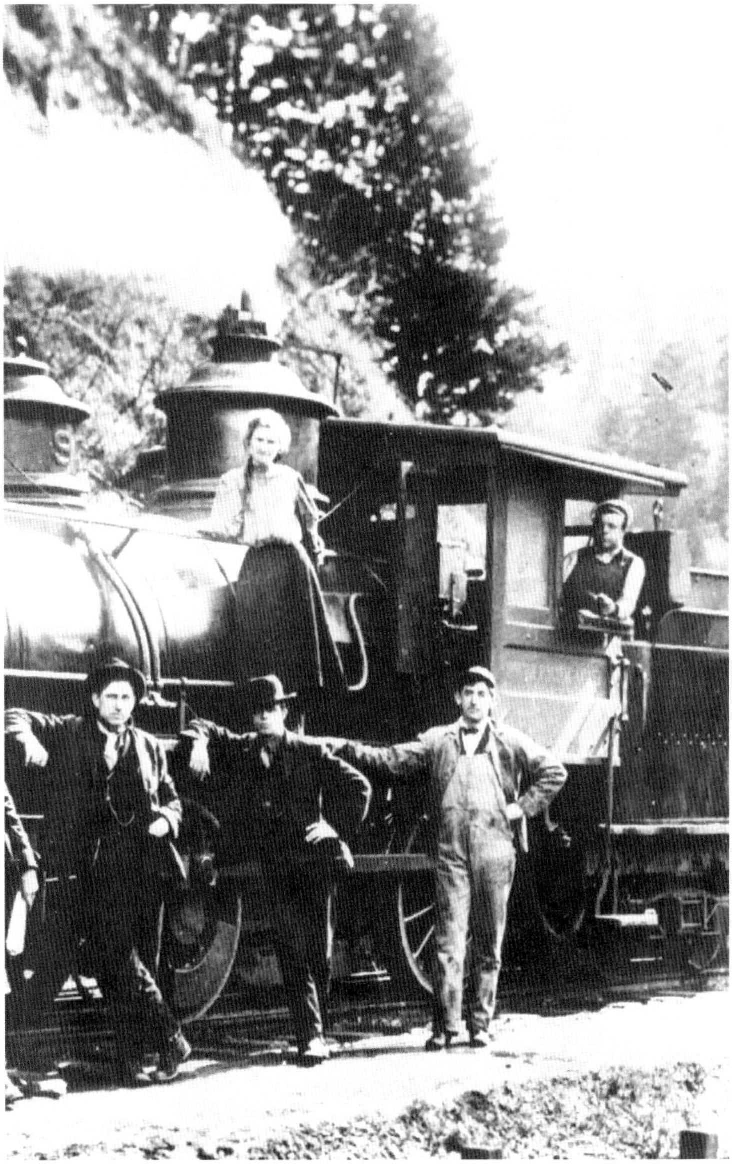

Alice Frances Matty (1878–1958)

Alice Matty grew up at Wrights Station in the mountains above Los Gatos. When the station agent was replaced in the early 1900s, young Alice was appointed to take over his position, becoming the first woman station agent hired by the Southern Pacific Railroad in California. Besides preparing waybills, Matty was the telegrapher and the ticket agent. Railroader Bruce MacGregor states that she would have handled the manual signal levers that threw the switches when trains needed to be taken off the main line and placed on sidings. And because Wrights was located in the bottom of a canyon, it had its share of flash floods, rock slides, and forest fires. It was up to Matty to telegraph for a repair crew to clear rocks from the track or shore up sagging roadbeds after heavy storms. As rail traffic increased so did the number of accidents, adding to the pressure of her job.

Matty never married but stayed at Wrights to look after her father, Anton Matty (1841–1922). In later years, she worked at the Bank of America in Los Gatos.

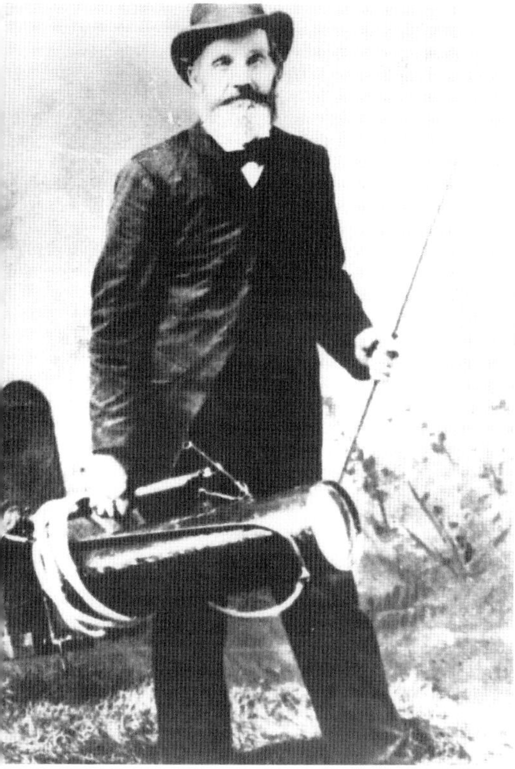

John Bean (1821–1909)

At the age of 62, John Bean was suffering from tuberculosis when he moved to Los Gatos. Like many before him, he felt the healthy climate would make life more comfortable. When his small orchard fell victim to the tree scale that plagued the area, he invented a high-pressure insecticide pump that was patented in 1904. The John Bean Manufacturing Company expanded to produce machinery for commercial and domestic use and merged with Anderson-Barngrover Manufacturing Company in 1928 to become Food Machinery Corporation (FMC).

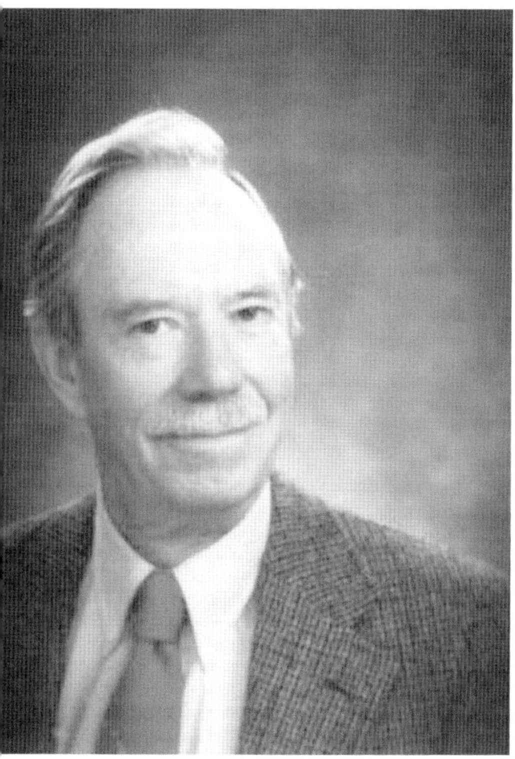

Charles Walton (1921–2011)

Born in England and educated in the United States, Walton became a US citizen while serving in the US Army Signal Corps in 1944. He moved to Los Gatos in 1960 after being transferred by IBM. In 1972, he left IBM to start his own company, Proximity Devices, where he received the first patent on his radio frequency identification devices (RFID) in 1983. Today, billions of RFID tags are used for inventory management in warehouses, libraries, and for many other applications. Walton was a peace advocate and supporter of local causes. Walton Lighthouse in Santa Cruz Harbor is named in honor of his father and brother.

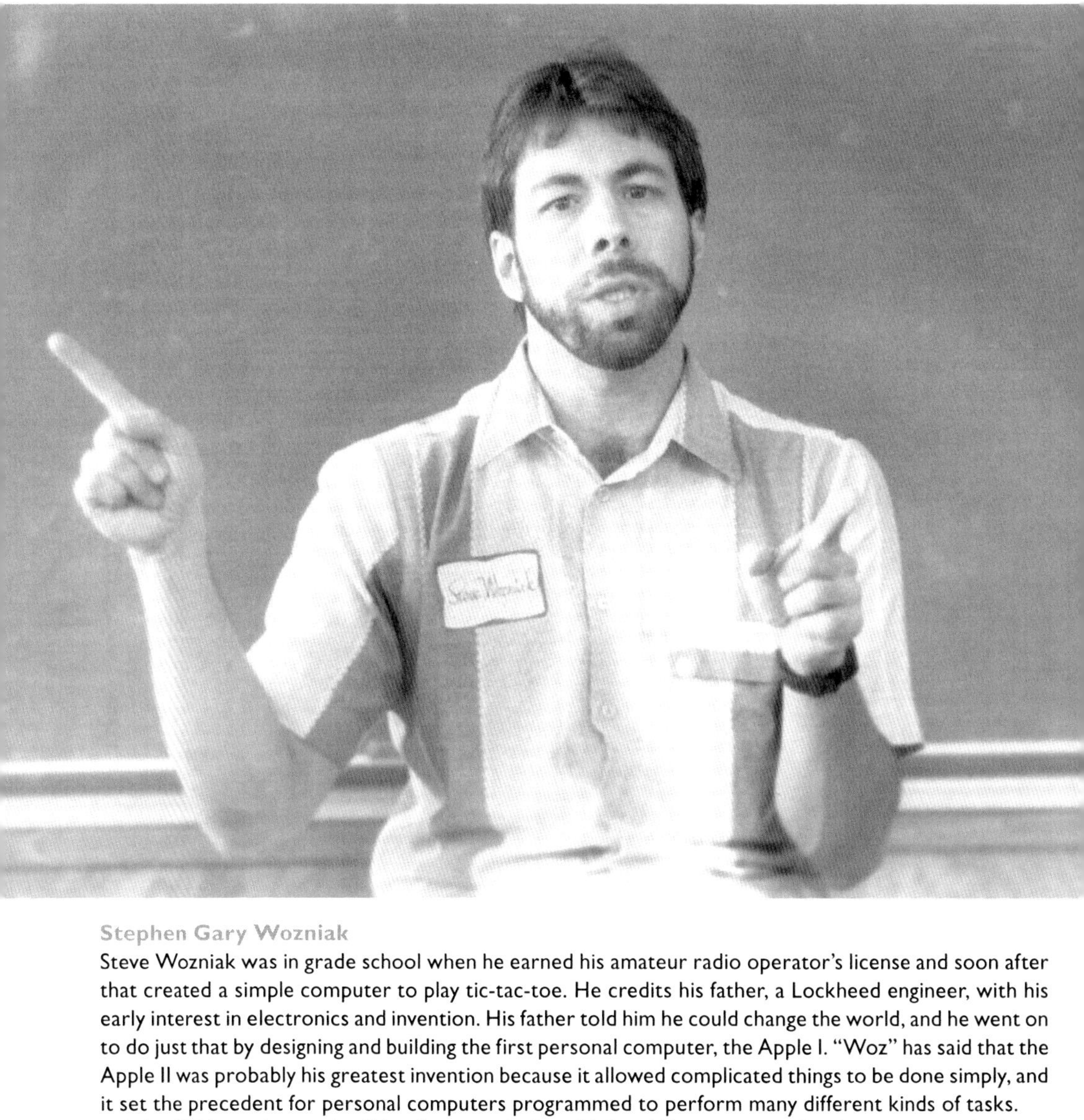

Stephen Gary Wozniak
Steve Wozniak was in grade school when he earned his amateur radio operator's license and soon after that created a simple computer to play tic-tac-toe. He credits his father, a Lockheed engineer, with his early interest in electronics and invention. His father told him he could change the world, and he went on to do just that by designing and building the first personal computer, the Apple I. "Woz" has said that the Apple II was probably his greatest invention because it allowed complicated things to be done simply, and it set the precedent for personal computers programmed to perform many different kinds of tasks.

In his 2006 autobiography, *iWoz: Computer Geek to Cult Icon*, Wozniak says, "If you're as lucky as I've been, then you'll get to live in a time when you're young just as a revolution is about to take off. Just like Henry Ford was there for the automotive industry, I was there to see and build the first personal computers." A longtime Los Gatos resident, he can sometimes be spotted riding his Segway around town.

CHAPTER THREE

The Catalysts

Commerce and community are two words with perhaps equal billing in the history of Los Gatos. Town father John Lyndon was a consummate businessman who built Hotel Lyndon to serve the community. Beyond being profitable and providing "strictly first class accommodations," it sat at the heart of the village and was the site of countless meetings, banquets, dances, and family celebrations. Some people made the hotel their home. Gertrude Atherton, writer of novels, boarded there in 1920. Society editor Caroline Earle Baggerly lived under the turret for a number of years.

The Los Gatans chronicled in this chapter tended to business and made things happen, even as they developed and valued strong community ties. That kind of local patriotism has endured for more than a century. George Green operated his drugstore on Main Street for 40 years but also found time to serve on the town council for 20 of those years. Sewell Brown built a three-story barn to process apricot pits but kept it open for community gatherings. Bank president Clarence Hamsher preserved historic photographs of the town taken in the 19th and early 20th centuries, images that otherwise would probably have been lost. Billy Jones used personal time, energy, and money to build the Wildcat Railroad, creating memories for thousands of children. Local businessman John Lochner has shepherded the town's fire bell for years, concerned with its preservation.

When the town put on its fabled pageants between 1919 and 1947, nearly everyone contributed to the effort. Leading roles were often taken by merchants. Service clubs, populated by people of enterprise, have consistently been an important part of Los Gatos culture. Community events such as the Los Gatos Children's and Holiday Parade, sponsored by the Lions Club and now in its fifth decade, are valued and enjoyed.

In modern times, architect Gary Schloh has worked tirelessly to maintain and update historic homes and protect the integrity of historic neighborhoods. The late builder Dave Flick was nearly a one-man redevelopment agency. He concentrated on quality work and saving what was valuable from the past, buildings that wore the patina of time.

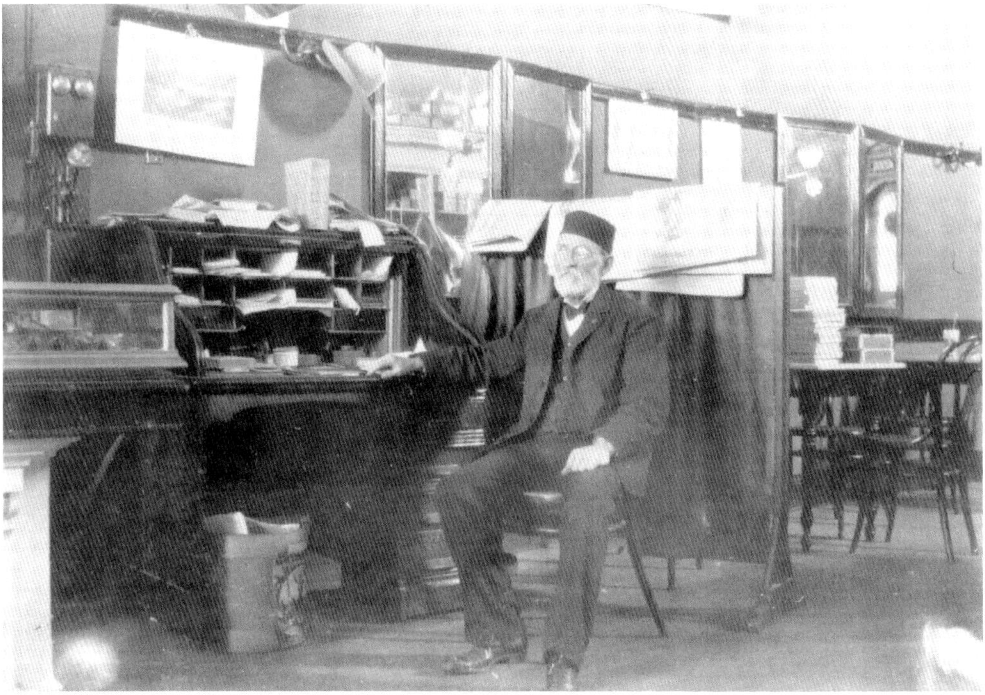

Henry Jewett Crall (1845–1926)

News of the firing on Fort Sumter by Confederate forces on April 12, 1861, traveled around the country by telegraph. Henry Crall "flew to arms" at the call for Union troops, among the first 100 men in Ohio to do so. He was 15 years old when he marched single file around the courthouse square in Bryan, Ohio, with his fellow recruits, and each received a small Bible from the women of the town. He served as a principal musician, first in the 14th and later in the 38th Ohio Infantries, a fact noted on his gravestone in Los Gatos Memorial Park. Four generations of Cralls operated a retail stationery business in Los Gatos from 1891 to 1981.

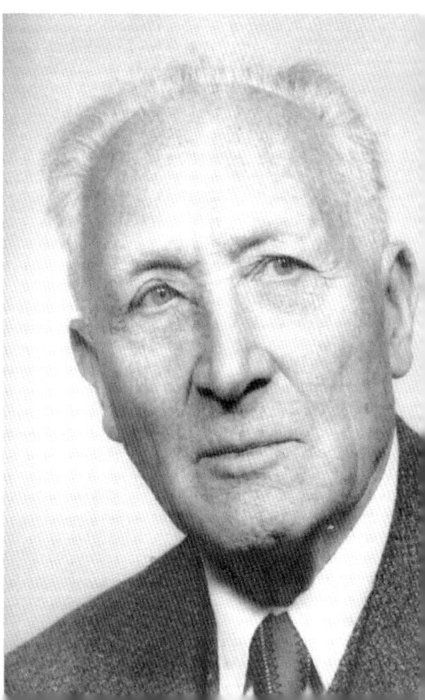

George A. Green (1873–1957)

Pharmacist George Green moved to Los Gatos in 1904 and purchased the Johns and Johnson Pharmacy in the Beckwith Block. In 1911, he moved his business to 11 East Main Street, next to the bridge, where Green's Pharmacy was in business for more than 40 years. Green served on the town council from 1922 to 1942 and became the first official mayor in 1927. Green and his wife, Edith Stahl Green, built a Craftsman-style cottage on Glen Ridge Avenue that still retains many of its original features.

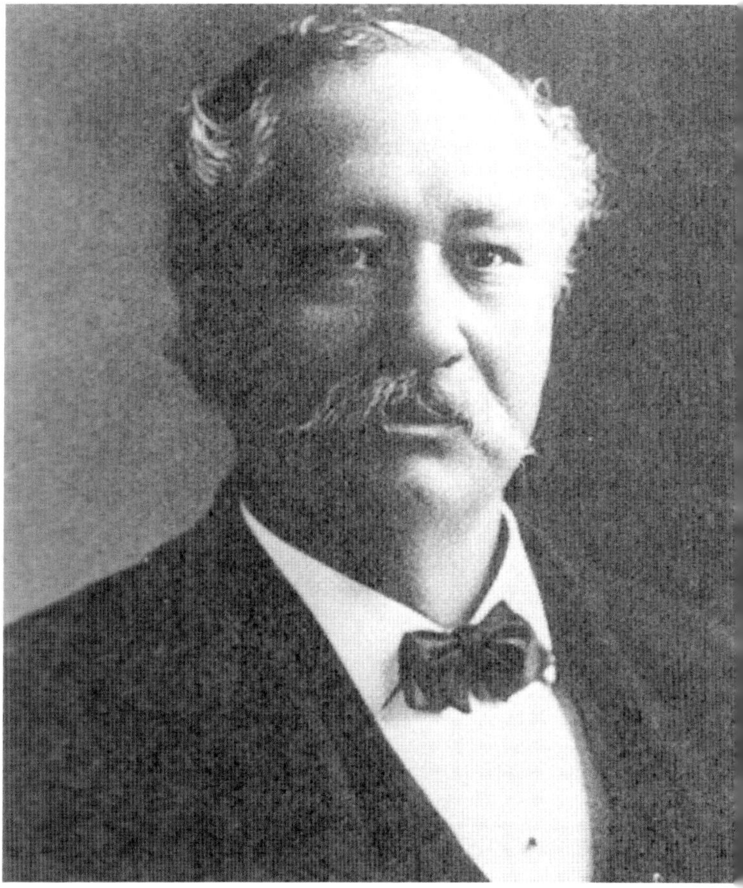

John Erickson (1844–1921)
Known as "the best wheelwright in Santa Clara County," John Erickson immigrated to the United States from Sweden in 1870. His wife, Wendla Nordstrom, arrived from Sweden in 1873. By about 1878, the family was settled in Los Gatos and John was building the Los Gatos Agricultural Works on East Main Street. When his building burned down on October 18, 1890, along with Seanor's Opera House next door, Erickson moved his business to 280 East Main Street, where he engaged in general blacksmithing, with horseshoeing as a specialty. He built carriages and fruit wagons to order. His son Andrew carried on the family business as Erickson's Garage, merging into the age of the automobile.

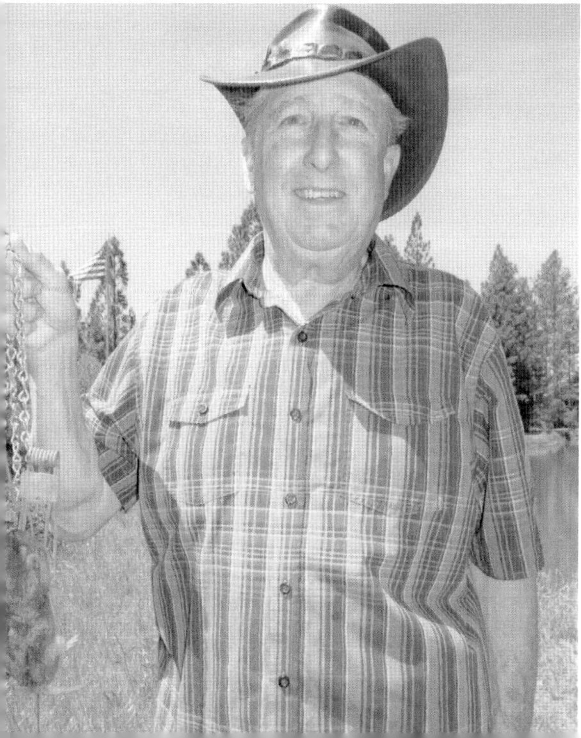

Ron Fink
In the summer of 1958, Ron Fink had just graduated from Los Gatos High School when he accepted part-time work at the Macabee Gopher Trap Company, the oldest business in town. He was appointed general manager of the company in 1963 and for more than 50 years has been the man in charge. Although manufacturing shifted to China in 2008, he continues to provide oversight and quality control for the product at 110 Loma Alta Avenue. His father, Lester Fink, was an apricot orchardist who had 33 acres off Shannon Road and also drove the school bus for many years. His mother, Alice Scott Fink, descended from Samuel and Mary Ann Scott, who came to the area in about 1890 and developed a notable peach orchard. (Courtesy Ron Fink.)

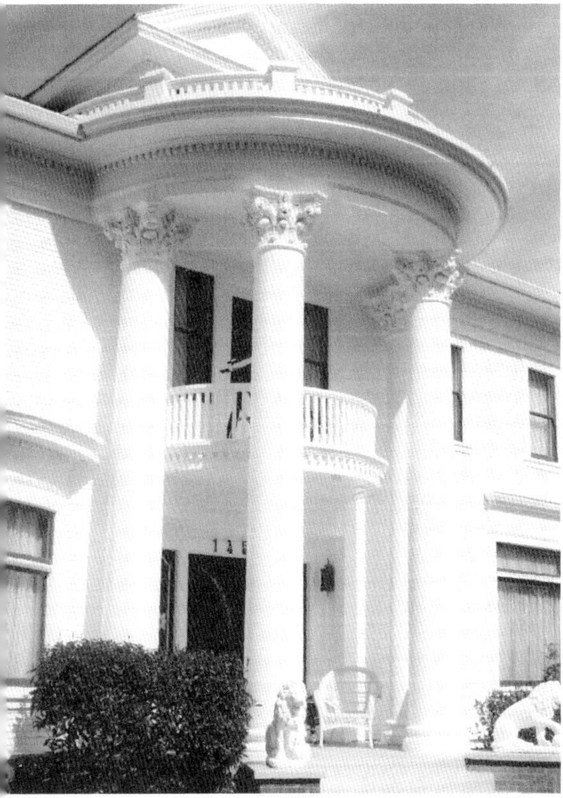

James Walter Crider (1889–1951)

J. Walter Crider purchased the Ford Opera House in 1916 and opened Crider's Department Store. He was known for supplying everything from Buster Brown shoes to elegant imported carpets from the Orient. The "Merchant Prince" of Los Gatos also had umbrellas for sale on the sidewalk hours before the rain arrived. Crider is remembered for his promotional stunts. He tossed turkeys off the store balcony at Thanksgiving and one year hired a dwarf to play Santa Claus. The store closed in 1957. Crider and his wife, Lydia Belle Curtner Crider (1888–1971), purchased this landmark 5,000-square-foot home at 145 Glen Ridge Avenue in 1920. Crider served as mayor from 1922 to 1924.

David Christian Crummey (1844–1928)

David Crummey enlisted in the 9th Battery, Michigan Light Artillery, in 1862 at age 18. He survived the Battle of Gettysburg and mustered out in 1865. He was married in 1874 to Addie Maria Bean (1854–1915), daughter of inventor John Bean. In 1888, the couple moved to Los Gatos, where Crummey became the first president of the Bean Spray Pump Company. His son, John D. Crummey, succeeded him and grew the enterprise. Stock in the company became available in 1928, and after acquisition of Anderson-Barngrover and Sprague-Sells, the business was renamed Food Machinery Corporation (FMC). David and Addie Crummey lived at 33 Glen Ridge Avenue.

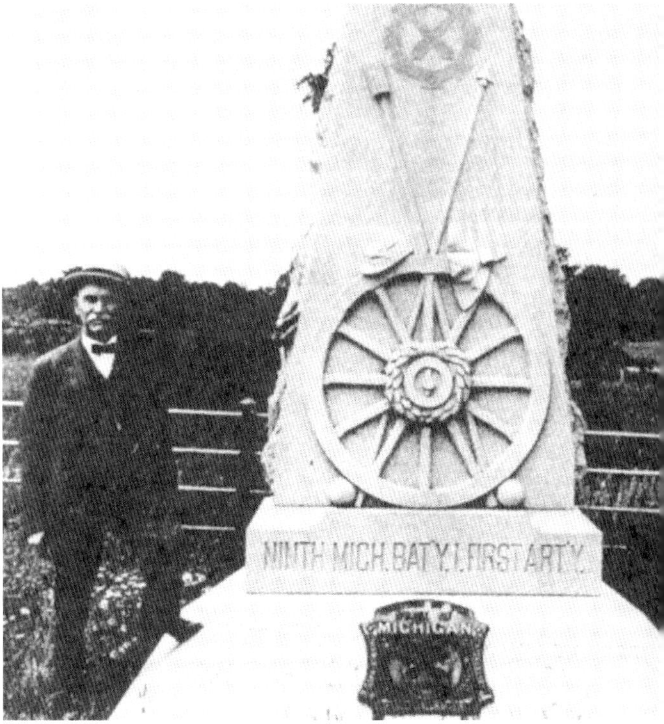

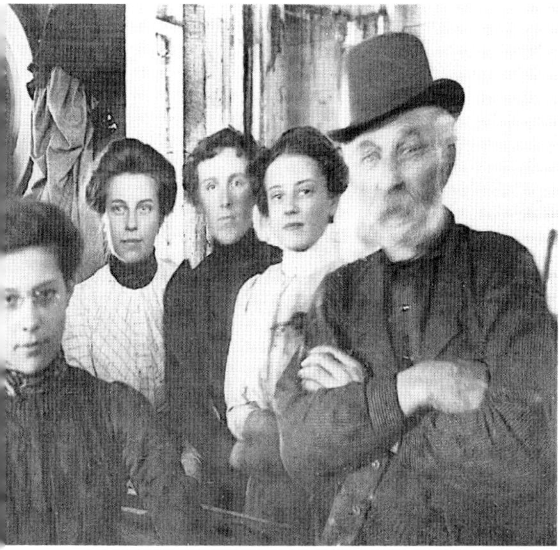

George Henry Hooke (1859–1949)
In 1894, George Hooke became president, principal stockholder, and manager of Los Gatos Canneries, where about one million cans of fruit were packed annually. He traveled to Europe to negotiate the sale of local fruit there and was instrumental in the foundation of the Los Gatos Fruit Growers Union. Hooke and his wife, Adelia Gibbs Hooke (1858–1943), often summered in Los Gatos but wintered in San Francisco, where he sang with and conducted the choir at Grace Cathedral. He opposed regulation of work hours for women and children, fearing some of the fruit crop would then go to waste. "Women consider it a holiday when they go to work in the canneries during the fruit season," he said.

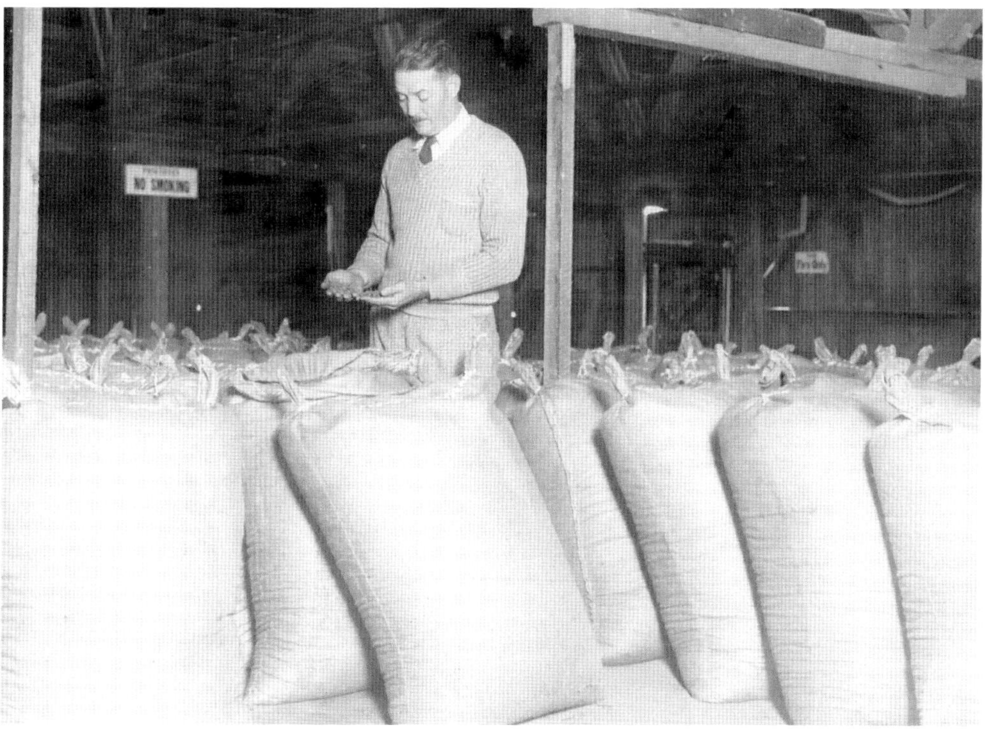

Sewell Solon Brown (1891–1952)
In the first half of the 20th century, California produced about 10,000 tons of apricot pits annually. The California Prune and Apricot Growers Association pioneered a process for salvaging precious oils from the pits, and that business was taken over by Sewell S. Brown and a partner in 1925. The apricot pit processing plant, located near Vasona Junction, was housed in a three-story, red-painted shed built by Brown in 1902. Brown was a community-minded man who kept the facility open for community gatherings. He founded Boy Scout Troop 39 and was instrumental in building a youth center in 1941. In 1916, Brown married Sue Rundle Bell, daughter of Judge R.R. Bell. The "pit works" burned to the ground in 1955. (Courtesy Jim Zetterquist.)

James A. Bacigalupi (1882–1950)

The son of Italian immigrants, James A. Bacigalupi was a brilliant young lawyer when he began his close association with A.P. Giannini and worked to build a bank for people who had never used such an institution before. The establishment of the Bank of Italy, later the Bank of America, and the Transamerica Corporation were landmark accomplishments. He married Mary Ellen Jones in 1909 and was the father of Louise, James Jr., Jeanne, and Mary Anne. During his years of residence in Los Gatos, he was active in civic affairs and a member of the La Rinconada Golf Club. (Courtesy Farwell family.)

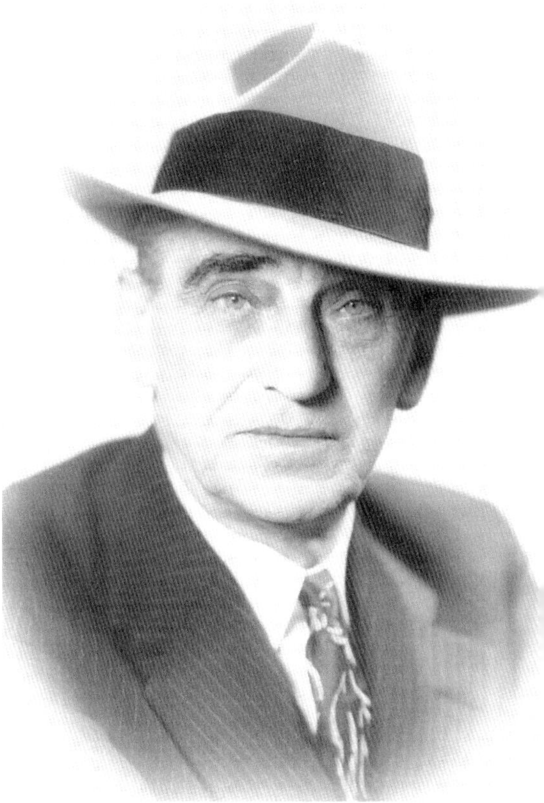

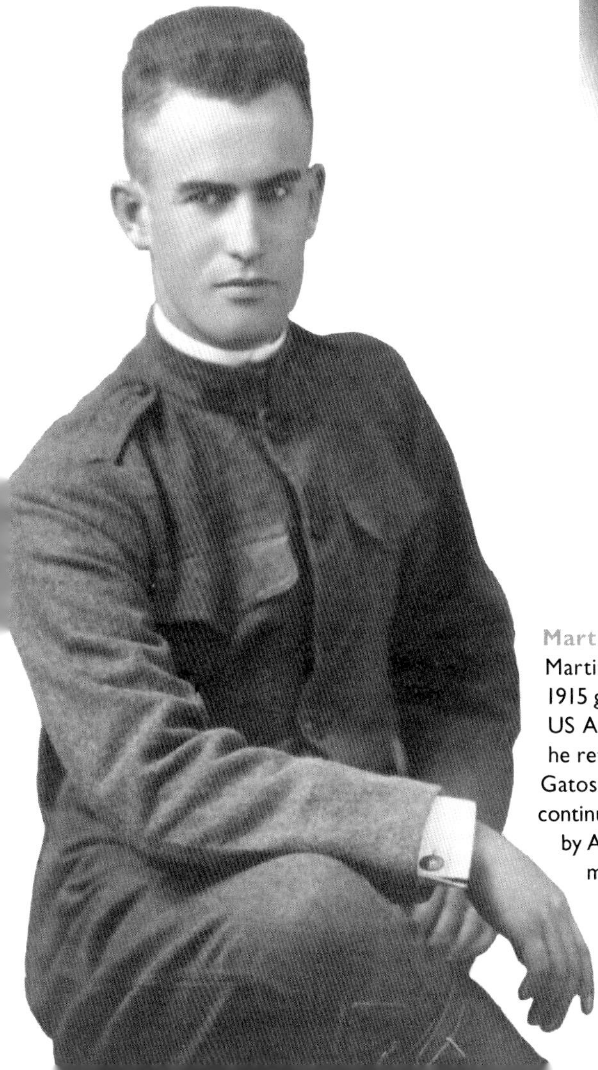

Martin Lyons LeFevre (1895–1954)

Martin LeFevre was the son of a Los Gatos shoemaker. A 1915 graduate of Los Gatos High School, he served in the US Army during World War I. Following the Armistice, he returned home and went to work for the Bank of Los Gatos. When it was acquired by the Bank of America, he continued with that organization, and in 1940, he was chosen by A.P. Giannini to manage the Los Gatos office. LeFevre married Patience Whitehouse Hostetter (1900–1997) in 1927. She played the lead role of Carmencita Riz in the 1924 Los Gatos pageant, *El Gato de Los Gatos*. (Courtesy Jan LeFevre.)

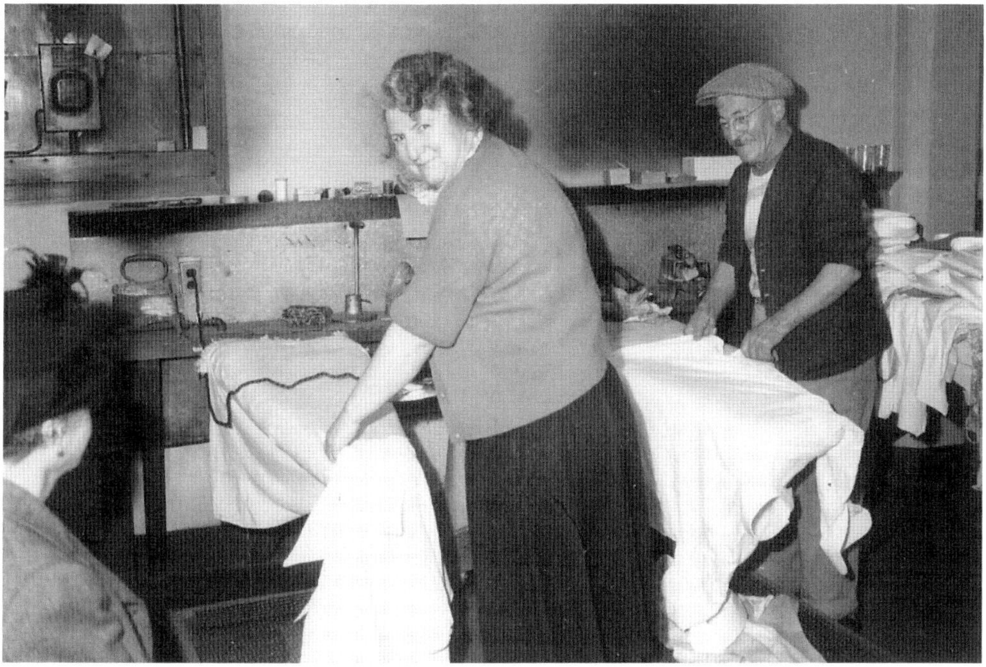

Jacques (1880–1961) and Therese Libante (1905–1996)
Natives of France, Jacques and Therese Libante immigrated to this country in 1904 and 1921, respectively. They were married in San Francisco, and after their son Andre developed asthma, they moved to Los Gatos because of its famed favorable climate. The Libantes operated a laundry on Johnson Avenue for a few months before they moved into the stone house at 15 University Avenue in 1930. They built the Art Deco building next door at 11 University Avenue in 1934 to house their Gem City French Laundry, which specialized in hand laundering fine fabrics and special garments. Jacques had a custom starch formula for each of his clients. (Courtesy Janet Libante Goodman.)

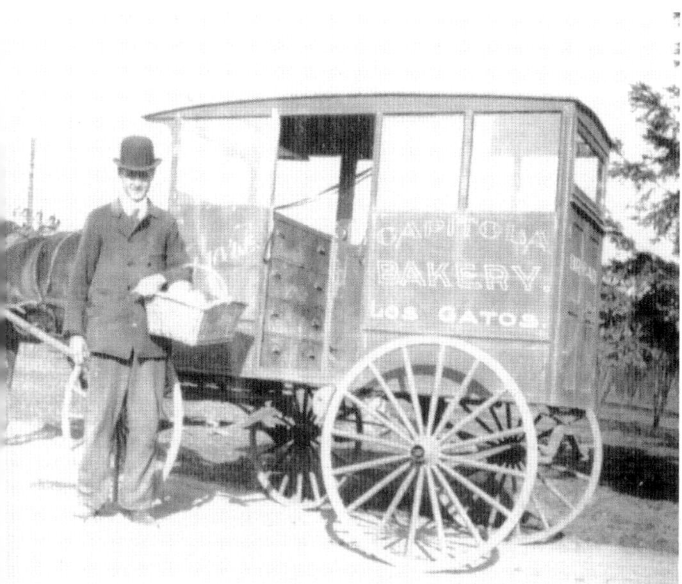

William J. (1872–1920) and Susie Walker Kyle (1875–1951)
William Kyle left Ireland in 1891 at age 19 and settled in Capitola, where he opened a bakery. Susie came to California by covered wagon in 1881. The couple married in 1898 and moved in 1900 to Los Gatos, where they opened Kyle's Capitola Bakery at 5 North Santa Cruz Avenue. The business offered home delivery of pies, doughnuts, and bread as far away as Quito Road. Pictured is employee Horace Ribble with the bakery wagon. (Courtesy Elayne Shore Shuman.)

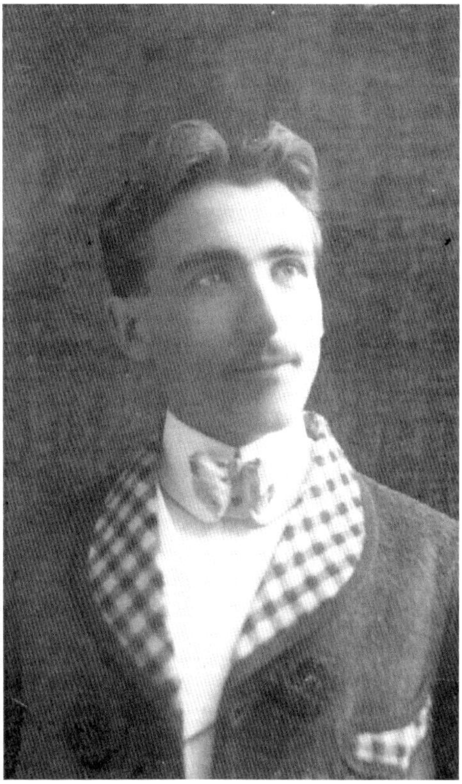

Arthur Wellington Templeman (1877–1954)

Born in Nova Scotia, Arthur Templeman moved to Los Gatos in 1902 to work in his uncle's business, A.W. Bogart Hardware. He bought the enterprise in 1916 upon the death of Bogart, and in 1926, he constructed a new home for Templeman Hardware at 24 North Santa Cruz Avenue, complete with the first freight elevator in town. Templeman married suffragist Laura Mae Hardwick (1881–1959) in 1904. Their only child, Mima Eulalia Templeman, died in 2009 at age 100. After nearly 53 years in the hardware business in Los Gatos, Templeman died when his automobile ran off Almaden Road and crashed into a tree. (Courtesy Mima Templeman Hardwicke.)

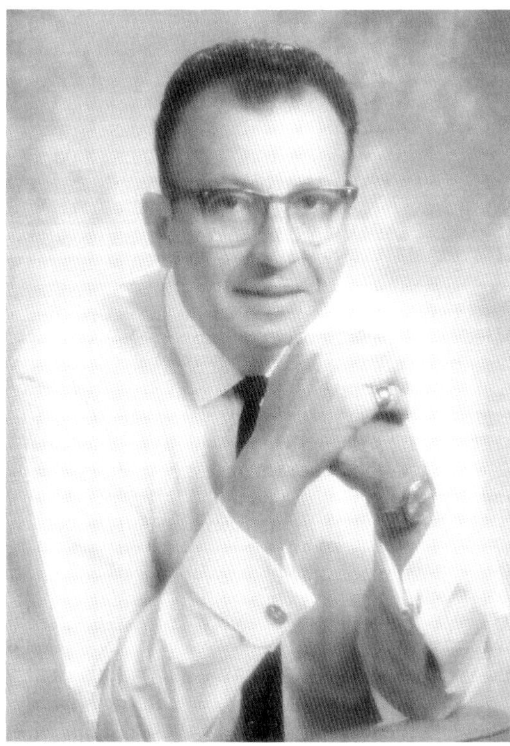

Frank Lazaneo (1928–2003)

Born of Croatian parents in San Francisco, Frank Lazaneo grew up in Los Gatos. He worked as a bag boy at the Los Gatos Market in his teens and at age 29 purchased the business. From 1957 to 1982, he operated his grocery store on Santa Cruz Avenue in a neighborly fashion, calling his customers by name. He was active in the community and happened to chair the annual Christmas parade committee the only year the event has ever been rained out. His friends called it "the year it rained on Frank's parade." (Courtesy Patty Hannegan.)

Francis Hepburn McCullagh (1853–1938)

Not long after his June 10, 1880, wedding to Mary Elizabeth Evans in Pennsylvania, Frank McCullagh and his bride came to Los Gatos. Money from a shipping business enabled him to buy 166 acres, which included two Victorian houses. Over the next few years, McCullagh sold off most of the property for development. The couple returned to Philadelphia in 1887 but shortly retraced their steps. They bought back 10 acres of the original property and in 1901 contracted with noted architect Willis Polk to remake the original houses into one large home. The result was La Estancia, where McCullagh is pictured in front of the gates of the estate.

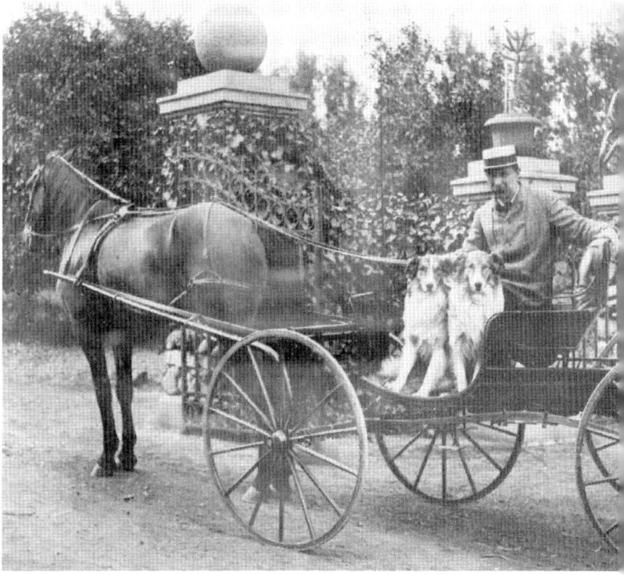

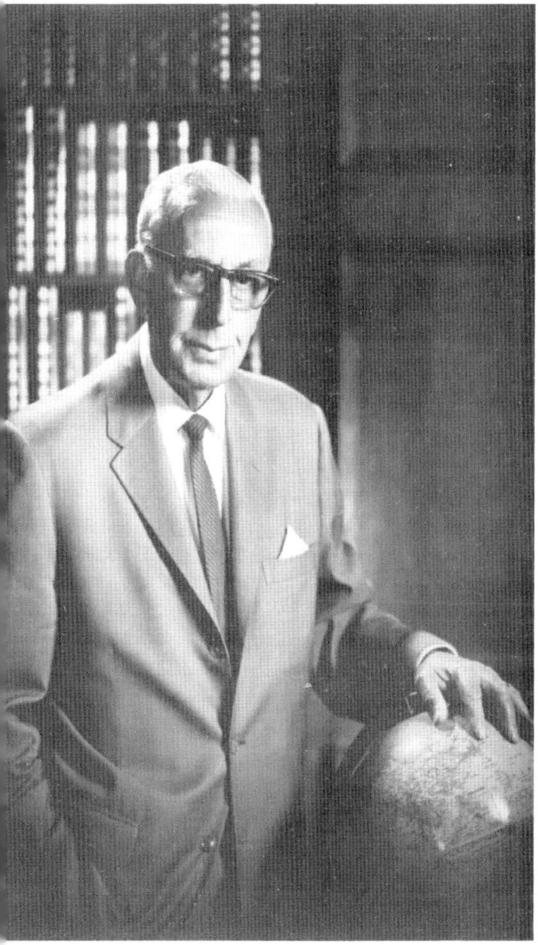

John Lincoln (1897–1972)

"Simply the Best—Since 1925." That is the slogan of the Lincoln Shoe Polish Company, founded by Los Gatan John Lincoln. He spent some years on the road selling rubber heels before he developed the formula for his high-gloss polish, so popular that at one time it was standard issue for US Marines. For many years, Lincoln traveled daily by train to San Francisco with other members of the Los Gatos Commuter Club. The company is now based in Sunnyvale. Lincoln's other accomplishments included his tenure as mayor from 1962 to 1966, during which time the old Southern Pacific Railroad right-of-way was converted to much-needed parking for local businesses and Vasona Park opened.

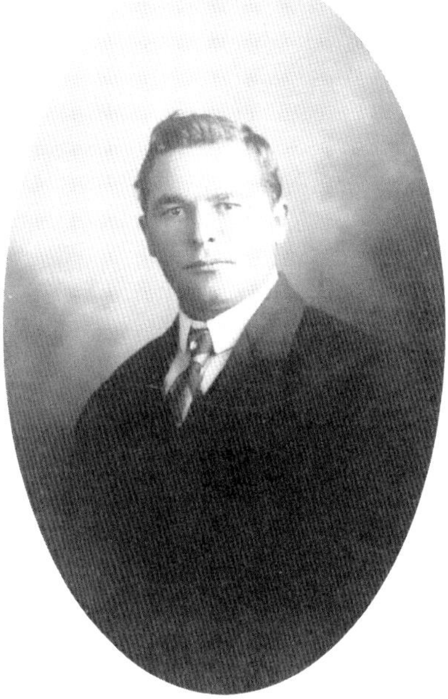

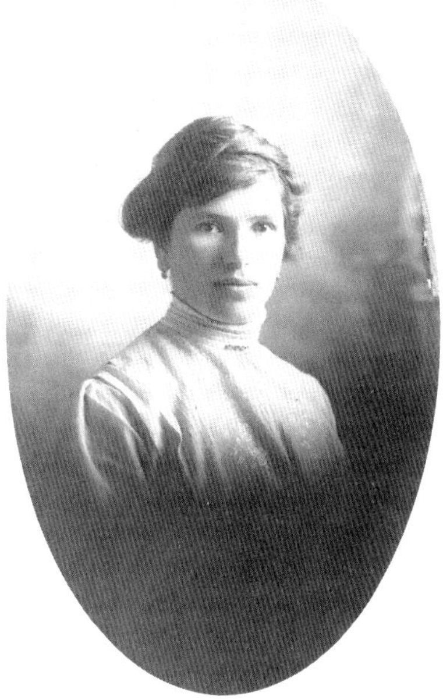

Giovanni (1877–1929) and Elizabetta Contardo Della Vedova (1880–1973)
John and Elizabeth Vedova immigrated to America from their native Tolmezzo, Italy, in 1907. They located in 1911 in Los Gatos, where John was a successful cement contractor. He constructed numerous sidewalks, including those that crossed the Main Street Bridge, and did the concrete work on many Los Gatos homes. His bungalow at 56 Villa Avenue was built around 1920. That same year, the Vedovas sent tickets to three young relatives in Italy, enabling them to come to the United States and escape the hardships after World War I. John Vedova passed away in 1929 after the shock of the stock market crash, which contributed to his demise. The Vedova home was demolished in 2011 to make room for the new library. (Courtesy Contardo, Pillinini, and Picone families.)

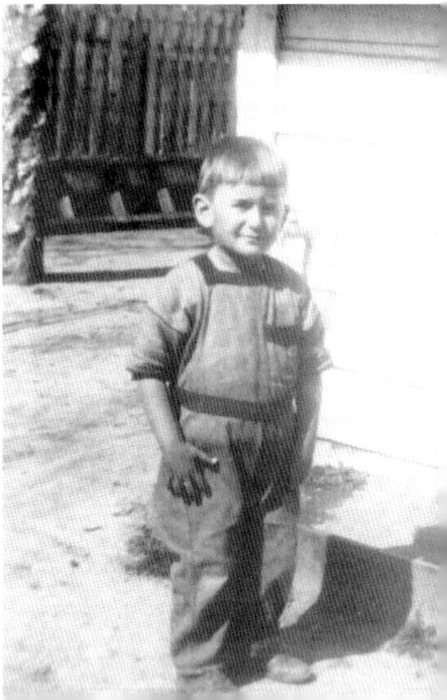

Amiel Zanardi (1918–2014)
"Aze" Zanardi is pictured here around 1923 at his home on University Avenue. His story is one that encompasses the possibilities of life in America. His parents, Giuseppe and Louisa, emigrated from northern Italy in 1911 and 1917, respectively. Giuseppe, or "Joe," quickly grasped the opportunity to partner in a fledging enterprise, the Los Gatos Scavenger Company. By age 22, Aze was in charge, and with hard work, perseverance, and good business sense, he built the company and secured a good life for his family. Aze married Antoinette Bortolussi (1921–2014) in 1940, and the couple had two sons, Jim and Joe. (Courtesy Amiel Zanardi.)

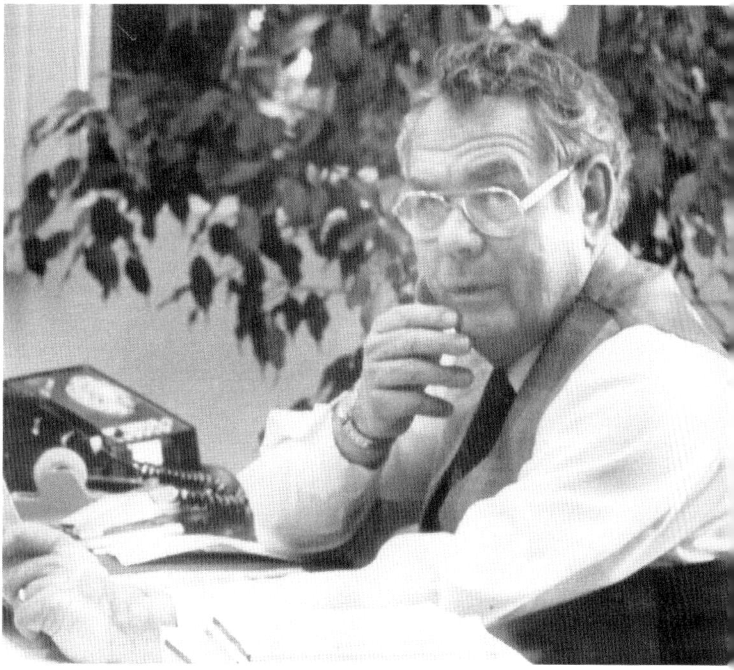

John Panighetti (1928–2003)
The Panighetti family immigrated to California from Italy in 1885. Grandfather Carlo Panighetti purchased 80 acres in the Santa Cruz Mountains and planted fruit trees. "Jack" Panighetti was born at home on Santa Cruz Avenue and went to work for the post office as a carrier at age 16. Promoted to postmaster in 1966, his career spanned 41 years. Panighetti was active in many town organizations and Scouting. He recalled one rainy day opening a letter box and discovering a small boy staying dry while eating his lunch. (Courtesy Peggy Panighetti.)

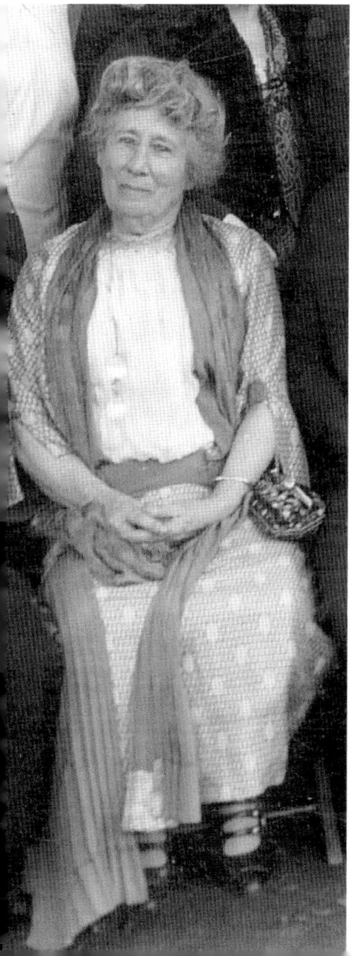

Emily Lucy Cohen (1857–1935)
Emily Cohen was born in New York City to English immigrant parents who arrived in 1856. Her father's requirement to register for the draft in 1863 at the height of the Civil War and the resulting violent draft riots may have been the impetus for the family's move to California. Emily arrived in Los Gatos before 1900. She was a charter member of the History Club of Los Gatos, served on the library board from 1905 to 1935, and created costumes for the 1919 town pageant. During World War I, she headed local Red Cross efforts to provide warm clothing for overseas soldiers. Emily married for the first time in 1929, at age 73, to composer Grenville Pettis (1871–1935). She was an enthusiastic gardener known for her tuberous begonias.

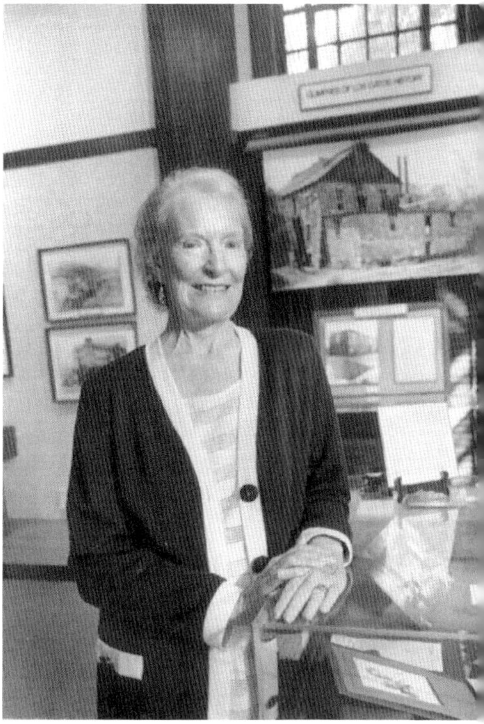

Mardi Durham Gualtieri Bennett Brick

Born in Reno, Nevada, Mardi came to Los Gatos in 1952 with her physician husband, who started a medical practice in town. The couple built a home at 58 Alpine Avenue after the house owned by John Whisenant burned down. She was a tireless volunteer and was instrumental in saving Forbes Mill from demolition in the 1970s. The first survey made of Victorian houses in Los Gatos was done in 1971, and in the summer of 1975, Mardi started the Bellringer Project. She served on the town council from 1976 to 1980 and as mayor in 1978. Author of *Images of Long Ago*, she also composed a song titled "To Los Gatos."

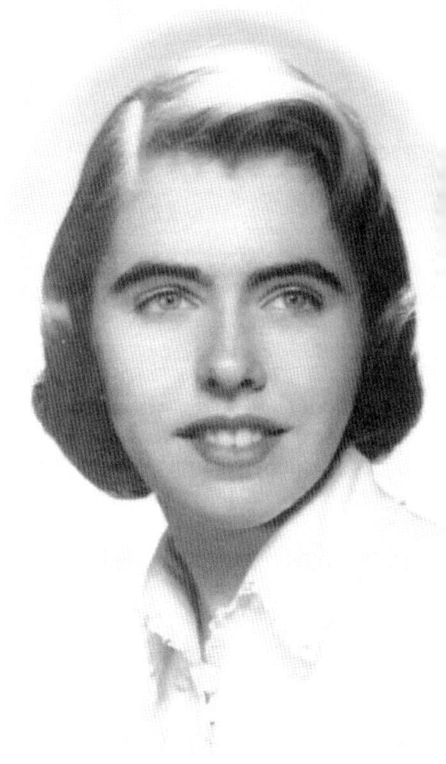

Patricia Ann Dunning (1941–2010)

When she was 16 years old, Pat Dunning talked her way into Cornell University and graduated with a degree in chemistry and math. She moved to California and commenced a 30-year career with IBM. Later, she earned a master's degree in anthropology and taught at San Jose State University. She organized the first archeological dig at Forbes Mill, which was staffed by her students. A longtime volunteer for the Museums of Los Gatos, Dunning cochaired the Historic Homes Tour, completing necessary research on the houses and the people who inhabited them.

70

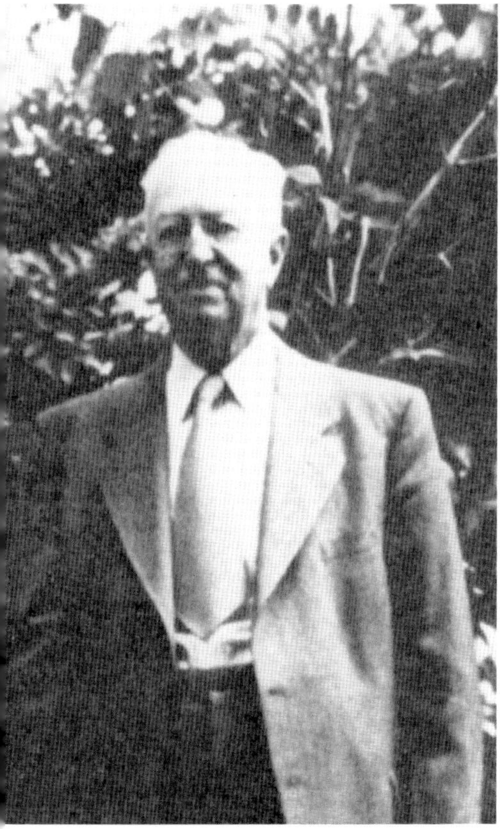

Clarence Ford Hamsher (1876–1950)

C.F. Hamsher was elected president of the First National Bank in 1927, but he was also an avid local historian with an intense interest in preserving the past. He wrote and collected history articles, and, perhaps most importantly, made copies of approximately 100 original historic Los Gatos photographs taken between the late 1860s and 1920. He collected the photographs from town pioneers, had them framed, and hung them on the walls of the bank building. When the bank was sold in 1955, the photographs were donated to the library, where the Hamsher Collection forms the core of the town's historical memory. The Hamsher family lived at 17940 Saratoga Road for about 30 years.

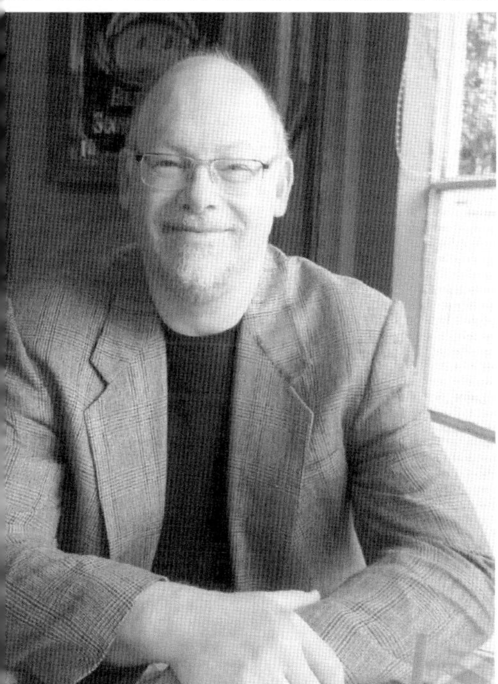

Alastair Dallas

Alastair Dallas is an information designer and architect whose experience includes six years at Walt Disney Imagineering. Additionally, he has worked for Lotus, Netscape, and a host of startups. He and his wife, Peggy, also an architect, have lived in Los Gatos since 1990. Dallas cares deeply for his community, and in 1999, he published *Los Gatos Observed*, a beautifully executed book chronicling the eclectic architecture and intriguing history of the town. In 2006, he pioneered a popular online news source called the *Los Gatos Observer*, and in 2011, he founded the blog *All Things Los Gatos*. (Courtesy Peggy Dallas.)

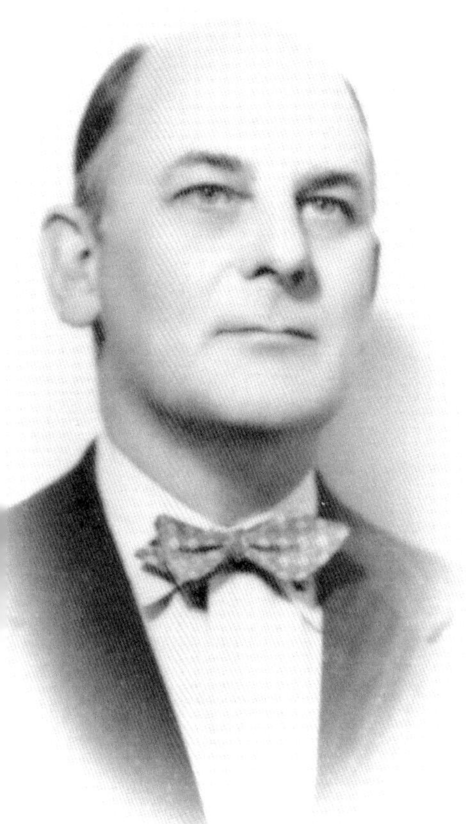

Frederic Horner Johnson (1892–1976)

Fred Johnson prospered first as an engineer and then as a securities broker before the Great Depression of the 1930s nearly wiped him out. In 1938, at age 46, he moved to Los Gatos with his wife and three children. The family purchased the former home of pioneering banker James A. Case at Massol and Saratoga Avenues, where a sizeable barn and the surrounding four acres of orchards and gardens allowed Johnson to indulge his pastime of fermenting mellow vinegars from local wines. He also grew herbs and gathered spices from around the world. In 1941, he founded the Spice Islands Company.

E. Gary Schloh

Many of the beautiful homes in Los Gatos have been touched by the magic of architect Gary Schloh. His work covers the whole spectrum, from complete tear-downs and building new from the ground up to updating historic homes for modern living. In his 35 years in Los Gatos, he has built or restored more than 350 homes, always cognizant of maintaining the character and history of the town's neighborhoods. Schloh came to Los Gatos in 1974 to work for architect Frank Laulainen, who designed Old Town. A longtime member of the parks commission and Lions Club, Schloh was a cofounder of the beautification committee. His legacy will be the beautification of the town.

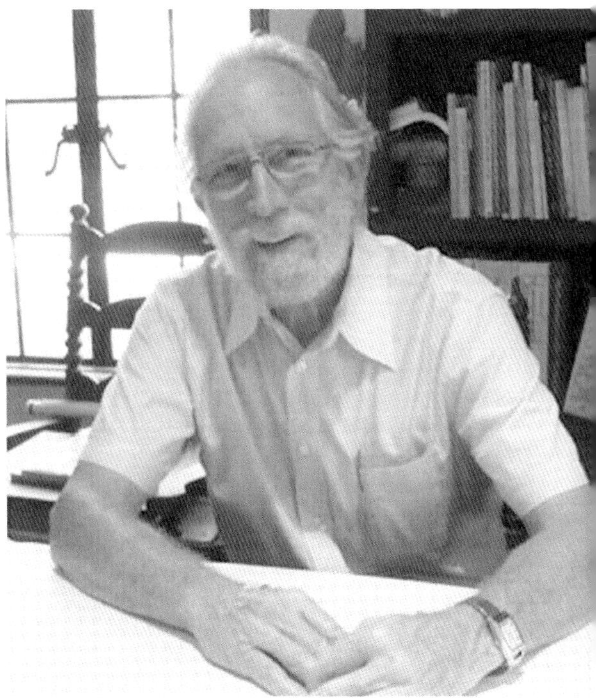

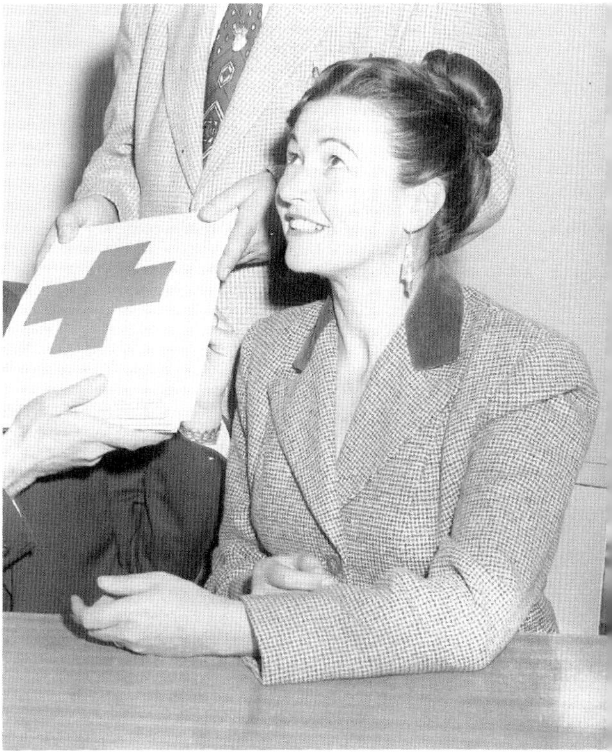

Clelles Rackham Ness (1911–1959)

Clelles Ness, called "Keddie," was born in Ogden, Utah. After earning her registered nurse certification and completing graduate work, Clelles moved to San Jose to work in the pediatric ward at Santa Clara County Hospital. There she met, and married, Ansten Ness, an intern at the hospital. During World War II, Dr. Ness served as an Army physician. Clelles and her family resided all over the country. At each base, Clelles became involved with local organizations, and at the war's end, in 1945, she continued this pattern when the family moved to Los Gatos. In 1947, she received a citizen of the year award for her contributions to town life. Childhood rheumatic fever contributed to her death at age 48. The Children's Garden at the new library is named in her honor.

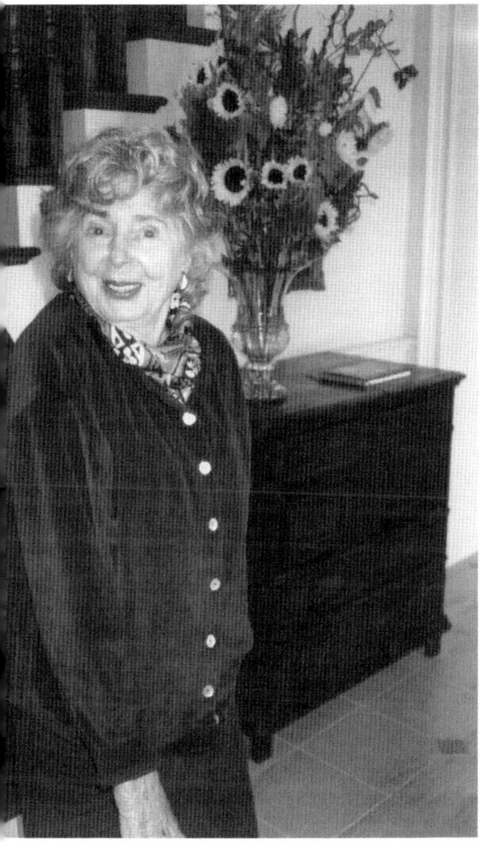

Susan Elizabeth McClendon (1914–2002)

"Betty" McClendon spent more than half a century teaching the youth of Los Gatos the graces of ballroom dancing and social deportment. Born in Lompoc, California, Betty's family settled in Los Gatos early in her life. She attended Los Gatos schools and left only once, for 10 years, to teach in New York at the Fred Astaire and Arthur Murray dance studios. "Miss Manners" held classes in various venues around town, including the Los Gatos History Club, Daves Avenue School, and the Saratoga Foothill Club. She counted among her students many prominent citizens, including a future high school principal, a town councilman, and a journalist. (Courtesy Joanne Rogers.)

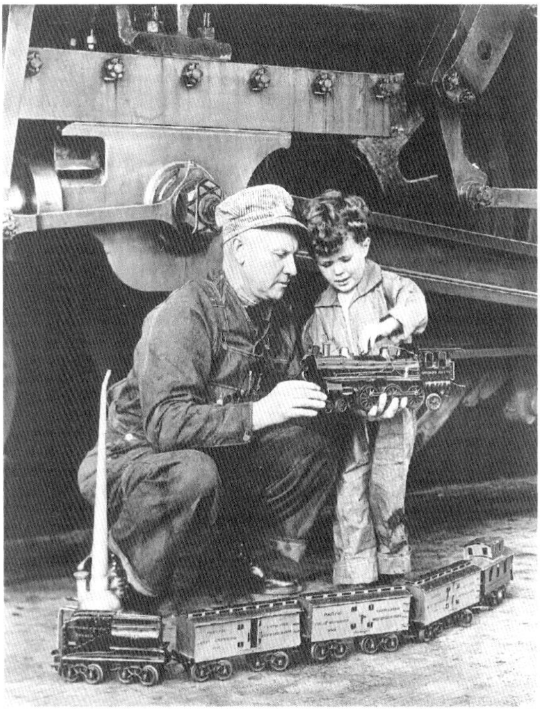

William Jones (1884–1968)

In Los Gatos, the name "Billy Jones" is synonymous with railroading. Jones went to work at age 13 as an engine wiper at the South Pacific Coast Railroad's roundhouse in Ben Lomond, his hometown. He moved quickly through the ranks and had a remarkable career before his retirement in 1949. But that was not the end of the line for Jones. He assembled a one-third-scale steam railroad on his Daves Avenue ranch. He called it the Wildcat Railroad, and it carried countless delighted children around his orchard. After Jones's death, the Wildcat was relocated to the Vasona–Oak Meadow Park complex, where it operates today.

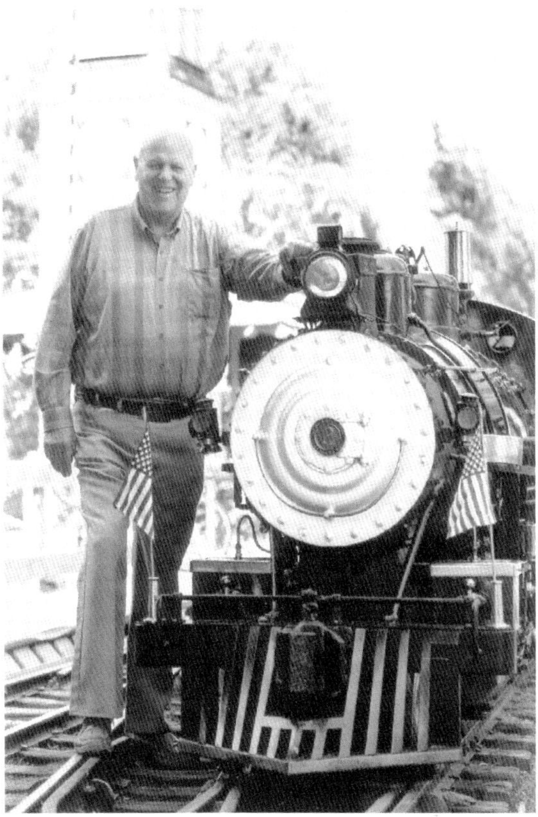

William E. Mason (1912–1990)

Bill Mason was an electrical contractor who had a love of railroads. After the death of Billy Jones in 1968, Mason became president of a nonprofit organization founded to relocate and operate the Wildcat Railroad. The group raised money to purchase the railroad from the Jones estate and transplant it to a corner of Oak Meadow Park and a portion of Vasona Park, where, since 1970, it has attracted more than a million visitors.
In 1980, the Billy Jones Wildcat Railroad Corporation purchased a historic carousel manufactured for use at the 1915 Panama-Pacific Exposition and shipped around the Horn from England. After 10 years of restoration, the ride opened to the public. It is located near the train station and named the William E. "Bill" Mason Carousel.

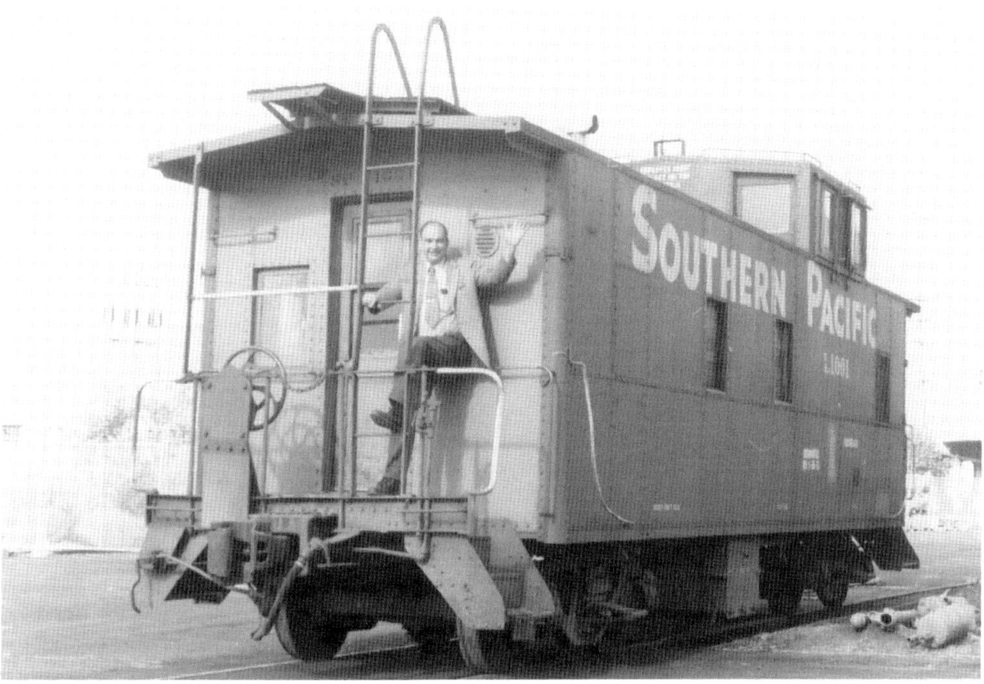

Albert B. Smith (1921–1993)
In 1962, Al Smith became president of Orchard Supply Hardware, which his father, Stanley Smith, helped establish as a farmers' cooperative in 1931. Smith taught agriculture classes and served on the town council from 1974 to 1978, including one year as mayor. He had a lifelong zest for railroading, nurtured by his childhood on a ranch at Vasona Junction, where he heard the whistles of passing steam locomotives. As a young man, he went to work for the Southern Pacific Railroad, but that career came to an abrupt halt when, at age 21, while walking along the tops of moving railroad cars, he fell onto the tracks and his left leg was severed below the knee. He used his belt as a tourniquet, training he had learned as a Boy Scout. (Courtesy Chuck Bergtold.)

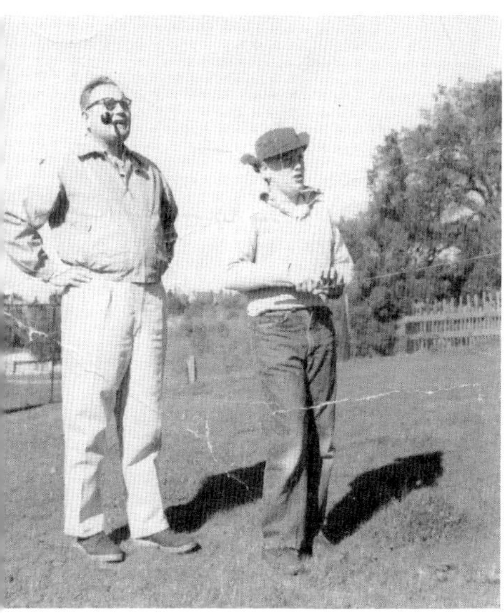

C. Lyman Bergtold (1914–1978)
Lyman Bergtold saved a piece of Los Gatos history. His parents, Charles H. Bergtold (1870–1926) and Louise Corkill Bergtold (1884–1967) came to Los Gatos around 1922 and settled on an idyllic acreage they named Placer Oaks Ranch. They operated a dairy on their land, which overlooked Los Gatos Creek. In 1916, when Forbes Mill was torn down, their neighbor Dr. Frank Knowles had one of the original grinding stones hauled to his ranch by mules, and it was cemented into the landing of his back step. When the stone was eventually chiseled out, Bergtold moved it to his land. In 2005, the Bergtold family donated the stone to the Los Gatos History Museum. Bergtold is seen here on the ranch with his son Chuck, who is flying a kite. (Courtesy Chuck Bergtold.)

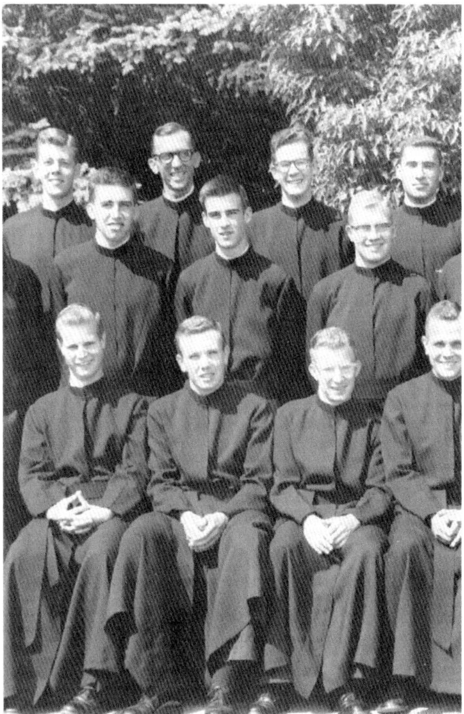

Edmund G. Brown Jr.

Gov. Jerry Brown, the "philosopher prince" of California politics, spent 3.5 years studying for the priesthood at the Jesuits' Sacred Heart Novitiate on the hills south of town. He is pictured here as a first-year novice in 1956, standing at center in the middle row. The son of California's popular 32nd governor, Pat Brown, who served from 1959 to 1967, Jerry Brown changed his mind about the priesthood and left Los Gatos. He subsequently graduated from Yale Law School in 1964 and went on to serve in a number of offices, including California secretary of state (1971–1975), mayor of Oakland (1999–2007), attorney general of California (2007–2011), and California's 34th and 39th governor. (Courtesy Jesuit Center.)

Mike Wasserman

Mike Wasserman moved to Los Gatos at age 14 and is a graduate of the University of Southern California. Kim Currie became his wife two days after their college graduation, and in 1982, they settled in the Almond Grove district. He coached youth sports, and they both worked on the restoration of Henry C. Crall's Norman French home on Broadway, now the Wassermans' residence. A local businessman, Wasserman entered politics in 2002 with a successful run for town council. He quickly became known for his integrity and concern for the common good. A two-term councilman, he served two years as mayor. Under his leadership in 2008, the town council voted to proceed with a new library and a new sports park. In 2010, he was elected Santa Clara County District 1 supervisor.

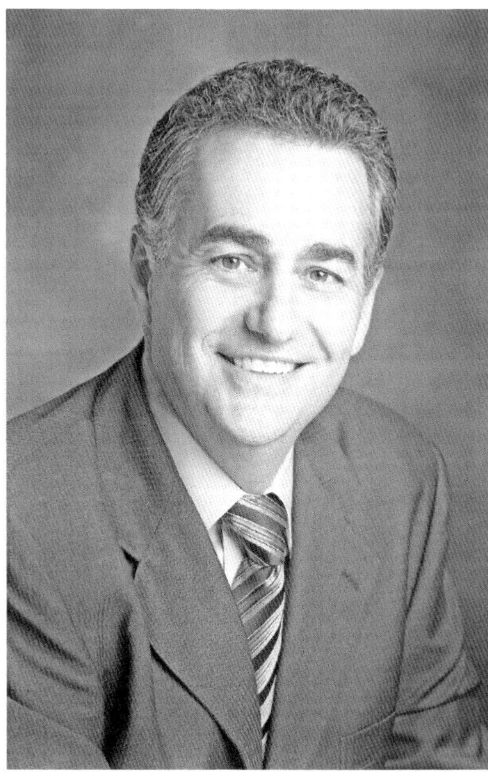

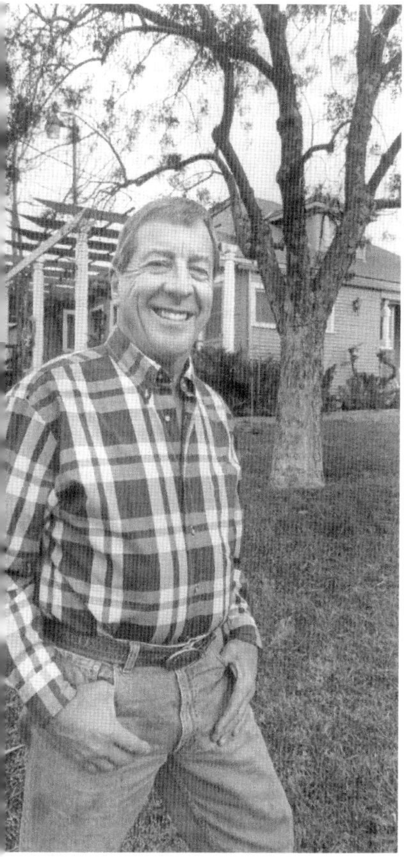

John Lochner

Sometime after the town's historic fire bell was sold to a chicken restaurant in Lodi, John Lochner was part of a group of concerned citizens responsible for the return of that historic artifact to town. He constructed the bell tower that stood at the corner of the town plaza for 15 years. Always an enthusiastic town supporter, Lochner served on the town council for two terms and was mayor in 1975 and 1980. He was elected citizen of the year in 1989. A well-liked member of the community, Lochner often raises spirits by leading singing at town events.

Randy Attaway

In January 1994, two months after being sworn in as mayor of Los Gatos, Randy Attaway learned that the Brazilian National Soccer Team had chosen Villa Felice as its temporary home while competing in the FIFA World Cup soccer tournament at Stanford University in June and July. Attaway appreciated the popularity of World Cup soccer. Los Gatos hospitality began with a welcoming ceremony on May 26, the day the Brazilians arrived, and culminated on July 4 with an impromptu street party that Los Gatos will never forget. That evening, an estimated 30,000 revelers came to celebrate. On July 17, Brazil won the World Cup by defeating Italy 3-2 on penalties at the Rose Bowl in Pasadena. Attaway is pictured with Sara La Berge. (Courtesy Randy Attaway.)

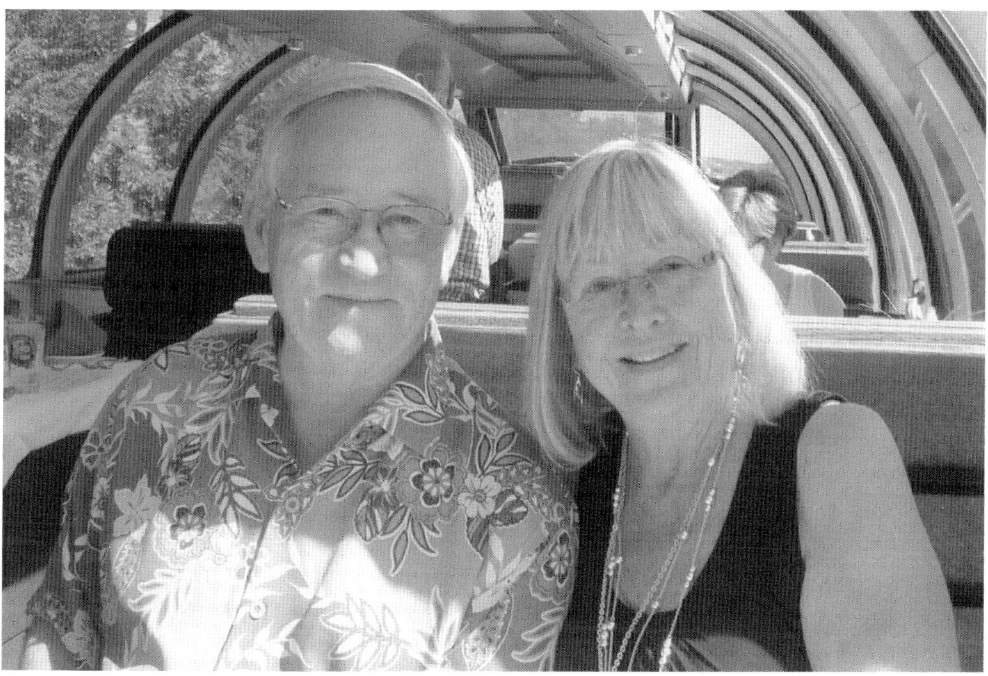

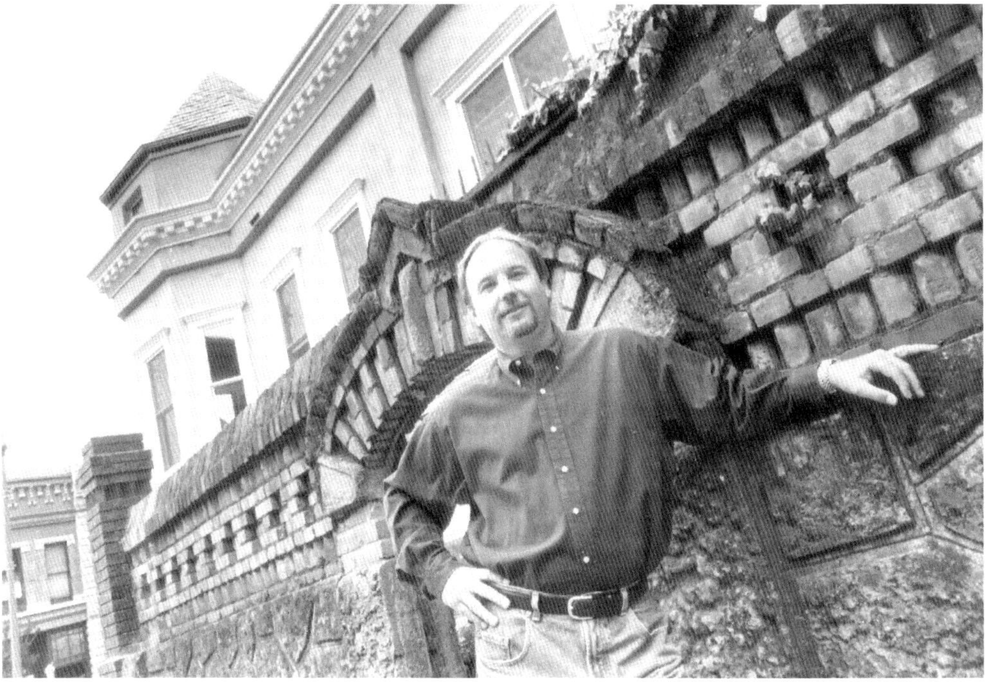

Dave Flick (1957–2011)

A master builder, Dave Flick had a love for the historical, for the quality and craftsmanship of things produced in the past. He honed his restoration skills by working on classic automobiles and then moved on to the development of high-end custom homes and the renovation of commercial buildings. His appreciation for the character and history of Los Gatos resulted in the rehabilitation of many downtown landmarks, including the Soda Works Plaza at East Main Street and College Avenue. He is pictured next to the brick and mortar wall commissioned by Luigi Mariotti in 1910 at that location, which he preserved and restored. Flick's projects were so admired that he did not advertise but simply relied on word-of-mouth.

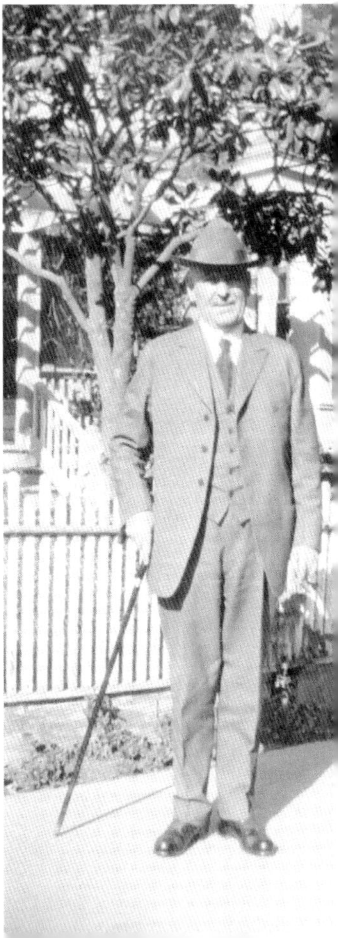

Richard Rundle Bell (1860–1935)

Judge Richard R. Bell helped shape the young town of Los Gatos. Arriving in 1888, he acquired a food and fuel business, which he renamed R.R. Bell Company. He studied at Hastings Law School and was accepted to the California State Bar in 1897. Later, he served as justice of the peace for Redwood Township. Bell contributed to the town as both mayor and town attorney and was known as a judge with a generous heart, one who would provide a helping hand to the down-and-out. Judge Bell walked to his office each day wearing his Homburg hat and carrying a cane, always careful to tip his hat to the ladies. (Courtesy Jim Zetterquist.)

CHAPTER FOUR

Authors, Artists, Athletes

Ambrose Bierce was the first author of national note to live in Los Gatos. He came seeking relief from asthma in 1895 and stayed for most of five years. Bierce lived in the big hotel at the northeast corner of East Main and Pleasant Streets, the El Monte. He must have spent time sitting on the wide, peaceful porch, watching the passing scene. But he had long-since earned the nickname "Bitter Bierce" for the caustic criticism he leveled at nearly everybody and everything as an editor and literary critic.

At age 18, Bierce enlisted in the Union army just days after President Lincoln first called for volunteers to save the Union. He survived battles at Shiloh, Chickamauga, and Missionary Ridge before he was struck in the head by a Confederate bullet at Kennesaw Mountain, which he also survived. His unflinching Civil War short stories are considered the best ever written.

Since their appearance in the 1880s, newspapers have held a prominent place in town life. The last two decades of the 19th century saw no less than six local publications. After 31 years running the *Los Gatos News*, irascible editor H.B. Trantham minced no words in his editorials. He once called a competing newspaper "a non-compos mentis sheet" and its publisher a "superannuated relic of typography."

Most Los Gatans have heard of Olivia de Havilland, and a few may have watched "Broncho Billy" Anderson perform in a 100-year-old Western movie filmed in the hills of Los Gatos. Fewer are probably aware of Richard Smart, an actor who lived in town and was heir to the largest privately owned ranch in Hawaii, the Parker Ranch.

Artists and graphic designers are an essential part of the cultural fabric and memory of Los Gatos, including John Pugh and the late Rick Tharp. Robert Treat Paine was the sculptor of the iconic cats which have stood guard south of town for 92 years. While a few of the town's outstanding athletes and Olympians are represented here, sports teams and players in Los Gatos are numerous and deserve a book of their own.

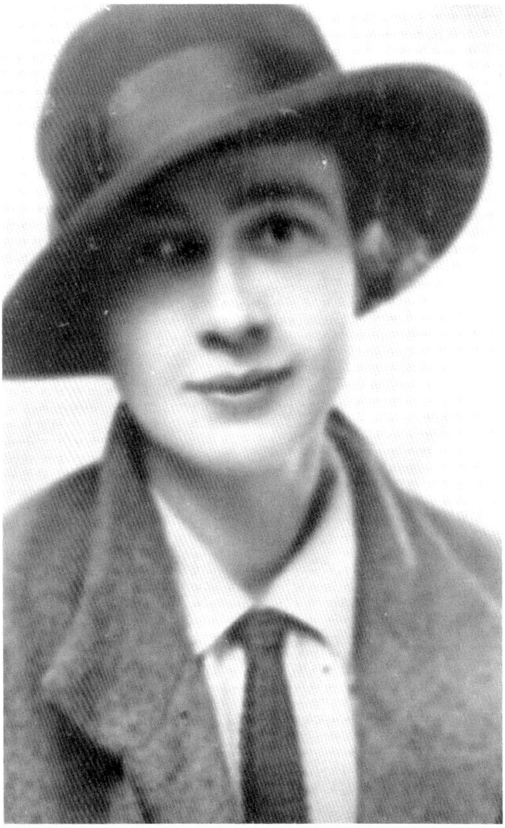

Maude Meagher (1895–1977)
Upon graduation from the University of California in 1917, Maude Meagher became a reporter for the *San Francisco Chronicle*, a foreign correspondent, and eventually a novelist. With partner Carolyn Smiley, she published *World Youth* magazine at Casa Tierra, the adobe home they built by hand. Completed in 1947, the house was reportedly the largest secular adobe in North America. In 1950, they published a booklet titled *How We Built an Adobe House*. (Courtesy Wendy Moreno.)

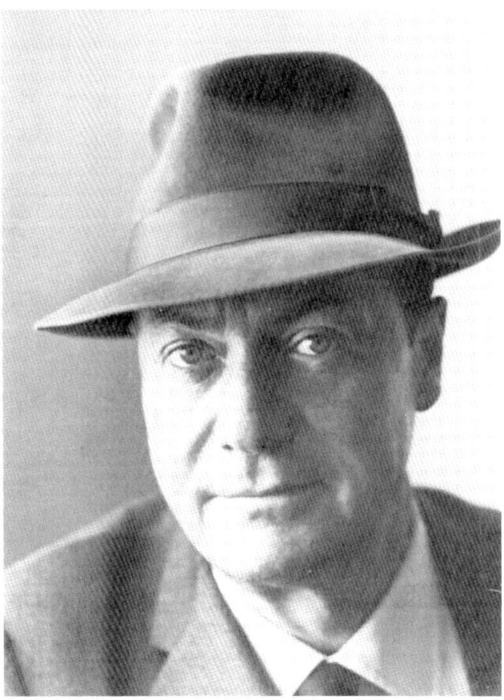

Kenneth Millar (1915–1983)
Kenneth Millar, who wrote under the pseudonyms John Macdonald, John Ross Macdonald, and Ross Macdonald, was born in Los Gatos but raised in Ontario, Canada. When Millar was three years old, his father abandoned him and his mother, which had a profound thematic significance in his novels. Millar was the successor of Dashiell Hammett and Raymond Chandler in the development of the hard-boiled detective story. He wrote two dozen novels between 1944 and 1976, 18 of them featuring Lew Archer, the character for whom he is best known, making him one of the most popular crime fiction writers in America.

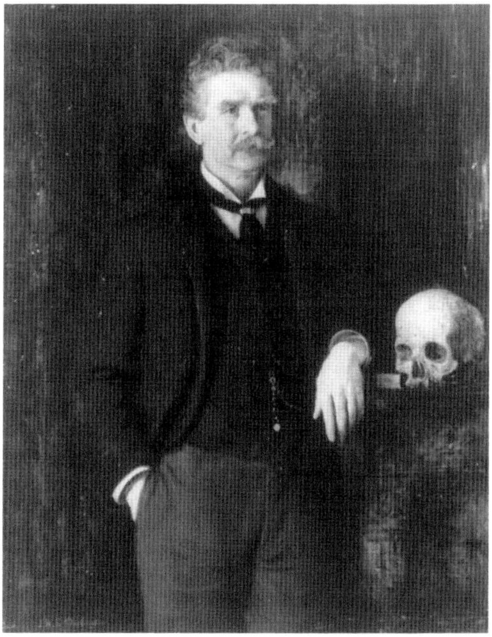

Ambrose Bierce (1842–1914?)

Ambrose Bierce was the best-known journalist and satirist of his day. Brilliant and controversial, he was famous for his caustic sarcasm. He attacked everyone—politicians, churchgoers, actors, and other writers. He is remembered for his most famous book, *The Devil's Dictionary*, and for his Civil War short stories, based on his own experiences in a number of horrific battles. Bierce first came to Los Gatos in the summer of 1895, hoping to find respite from his severe asthma. He checked into the Hotel El Monte. He returned in 1897 and spent the better part of three years at the same location. He then moved to the mountain community of Wrights, where he was often visited by local poets, writers, and fans. He died somewhere in Mexico, date unknown. (Courtesy Library of Congress, LC-USZ62-20182.)

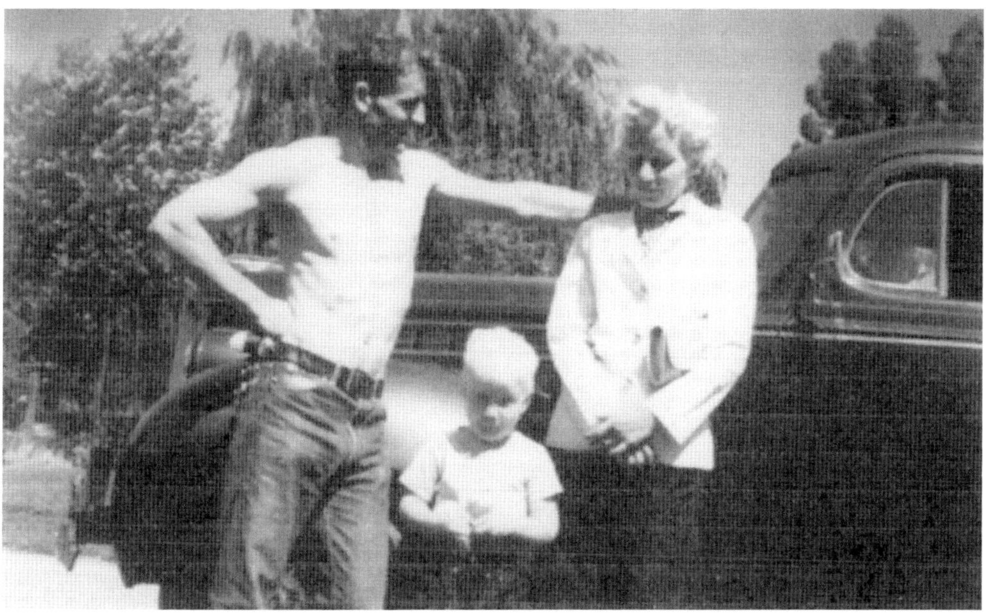

Neal (1926–1968) and Carolyn Cassady (1923–2013)

Neal and Carolyn Cassady purchased a house on Bancroft Avenue in 1954. Cassady was an icon of the Beat Generation and is most famous as the model for Dean Moriarty in Jack Kerouac's novel *On the Road*. As a member of Ken Kesey's Merry Pranksters, he drove the psychedelic school bus dubbed "Further" across the country. Cassady never overcame his addiction to drugs and served two years in San Quentin State Prison, accused of trafficking marijuana. Carolyn Cassady was appreciative of the support that she received from the community despite her husband's unconventional life, and she provided costume design and makeup artistry for local theatrical productions. The couple is pictured here with their son, John. Neal Cassady died a few days short of his 42nd birthday in Mexico.

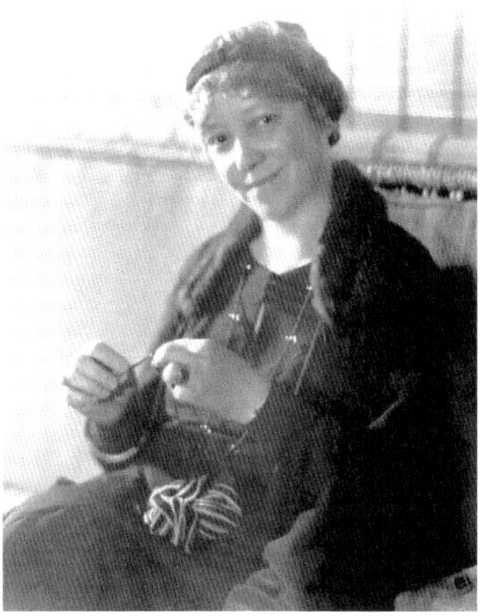

Ruth Comfort Mitchell (1882–1954)

Ruth Comfort Mitchell was a noted author who produced scripts for the Los Gatos pageants in 1929, 1930, and 1937 and acted in a number of the productions. She married Sanborn Young in 1914 and spent time on Young's 2,000-acre dairy farm near Fresno. There, she observed the hard work and risks involved in farming, and she was angered by John Steinbeck's *The Grapes of Wrath*, told from the migrant workers' point of view. In 1940 her novel, *Of Human Kindness*, was published to refute Steinbeck's work and to tell "the other side of the story." Although Steinbeck and Mitchell lived less than four miles apart in Los Gatos, they moved in completely different circles, and it is doubtful they ever met.

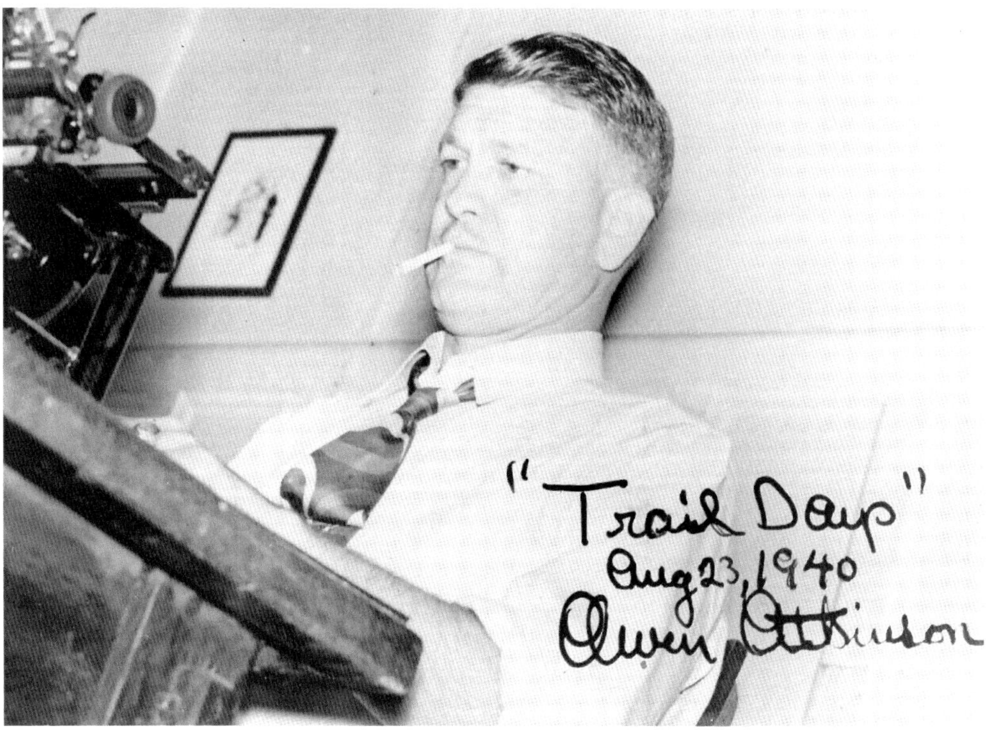

Marion Owen Atkinson (1898–1962)

Owen Atkinson was a native of Missouri who served in World War II. He got his start writing melodramatic pulp magazine thrillers in the 1930s and turned one of those stories into a screenplay that was filmed as *The Pool Where Horror Dwelt*, starring Wallace Beery and Mickey Rooney. He coauthored the story for the movie *20 Mule Team*, wherein two scoundrels plan to jump a valuable borax claim. Filmed by MGM in 1940 in the beautiful changing light of Death Valley, it starred Anne Baxter in her silver screen debut. In Los Gatos, Atkinson penned *Trail Days* for the 1940 town pageant. He and his wife, Kathleen, named their property on Foster Road Tilted Acres.

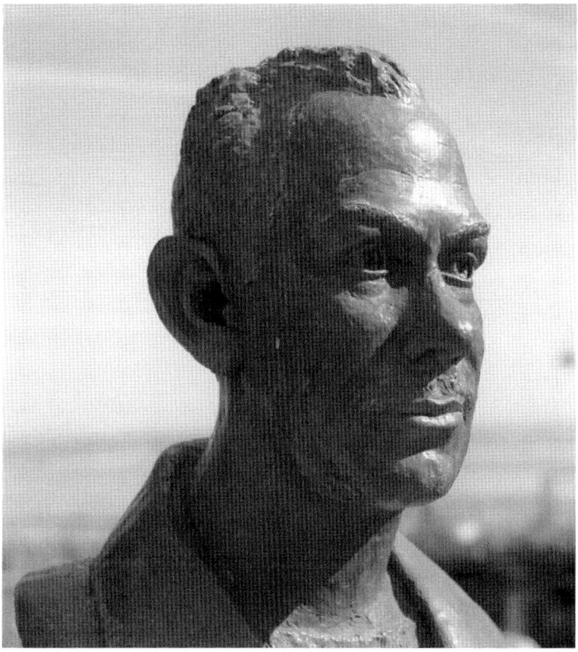

John Ernst Steinbeck (1902–1968)
John Steinbeck was a man of high social conscience and great empathy. He was only 36 years old when he decided he must "throw out the world" and sequester himself in his little house on Greenwood Lane in Los Gatos to write a novel addressing the plight of dust bowl migrants arriving in California. For three years, he had lived on and off with the Okies, and he was indignant, angry, and heartbroken by what he saw. At the suggestion of his wife, Carol Henning, he titled his book *The Grapes of Wrath*. Sculptress Carol Brown created this bronze bust of Steinbeck, which stands midway along Cannery Row in Monterey.

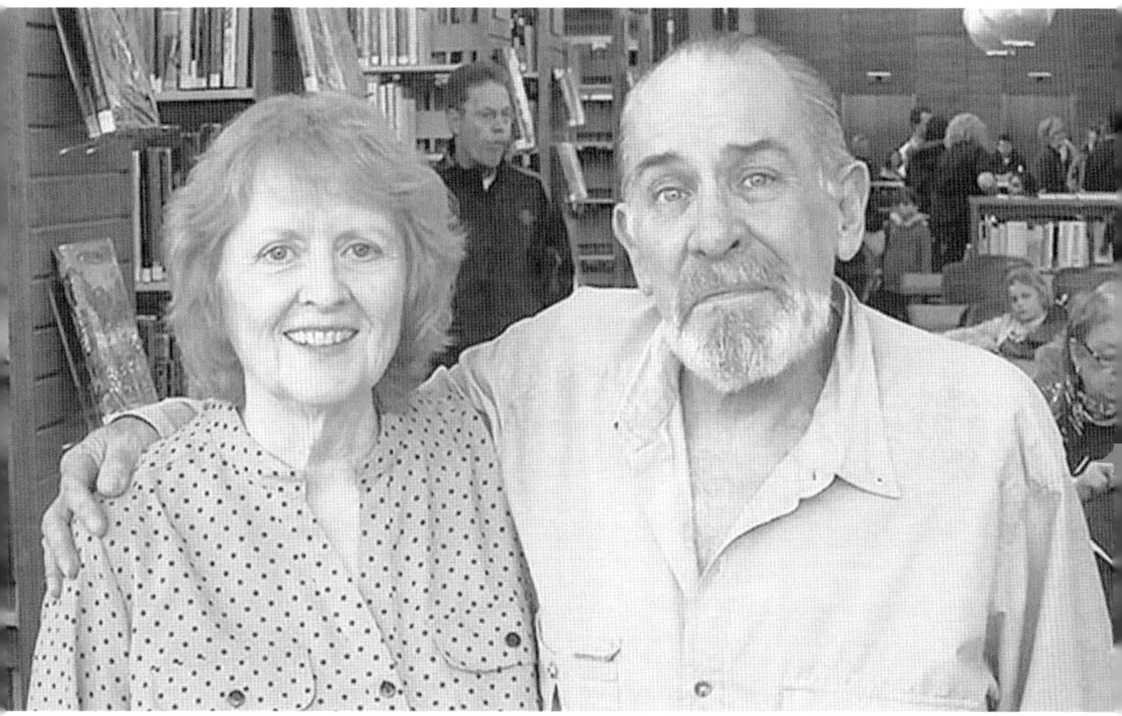

The Steinbeck Legacy
John Steinbeck did some of his most important writing during his Los Gatos years. The community was pleased to welcome his oldest son, Thom Steinbeck, as a guest speaker at the opening of the new Los Gatos Public Library on February 11, 2012. He is pictured here with Peggy Conaway Bergtold, who served as library director from 2000 to 2010. (Courtesy Valerie Archer Wainwright.)

Hiland L. (1870–1944) and Caroline Earle Baggerly (1874–1959)

"Hy" Baggerly spent more than half a century in journalism and was dubbed "the dean of Santa Clara County newsmen." He began as a reporter on the *San Francisco Call* before moving to the *San Francisco Bulletin*, where he worked for his sister Cora's husband, Fremont Older, and was one of the colorful sportswriters of his day. He purchased the *San Jose News* in 1916 and the *Los Gatos Mail-News* in 1927. Caroline was society editor for her husband's newspapers and spent the last 13 years of her life living under the turret at the Hotel Lyndon. The couple is pictured on a 1937 cruise.

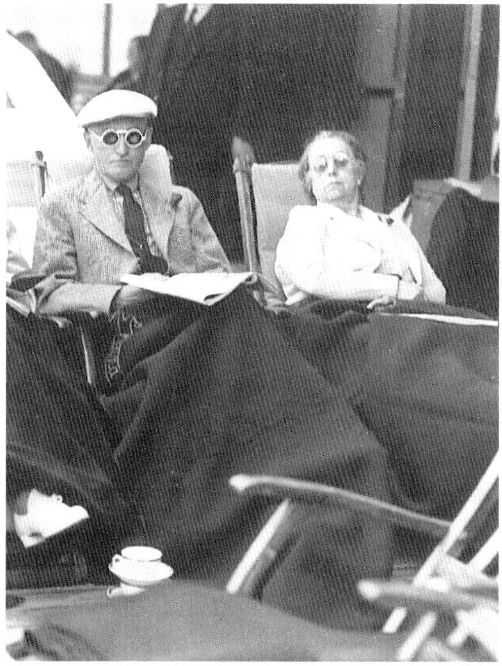

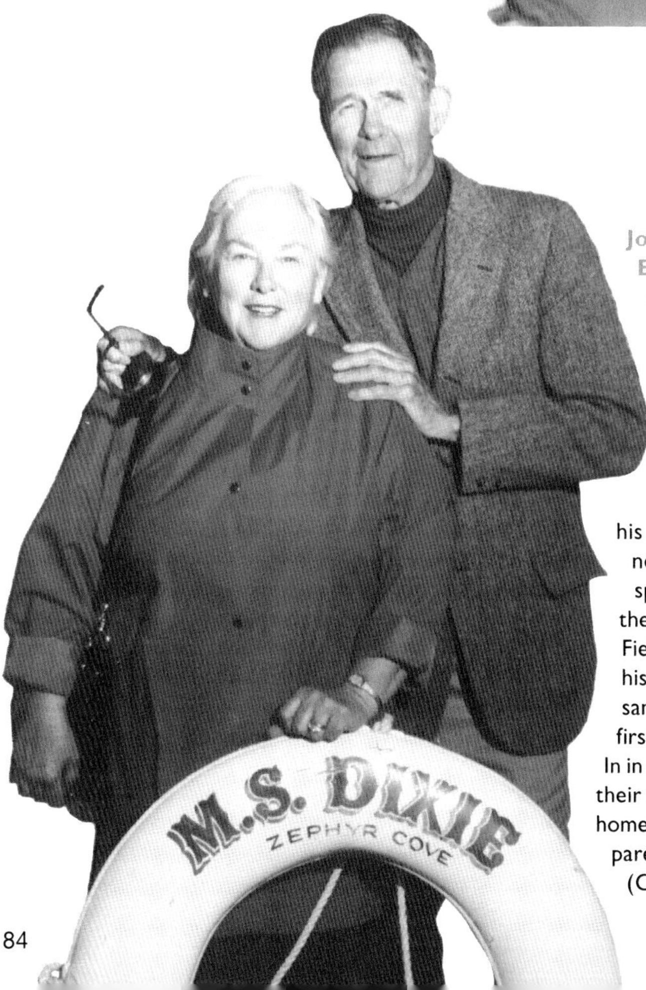

John S. (1915–2002) and Barbara Gibson Baggerly (1919–2013)

John and Barbara Baggerly met when they played lead roles in the 1940 pageant *Trail Days*. Married in 1944, just after John returned from service with the US Army in Iran, their marriage endured for 58 years. John soon developed his reputation as a consummate local newsman, with a special interest in sports. He was a tireless advocate for the youth of Los Gatos, and Baggerly Field on Blossom Hill Road is named in his honor. As a young woman, Barbara sang with her father's band and was the first waitress hired by the 5-Spot Drive-In in the late 1930s. The Baggerlys raised their four children in the Johnson Avenue home that had belonged to John's adoptive parents, Hiland and Caroline Baggerly. (Courtesy Barbara Baggerly.)

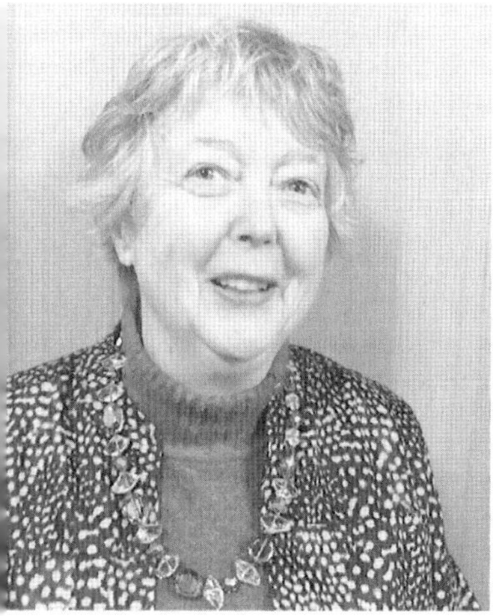

Mary Ann Cook

Mary Ann Cook graduated from Indiana's DePauw University, where she was editor of the college newspaper. She began her professional career in Texas. Cook came to Los Gatos in 1979 and was named editor of the *Los Gatos Times-Observer* in 1983. Her popular "Main Street" column was a mainstay of the *Los Gatos Weekly-Times* and the *Saratoga News*, and she has authored a number of one-act plays performed in local theaters and at the Edinburgh Fringe Festival.

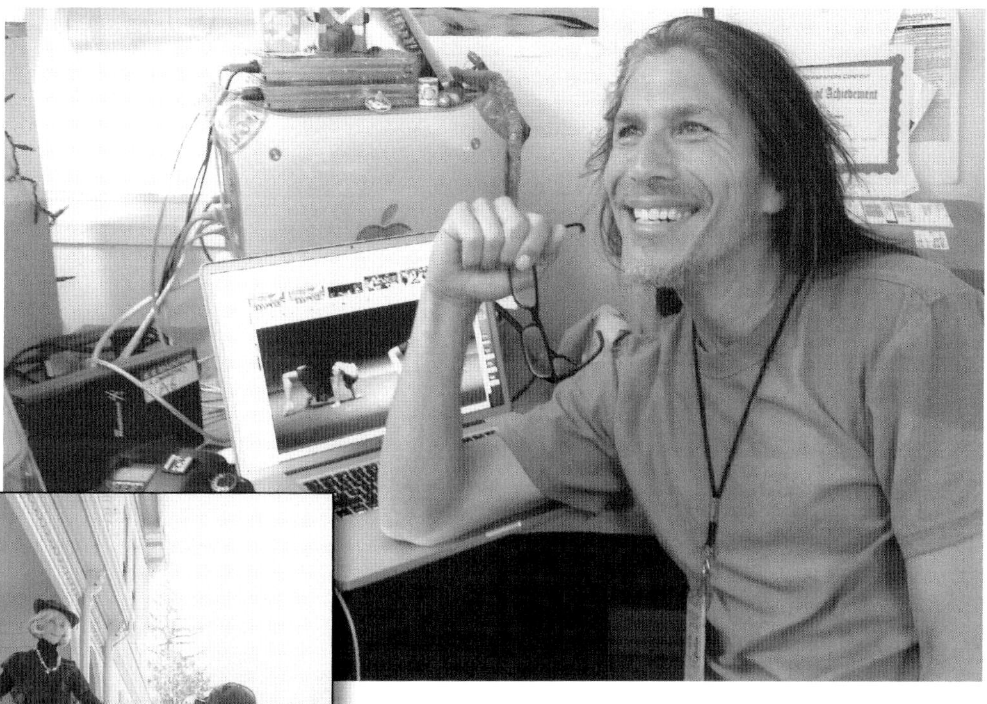

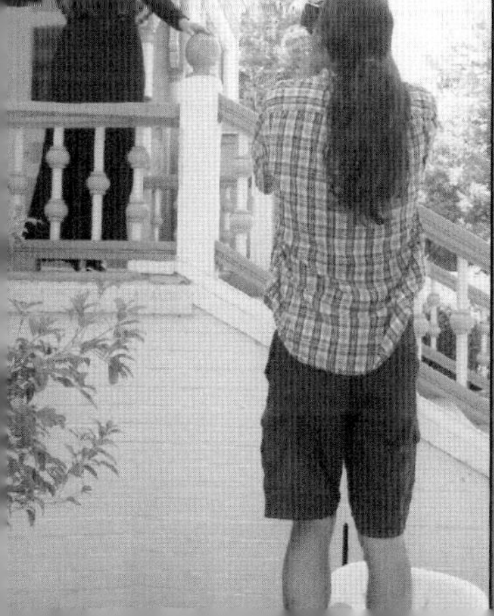

George Sakkestad

George Sakkestad has said that his goal is to evoke emotion in those who see his photographs. For nearly two decades he has documented the lives of the Los Gatos community. He has recorded major disasters such as the Loma Prieta earthquake and the Cats Fire but has also pointed his lens at memorable moments in everyday life, such as children playing or nature at its best. At left, Sakkestad is shown capturing an image of Sandy Decker dressed as Mary Coggeshall for a museum fundraiser. This award-winning photojournalist is truly the eyes of Los Gatos. (Above, courtesy George Sakkestad; left, courtesy Stephanie Mathews.)

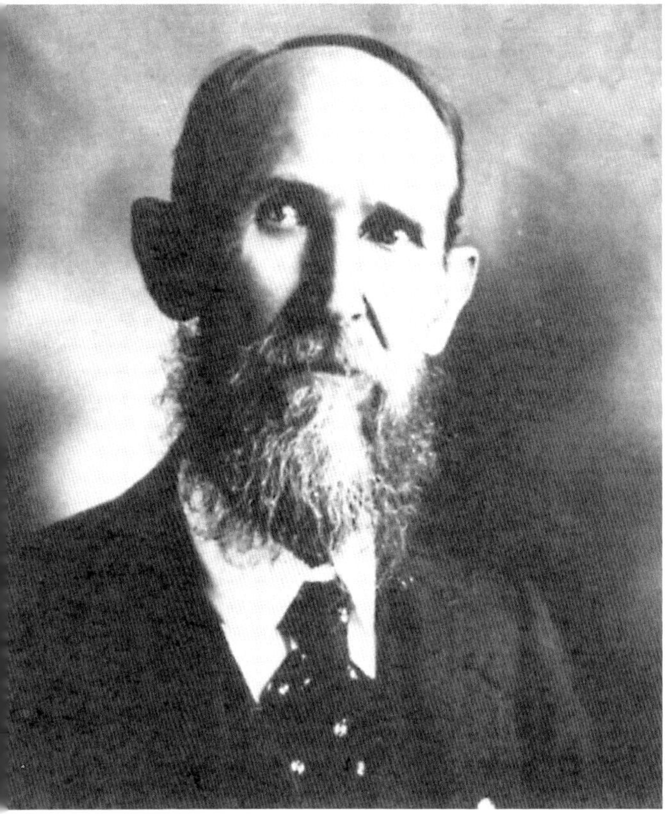

William Henry Benton Trantham (1847–after 1920)

Pioneering newsman W.H.B. Trantham was born on a farm in Missouri. He arrived in Los Gatos in 1884 and was one of the signers of the petition to incorporate the town in 1887. A former schoolteacher and principal, he was civic-minded and conservative. As publisher of the *Los Gatos News* for 31 years, he included this motto under the masthead on the front page: "Largest, Best, Cheapest. Read It." He wrote that publishers "worked early and late, for small pay and often on long credit."

Dick Sparrer

A longtime editor of the *Los Gatos Weekly-Times*, Dick Sparrer got his start in journalism when John Baggerly provided him with the opportunity to write sports stories for the *Los Gatos Times-Observer.* Sparrer has followed the lead of his mentor with outstanding coverage of all youth and high school sporting events in town, focusing on everyone who participates, not just the stars. In 2003, Sparrer was a member of the original selection committee for the Los Gatos High School Athletic Hall of Fame, which was established in remembrance of Baggerly. (Courtesy Dick Sparrer.)

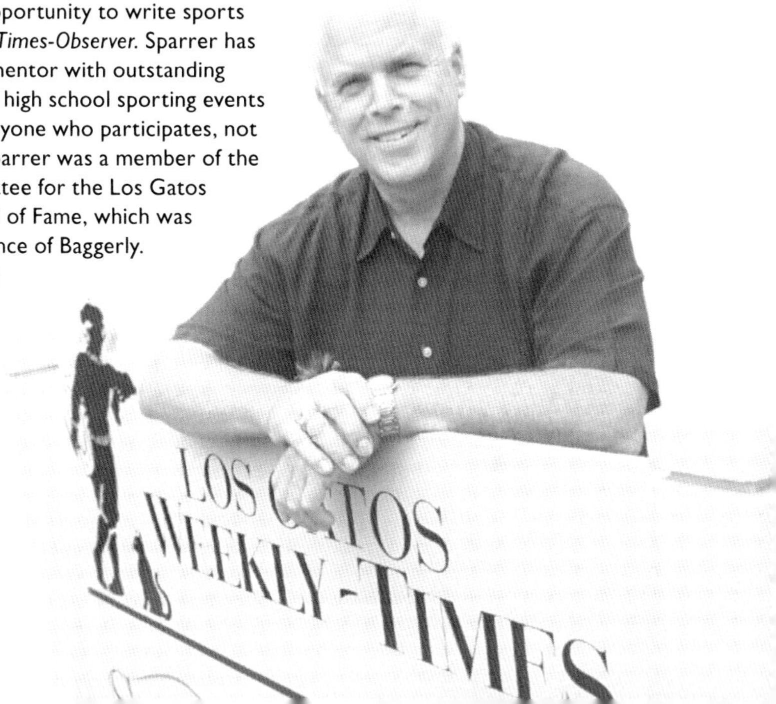

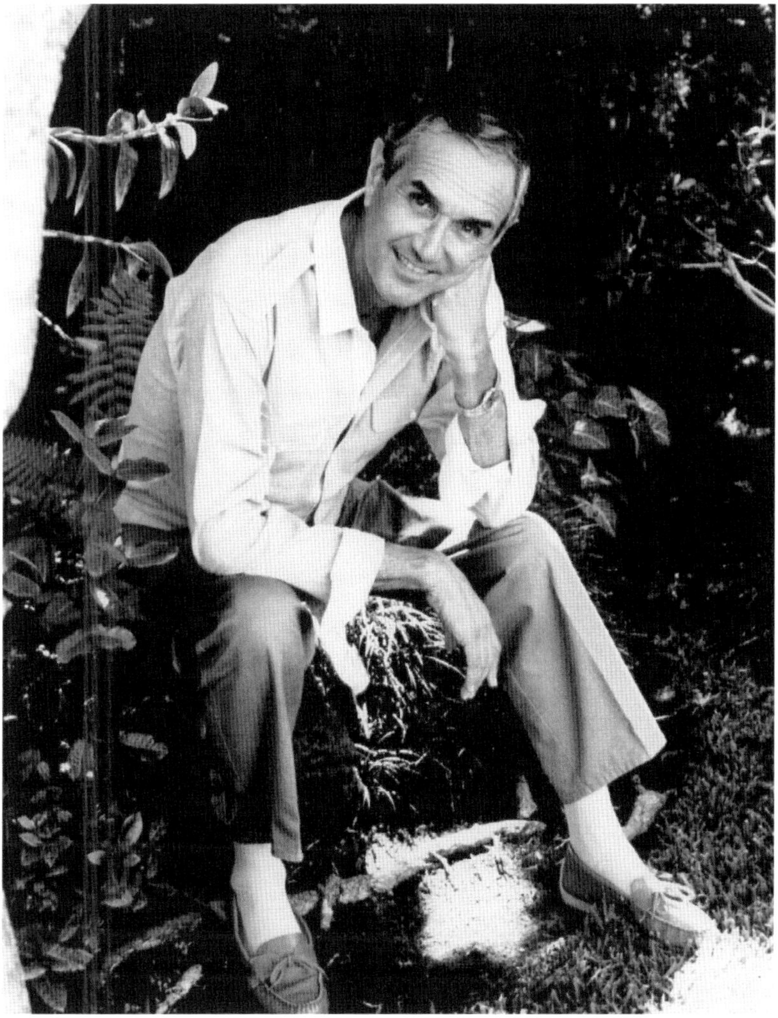

Richard Palmer Kaleioku Smart (1913–1992)
Richard Smart was born in Honolulu, Hawaii. In 1914, he lost his infant sister and then his mother, Annie Thelma Kahiluonapuaapi'ilani Parker, died from tuberculosis. In 1915, his father also died, leaving him heir to the largest privately owned ranch in Hawaii, the 500,000-acre Parker Ranch. He was raised by his part-Hawaiian maternal grandmother, Elizabeth Knight, in San Francisco and Los Gatos. While attending Los Gatos High School in 1930, he became interested in acting, which led to a 30-year career as a nightclub singer and actor. He appeared on Broadway and in many other venues as "Dick Smart."

While pursuing his acting career, Smart kept in close contact with his ranch manager and made annual visits to his property. During World War II, the US Marine Corps leased 40,000 acres of the ranch to use for Camp Tarawa. In later years, Smart took a more active role in managing the ranch, and in 1960, he returned for good. He built the Parker Ranch Visitor Center and Museum in Waimea and opened the Kahilu Theater to encourage tourism. He leased and sold coastal ranch land to resort developers, land that was too dry for his 30,000 head of Hereford cattle. In 1990, his wealth was estimated at $400 million.

Richard Smart was a sixth-generation descendant of John Palmer Parker, a New England sailor who founded the ranch in 1847. Smart died on Oahu in 1992 and left his estate in trust to support health care, education, and charitable giving. Author James Michener noted that Smart was respected by the local people, especially the native Hawaiians who worked for him. (Courtesy Parker Ranch.)

Grace Hyde Trine (1874–1972)

Grace Trine wrote and directed the town's 1923 pageant, *The Mesa Trail.* A Hopi Indian village was recreated on stage in front of 5,000 seats for the town's fifth annual outdoor production. A poet, lecturer, and dramatic reader, Grace and her husband, Ralph Waldo Trine, were deeply interested in the metaphysical. Originally from New York State, the couple lived locally while their son Robert attended Montezuma School.

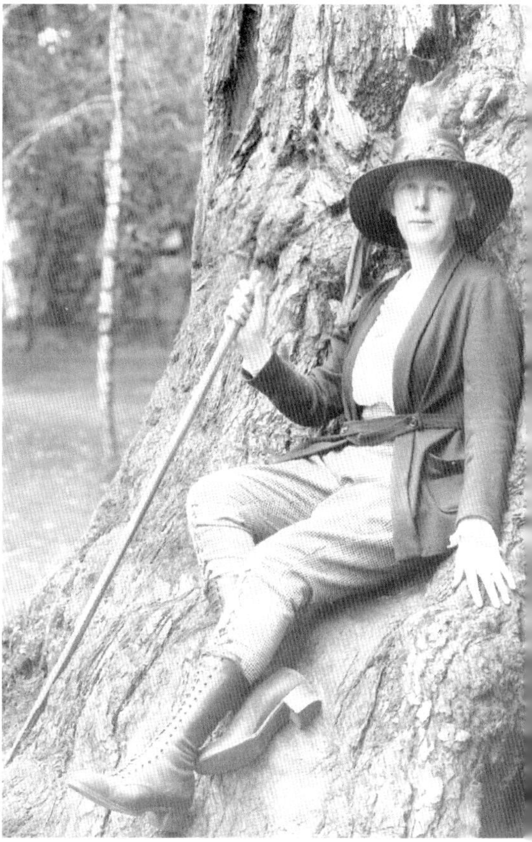

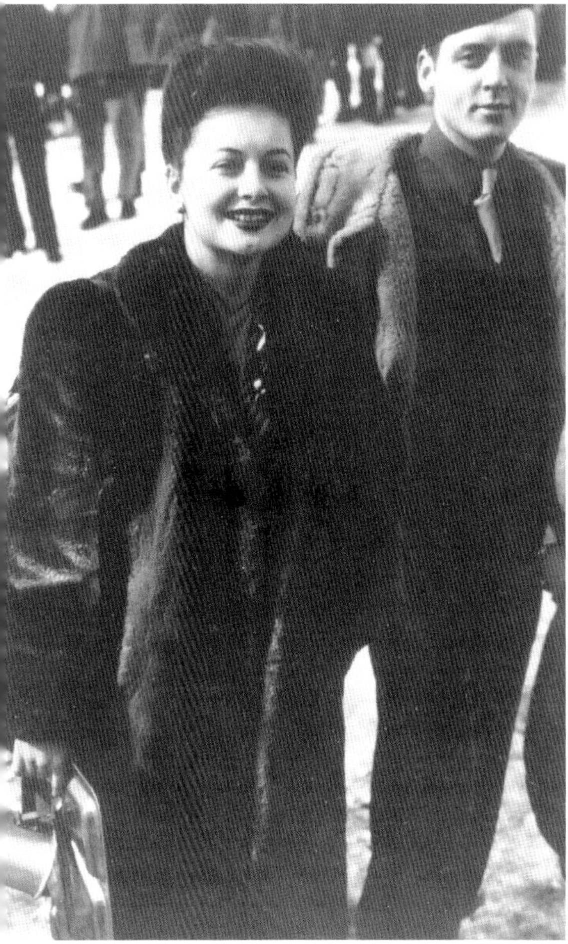

Olivia Mary de Havilland

Olivia de Havilland was born in Japan, grew up in Saratoga, and graduated from Los Gatos Union High School in 1934. She was not quite 18 when she signed a contract with Warner Bros. Studios. Her most famous role was that of Melanie Hamilton in David O. Selznick's *Gone with the Wind* (1939). She is shown here on a morale-boosting trip to visit wounded soldiers in the Aleutian Islands in 1944. She has made her home in Paris since 1956.

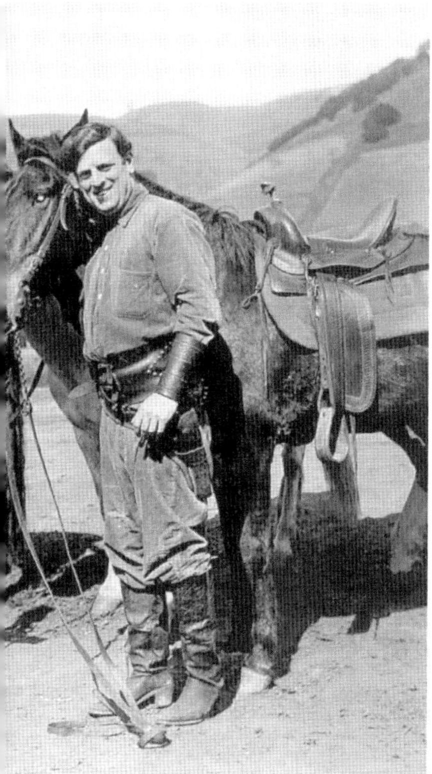

Gilbert M. Anderson (1880–1971)
"Broncho Billy" Anderson, born Maxwell Henry Aronson, left Arkansas at age 18 headed for New York City and a career in vaudeville. In 1903, he was hired to play several roles in the early motion picture *The Great Train Robbery*, and he decided the emerging film industry was for him. He partnered with George K. Spoor in 1907 to form the Essanay Film Company. Anderson arrived in Los Gatos in October 1910 with a troop of actors, and they all checked in to the Hotel Lyndon. College Avenue was used to shoot stagecoach footage, and at day's end, he and his crew relaxed on the rambling porch at the Lyndon. In 1957, Anderson was recognized with an Oscar for his pioneering work in film.

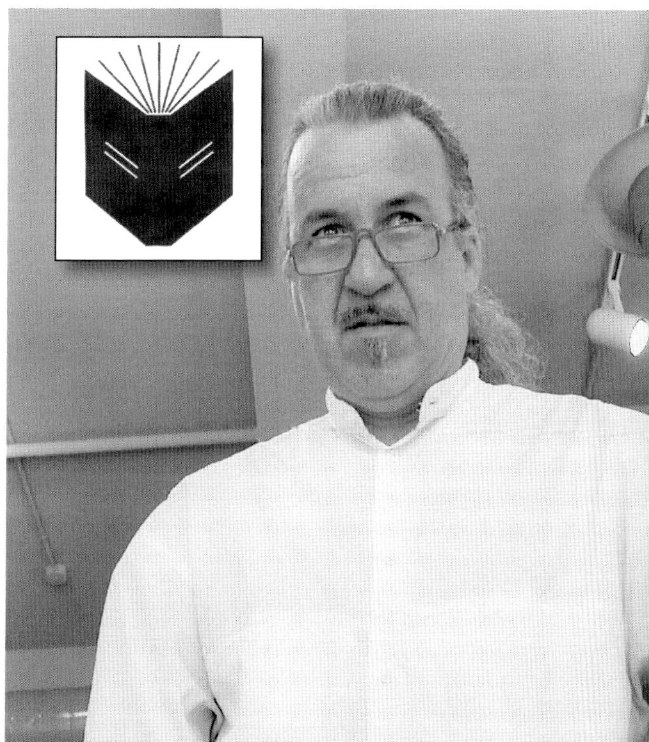

Rick Tharp (1952–2005)
Rick Tharp was an award-winning graphic designer recognized for innovation and the use of humor in his work. His design studio, Tharp Did It, was established in Los Gatos in 1975 and produced work ranging from business logos to advertising campaigns to wine labels. Over three decades, Tharp's enormous contributions to the Los Gatos community included the masthead for the *Los Gatos Weekly-Times*, street signs and banners, and advertisements, programs, and posters for community events. He often donated his design services to organizations in town, including this logo for the Library and Museum History Project. (Courtesy Ken Eklund.)

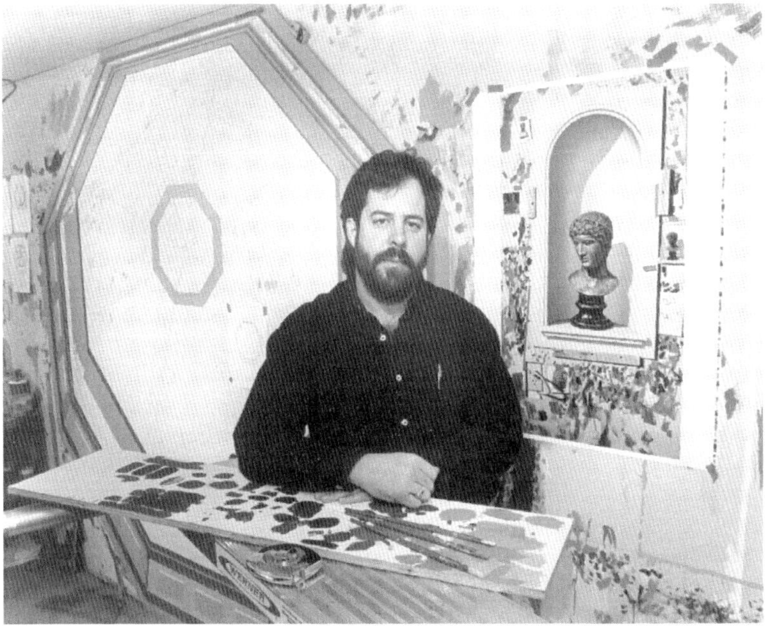

John Pugh

John Pugh is recognized as a master illusionist, his large-scale trompe l'oeil murals acknowledged across the country and abroad for their architectural, scholarly, and sometimes humorous content. Pugh started to paint his three-dimensional works of art in the late 1970s, and his ability to "trick the eye" is unsurpassed, to the delight of the thousands of people who have viewed his work. The narrative aspects of his work are often intriguing. "The storytelling ability of my murals is their very essence," he states. An example of the layered meaning in his designs can be seen on the side of a commercial building on East Main Street. The mural (shown below) is titled *Siete Punto Uno* and pays homage to the 7.1 Loma Prieta earthquake of October 17, 1989, that devastated Los Gatos and much of the Bay Area. Two large stone jaguars, recalling the Los Gatos cats, are shown in an ancient pre-Columbian Mexican temple motif. The wall of their inner sanctum is shattered, but the "Butterfly God" in a niche above the doorway is a symbol of rebirth, an optimistic statement about the future.

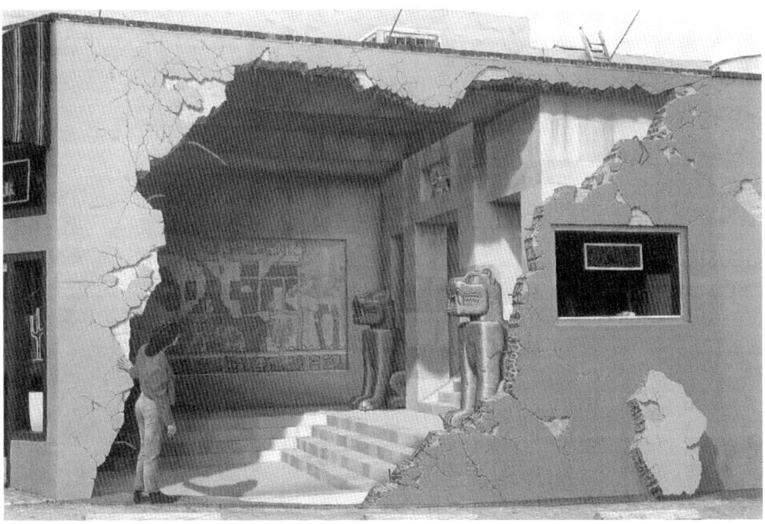

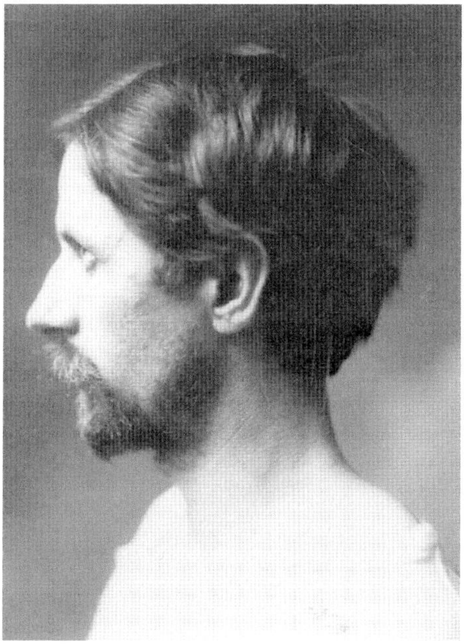

Robert Treat Paine (1869–1946)

Just on the outskirts of Los Gatos stand two colossal cats sculpted in 1922 by Robert Treat Paine. The sphinx-like creatures stand guard at the entrance to the former estate of Charles Erskine Scott Wood and have come to represent the town. Although many people assume the cats are made of stone, Paine created them by pouring cement into carefully crafted plaster molds. Paine studied at the Chicago School of Art with Augustus Saint-Gaudens, a sculptor known for his simple, naturalistic style. This photograph of Paine was taken while he was posing for Saint-Gaudens, his mentor, for a portrait of Christ. (Courtesy Janet Tam and Kit Ratcliff.)

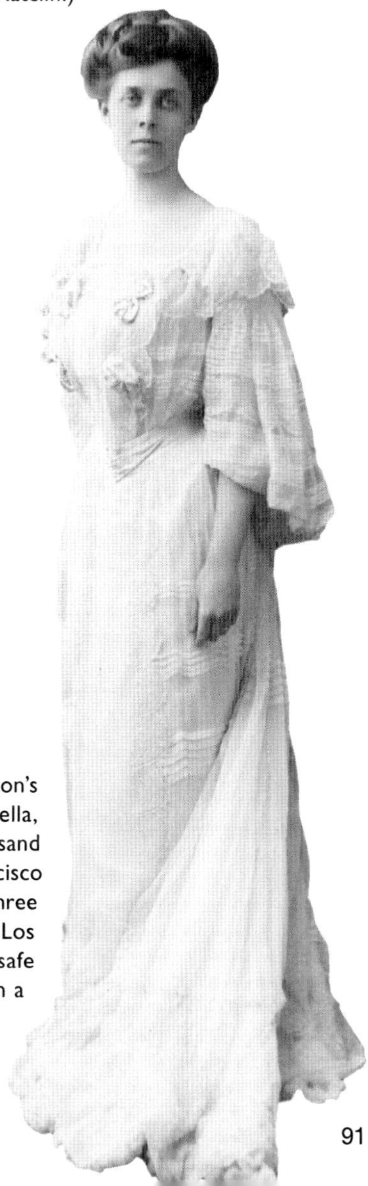

Clara Leonora (Peggy) Huntington (1878–1965)

Born into a famous American railroading family, Clara Huntington's father, Henry Edwards Huntington, and his second wife, Arabella, founded the Huntington Library in San Marino, California. A thousand long-stemmed Easter lilies decorated Trinity Church in San Francisco when Clara married Gilbert B. Perkins in 1902. The couple had three children, but the union ended badly in 1917 when Clara fled to Los Gatos after suing her husband for removing bonds from her safe deposit box. In 1919, she commissioned Julia Morgan to design a 5,000-square-foot Italianate home near Fairview Plaza that still stands. Clara was a well-regarded sculptress who studied in Europe. (Courtesy Huntington Library.)

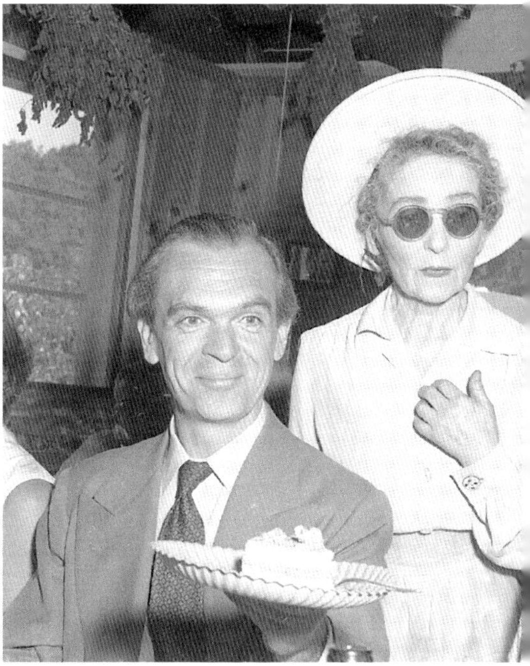

Yehudi Menuhin (1916–1999)

A world-class violinist, Menuhin first came to live in Los Gatos in May 1936 with his parents, Moshe and Marutha, and his sisters, Hephzibah and Yaltah. He was "on sabbatical" from an intense schedule of performances that began when he was a child. He celebrated his 40th birthday in Los Gatos, shown here, with his mother standing behind him. In 1985, Menuhin became a British citizen.

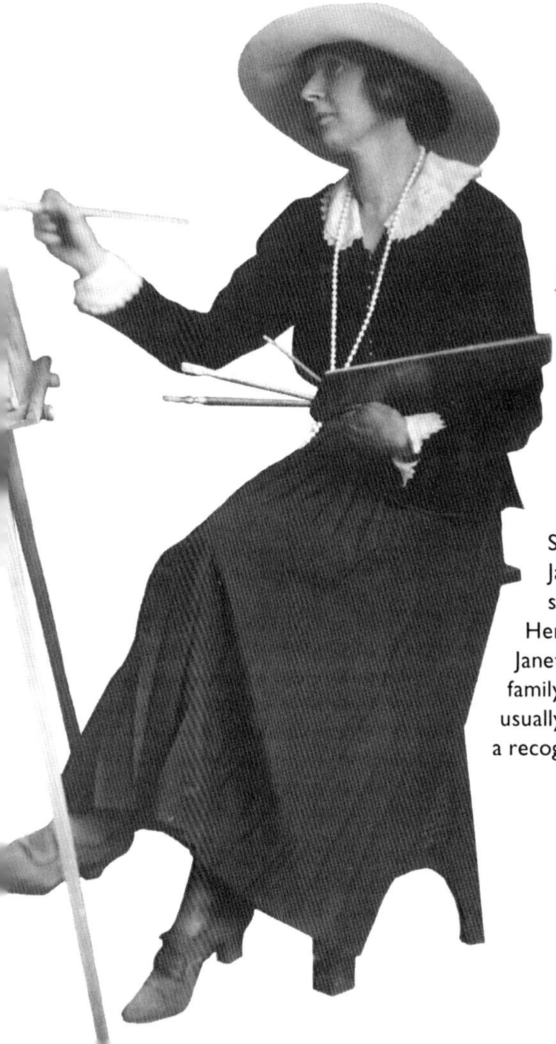

Janet Agnes Tobin (1879–1946)

Janet gained local recognition in 1897 when she sketched the cover of the first Los Gatos High School annual. Before long, her whimsical artwork appeared in newspapers and on greeting cards and "postals." She also produced illustrations for Hale Brothers Department Store in San Jose and was noted for her watercolor images of children.

The Tobin family lived in a modest home at 128 East Main Street, which also served as the town's first news depot. Janet's father, John F. Tobin, was an Irish immigrant who served in the Union army as a hospital steward for four years. Her mother, Isabella Kirkpatrick, was a Scottish immigrant. Janet and her sisters, Mary and Helen, spent quiet days at the family home, writing, gardening and painting. The US census usually listed Janet as "unemployed," but she was and remains a recognized artist. She died at Agnews State Hospital.

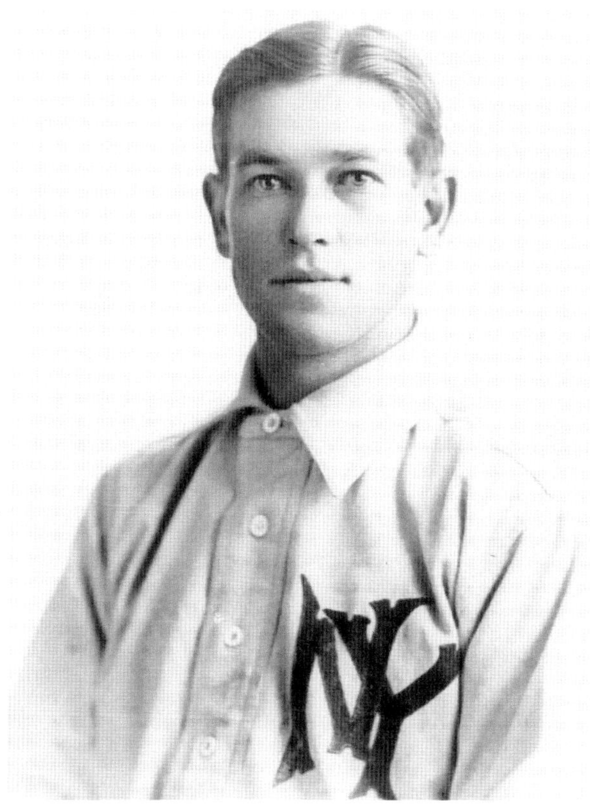

Harold Homer Chase (1883–1947)

Hal Chase was born in Los Gatos to a native of Maine, James E. Chase, who immigrated to the local area in 1869 to join the family lumber business. His mother was Mary Cavanee Chase, born in Ohio. The couple married in 1870. Hal Chase showed athletic talent at an early age and played for semiprofessional baseball teams and Santa Clara College before being signed by the Los Angeles Angels in 1903. He played for the New York Yankees from 1905 to 1913 and was their first captain. His finest season in the majors was in 1916 with the Cincinnati Reds, leading the National League batting average at .339.

"Prince Hal" was a great natural ballplayer and a complex person. He was widely regarded as the finest defensive first baseman ever to play the game, his brilliance with the glove unmatched. Unfortunately, much of his career was overshadowed by accusations of bribes, bets, and throwing games. (Both, courtesy Chase family and Chris Goode.)

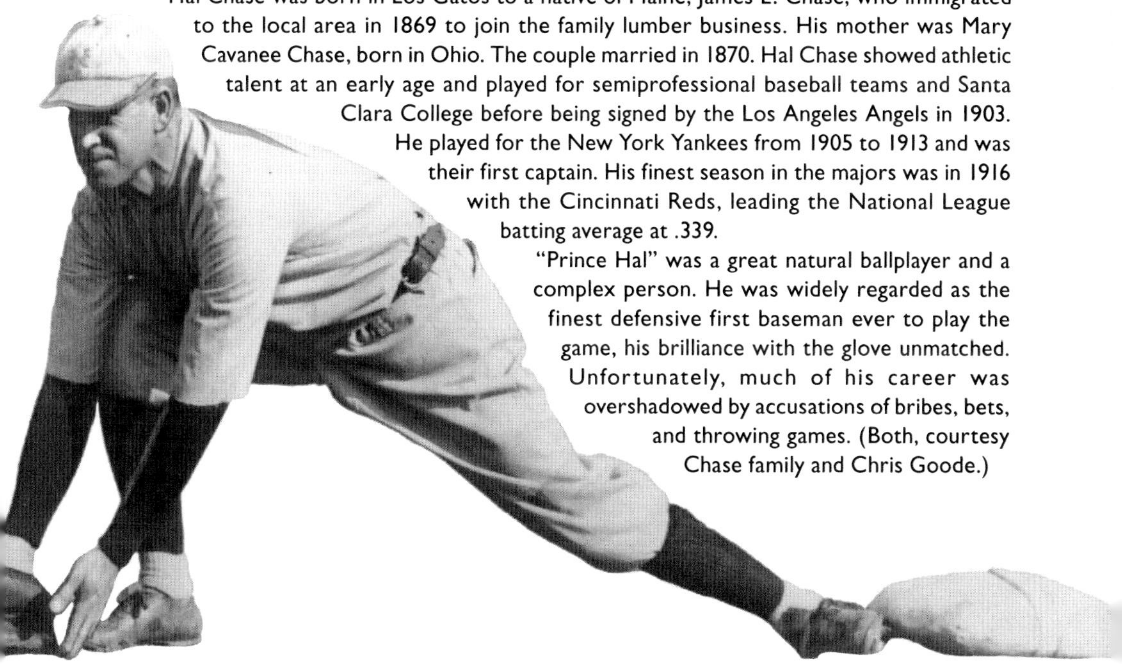

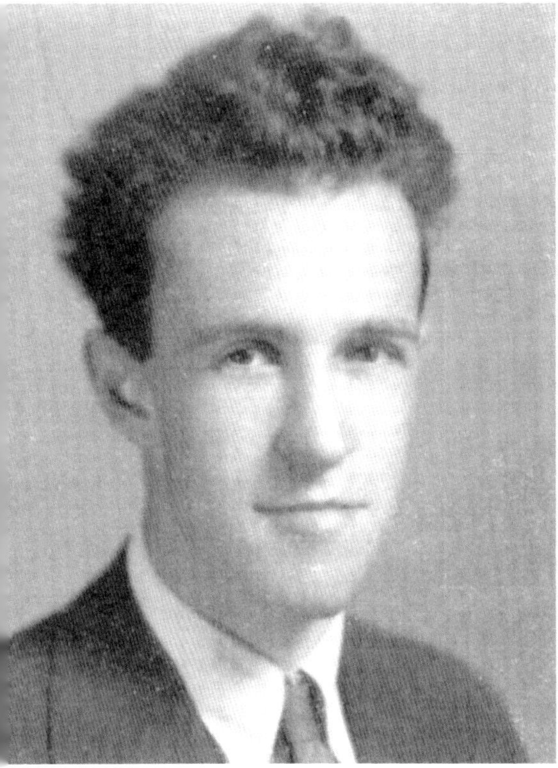

Douglas White Helm (1902–1953)

During his 25-year career at Los Gatos High School, Doug Helm was a history teacher, coach, and vice principal. The 1929 yearbook was dedicated to him "in recognition of his qualities of leadership and sagacity." Helm was the high school's football coach from 1927 to 1944 in addition to his duties as a one-man boys' physical education department. He was once quoted in the local newspaper saying, "The psychology of a football team is about as undecided as a woman's skirt. No matter how much you study it you never can tell what's coming next." The lighted turf field with all-weather track at the high school was named for him shortly after his untimely death.

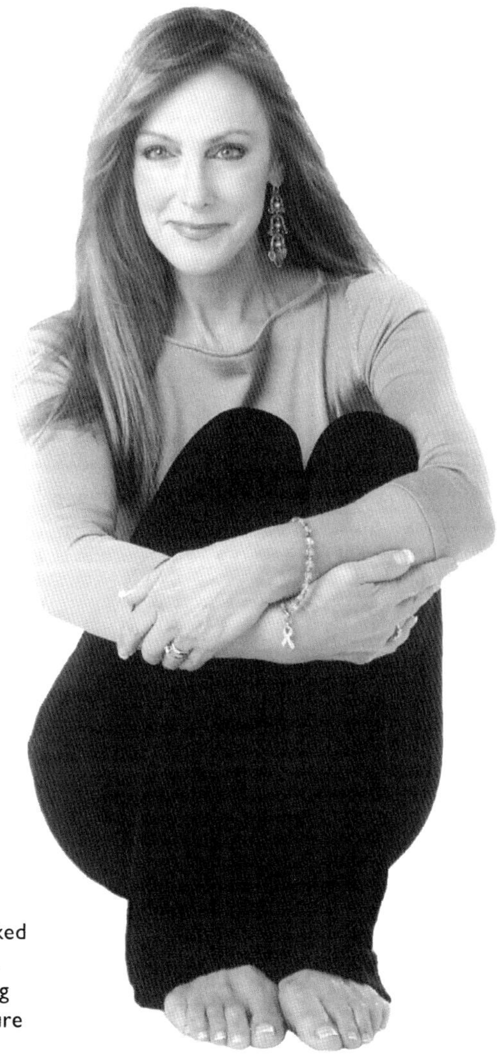

Peggy Fleming

For more than 30 years, Peggy Fleming and her husband, Dr. Greg L. Jenkins, have lived in the hills of Los Gatos. During her stunning career, Fleming captured five United States and three world figure-skating championships and an Olympic gold medal at the 1968 Grenoble Winter Games. Known for her elegance on the ice, she went on to star in television specials, worked as an on-air analyst for ABC Sports, and became a spokesperson for breast cancer awareness. Fleming Jenkins Vineyards & Winery was a successful venture during the last decade. (Courtesy Peggy Fleming.)

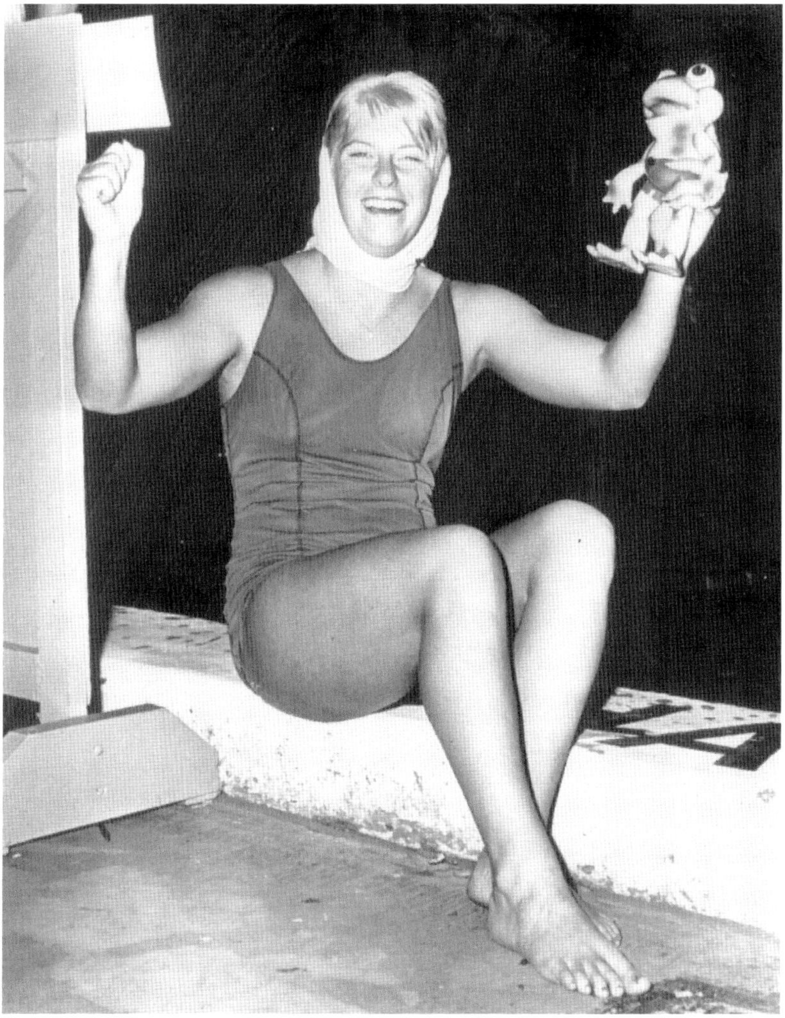

Susan Christina von Saltza

In 1958, when Chris von Saltza was 14 years old, *Sports Illustrated* magazine called her "the best freestyle swimmer ever developed in America." She lived up to her advanced billing. As a member of the Olympic swim team in 1960, competing in Rome, Italy, she brought home three gold medals and one silver medal. That same year, she appeared on the magazine's cover.

Von Saltza joined the Santa Clara Swim Club when she was 11 years old. She trained under coach George Haines and, at age 12, set her first world record. Later that year, she tried out for the 1956 Olympics but missed making the team by a heartbreaking few seconds. At that time, she set a personal goal to make the 1960 team.

Von Saltza was 16 years old and between her junior and senior years at Los Gatos High School when she traveled to Rome. Her performance there was remarkable, and when she returned to school in the fall for the first day of classes, the entire student body turned out to welcome her home. She was escorted up the long front walkway by Jim Wanless, student body president.

A gifted student as well as a gifted athlete, von Saltza went on to Stanford University, where she earned her degree in Asian studies. Unfortunately, no opportunities existed at that time for women's competitive sports at the college level. She worked as a systems engineer for IBM for 30 years. The photograph above, dated 1961, shows von Saltza with a rubber frog, a team mascot through the years.

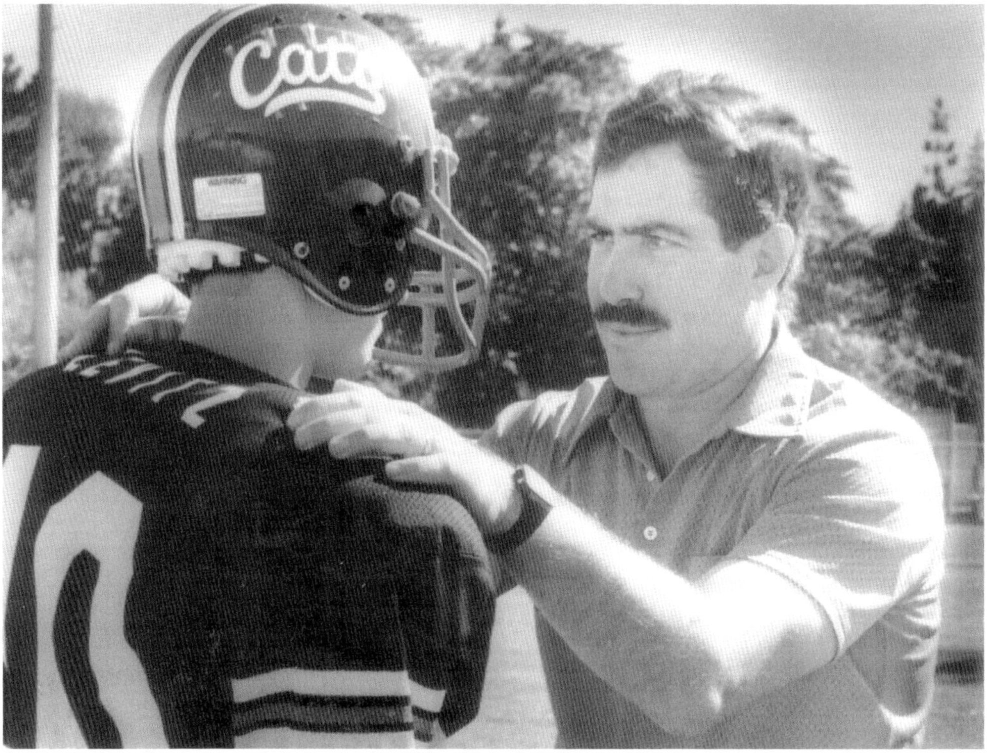

Horace "Butch" Cattolico

For 36 years, Butch Cattolico served as a respected math teacher and football coach at Los Gatos High School. Cattolico retired in 2013 with an impressive 264-62-5 record in his role as head football coach since 1986. Beyond his success on the football field, he believed in the importance of academic excellence, and he promoted the development of leadership skills and solid character. He expected the best of his football players, but even his reprimands ended with words of encouragement. His players came to call that "Cattolico Love." A scholarship in his name has been established to ensure that his legacy lives on.

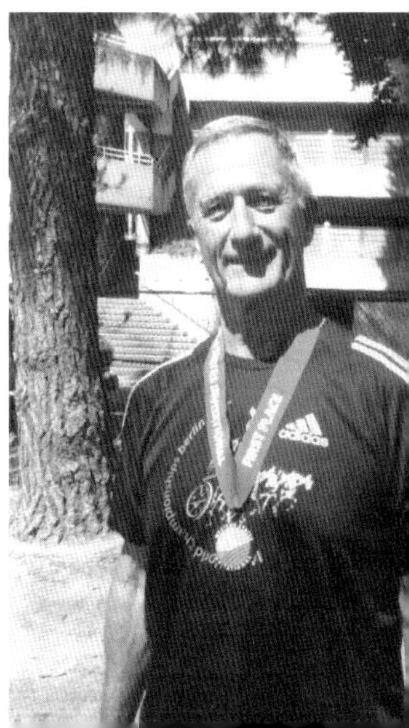

Ed Burke

For more than five decades, Ed Burke has competed in the hammer throw, setting records and receiving accolades for his athletic accomplishments. He is a three-time Olympian, contending in 1964, 1968, and 1984. In 1974, Ed and Shirley Burke settled in Los Gatos and opened the Los Gatos Athletic Club. Burke's love for his sport led him to coach young throwers, and he was instrumental in the addition of Junior Olympics development to many sports programs. His decision to resume training in order to compete in the 1984 Olympics at age 44 seemed foolish to some, but he qualified for the team and was selected to carry the American flag as the athletes circled the track for the opening ceremonies. (Courtesy Ed Burke.)

CHAPTER FIVE

Dynamic Duos

There have been many notable partnerships in Los Gatos history. The great love affair between Charles Erskine Scott Wood, a prominent lawyer, and Sara Bard Field, a poet and suffragette, is a dramatic story of abundant joy mixed with pain and suffering. They were willing to defy convention and sacrifice almost anything they possessed in order to be together. They built their home on a hill south of Los Gatos to live in a peaceful, beautiful place and find the solitude to write.

A different kind of partnership existed between the Joseph Doetsch Sr. family, who ranched north of Los Gatos, and their longtime employees, the Riichi Nishimura family. The Nishimuras were evacuated to Heart Mountain Relocation Center in 1942. When the ban was lifted, Doetsch did everything possible to help the Nishimuras reestablish their lives. He solved a desperate housing situation by scraping together scarce building materials to construct temporary housing for their use.

When the Irish come to town, which they do every March, they are celebrating a sister city partnership between Los Gatos and Listowel, County Kerry, Ireland. A visit to C.B. Hannegan's Irish Pub is mandatory, where they receive "a hundred thousand welcomes." A connection also exists between Los Gatos and Walt Disney Productions. Marcellite Garner Wall, who raised her children on Johnson Avenue in the 1940s, was the voice of Minnie Mouse in more than 40 early cartoons.

Charlie and Lucy Wedemeyer may have been the most inspiring duo in town. When Charlie was diagnosed with Lou Gehrig's disease at age 30, the "power of two" took over. With truly remarkable strength and perseverance, these soul mates worked together to enable Charlie to continue coaching football at Los Gatos High School.

On a lighter note, while Los Gatos didn't have Laverne and Shirley, it did have Shirley and Denise, mother and daughter, who ran their little Antiquarium antiques emporium in a corner of the Fretwell Block. One didn't have to collect antiques to pay a visit to these two likeable ladies who would raise customers' spirits and catch them up on what was happening around the town.

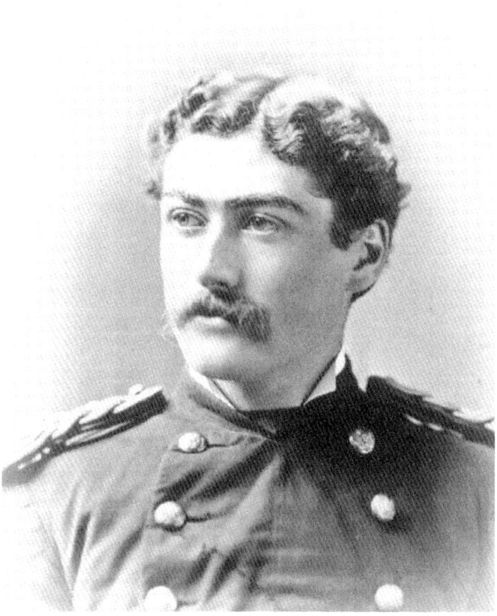

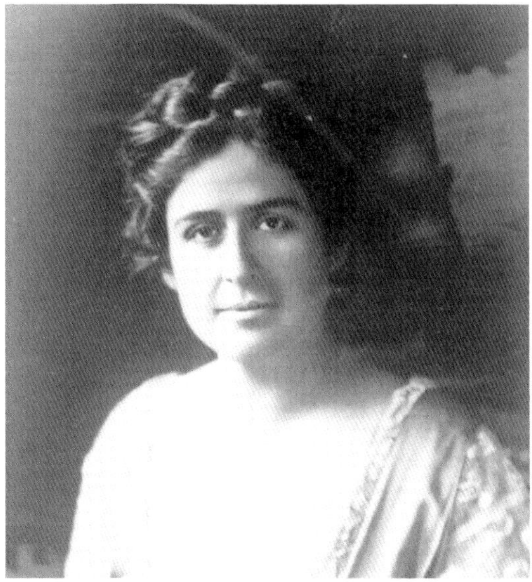

Charles Erskine Scott Wood (1852–1944) and Sara Bard Field (1882–1974)

The Bohemian enclave of C.E.S. Wood and his consort, Sara Bard Field, in the hills south of town intrigued the people of Los Gatos. From 1926 to 1944, the Cats Estate was a gathering place for artists, intellectuals, and radical thinkers. The occupants held themselves somewhat apart from the inhabitants of the little town located less than one mile away.

Wood was a West Point graduate, class of 1874, but a reluctant soldier. Stationed at Fort Vancouver, Washington Territory, he took a leave to travel to Alaska. He was recalled to his unit to participate in campaigns against the Nez Perce and Bannock Indians, which he sorely regretted later in life. In 1878 he went east to marry Nanny Moale Smith, a Washington, DC, socialite. Realizing he wanted to escape the Army, he secured another leave, this time to enroll in Columbia University Law School. He resigned from the Army in September 1884 and by 1885 was settled with his family in Portland, Oregon, and had set up his law practice.

Field was raised in a strict Baptist family and was just 18 when she married a fundamentalist Baptist minister twice her age, Albert Ehrgott, and accompanied him on a mission to Rangoon, Burma. In 1910, the Ehrgotts, now the parents of two children, also settled in Portland. The lives of both Wood and Field changed forever when they were introduced by Clarence Darrow. Within a year, they were deeply in love.

Field's 1914 divorce was bitterly contested by her husband. Wood's wife, Nanny, simply refused to grant him a divorce. The couple finally married in 1938, four years after Nanny's death and many years after they had settled at the Cats Estate.

Field became a national leader for women's suffrage. In 1915, she made a transcontinental journey by automobile, making speeches and collecting thousands of signatures along the way to present to Pres. Woodrow Wilson in Washington, DC, in favor of granting women the vote.

Wood and Field began living together in San Francisco in 1918. Nanny Wood continued to reign as the grande dame of Portland society and until the day she died never stopped hoping her husband would return to her. Reverend Ehrgott exploded with fury and indignation, feeling that his wife had chosen to enter a "life of sin" and embrace "free love." (Courtesy Huntington Library.)

A Compelling Love Affair

Both C.E.S. Wood and Sara Bard Field were singular, unusual people, and each lived to the age of 91 years. Their seemingly enchanted lives in fact included difficult, entangled relationships and tragedy. Field's son Albert, age 17, was killed when she accidently backed her car off a cliff in Marin County. Sara's leg was partially severed, and her grief caused a nervous breakdown. Wood's son Maxwell, a brilliant and handsome man, died a few years later of blood poisoning at age 37.

Wood was a polished man and a dichotomy. In his law practice he defended radicals, underdogs, powerful corporations, and wealthy people. He was unconventional enough to both enrage and charm those he met. A self-described philosophical anarchist, his friends included Emma Goldman, Margaret Sanger, and Mark Twain.

During their Portland years, Wood and his first wife, Nanny, were prominent members of society and lived in a large art-filled home. They were parents to six children. Wood's legal work eventually provided him with financial independence and enough money to set up trust funds for his Portland family so that he could retire and move to California to be with Field.

In 1919, Wood and Field traveled to Los Gatos in search of a "brooding place." Real estate salesman Zedd Riggs helped them find the 34-acre plot that became the Cats Estate. Until their home was finished in late 1925, they couple used a little cabin on the land as a weekend retreat. They lived on their own terms. Sara said later that "We were willing to make almost any sacrifice on earth to establish a life together," and that is what they did. Beyond their intense love for each other, they practiced literary collaboration and had a mutual interest in social justice. They read and edited each other's work and were both successfully published. Their home became a salon visited by the likes of John and Carol Steinbeck, Ansel Adams, and Carl Sandburg, encouraging their own creativity. Wood died in 1944, and Field sold the estate in 1955. She moved to Berkeley to be near her daughter's family. (Courtesy Wood family.)

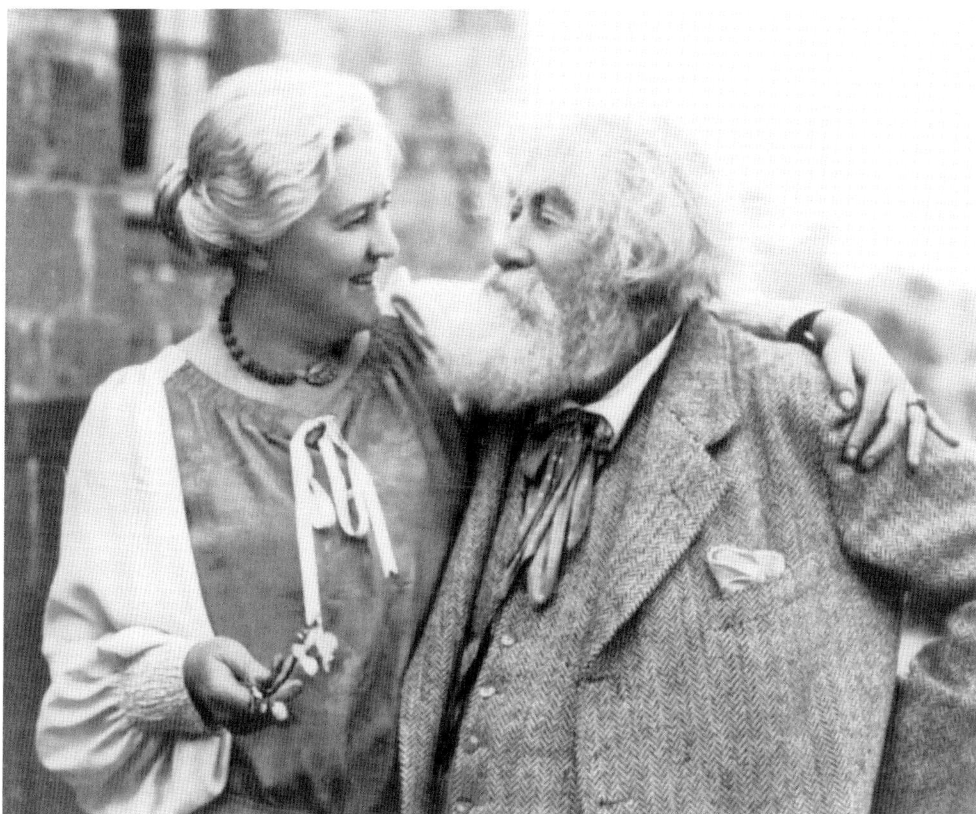

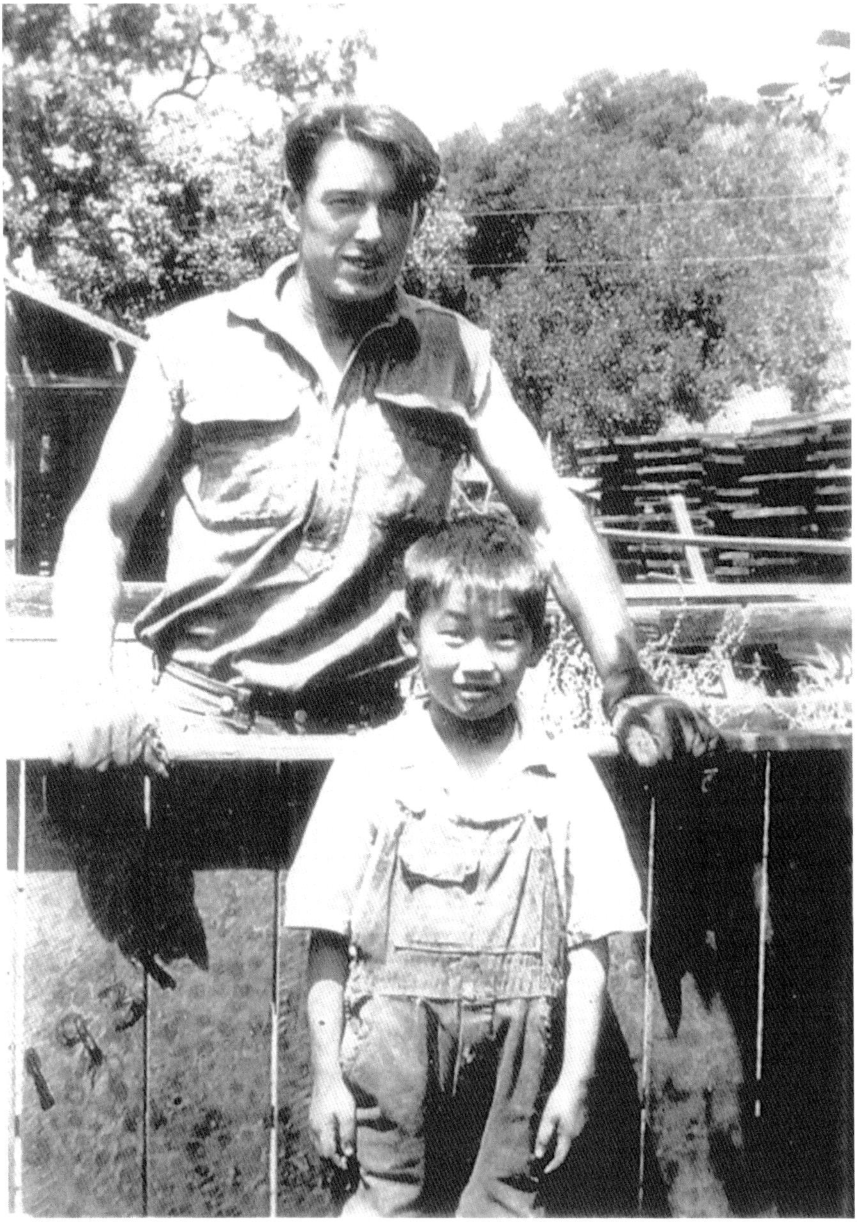

Joseph P. Doetsch Jr. (1907–2009) and Joe Nishimura

Joe Doetsch grew up on his family's orchard land, which they called Vasona Junction Farm. The family home was on land now occupied by the Santa Clara County Fire Department on South Winchester Boulevard. On the day in 1931 that Joe graduated from Santa Clara University with an engineering degree, he returned home, put on his work clothes, and set to work washing out wooden apricot trays. Young Joe Nishimura stands at his side in this image, symbolic of the long relationship between the two families. With the help of the Nishimuras, the Doetsch farm had a yearly production of 400 tons of apricots, prunes, almonds, grapes, and strawberries. During World War II, the Nishimura family was interned at Heart Mountain, and when they returned, the Doetsch family helped them reestablish their lives. (Courtesy Joseph P. Doetsch Jr.)

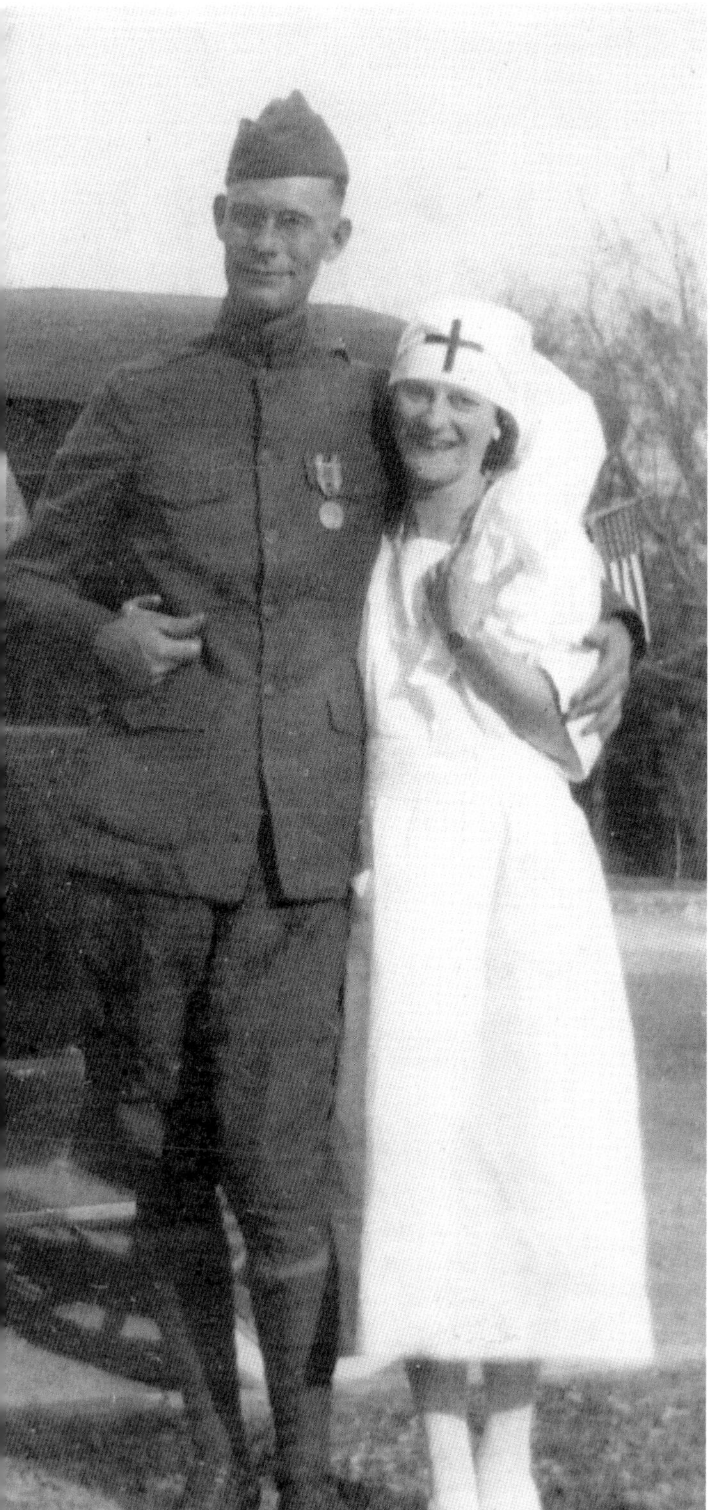

Paul E. Curtis Sr. (1888–1965) and Blanche Arnold Lidley (1894–1981)
Paul E. Curtis Sr. served in France and Germany during World War I, and when he returned, he was prominent in the business and financial circles of Los Gatos for more than 50 years. He owned a local hardware store, managed Redwood Estates properties as they developed, and, in the early 1930s, joined the First National Bank of Los Gatos, eventually becoming president. His wife, Blanche, was never a nurse but is dressed here for a Memorial Day observance. She is remembered for her participation in the Los Gatos pageants, starting with the first production in 1919 when she played the Spirit of Water. Their only child, Paul Curtis Jr., was a well-known local dance instructor who founded the Los Gatos Academy of Dance in 1954. (Courtesy Paul Curtis Jr.)

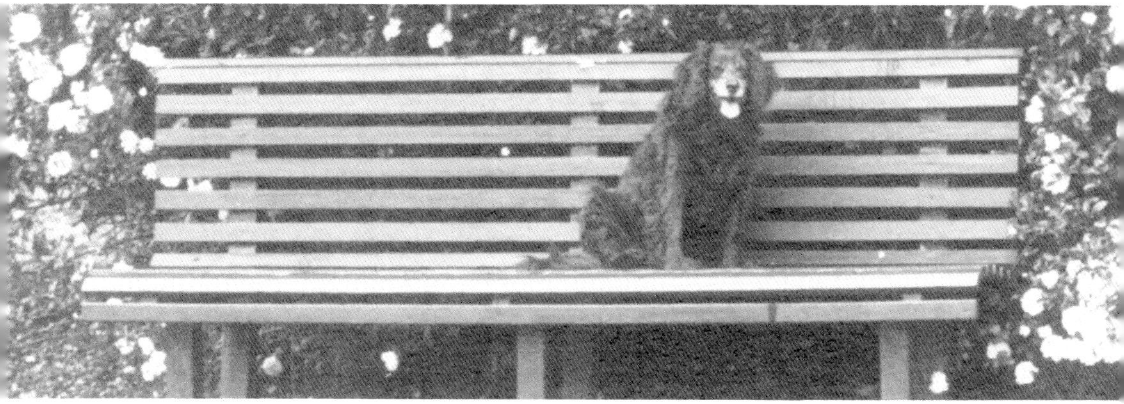

Rags

During the early 1900s, Rags became the unofficial town dog. The friendly cocker spaniel loved the local children and greeted them every morning on their way to school and visited them again during recess. This self-appointed guardian of the town's prominent citizens often accompanied his charges on their journey to the train station. Rags appeared in many of the town views documented by professional photographer Alice Wagner, and when he died in 1920, his obituary appeared in the *Evening News*.

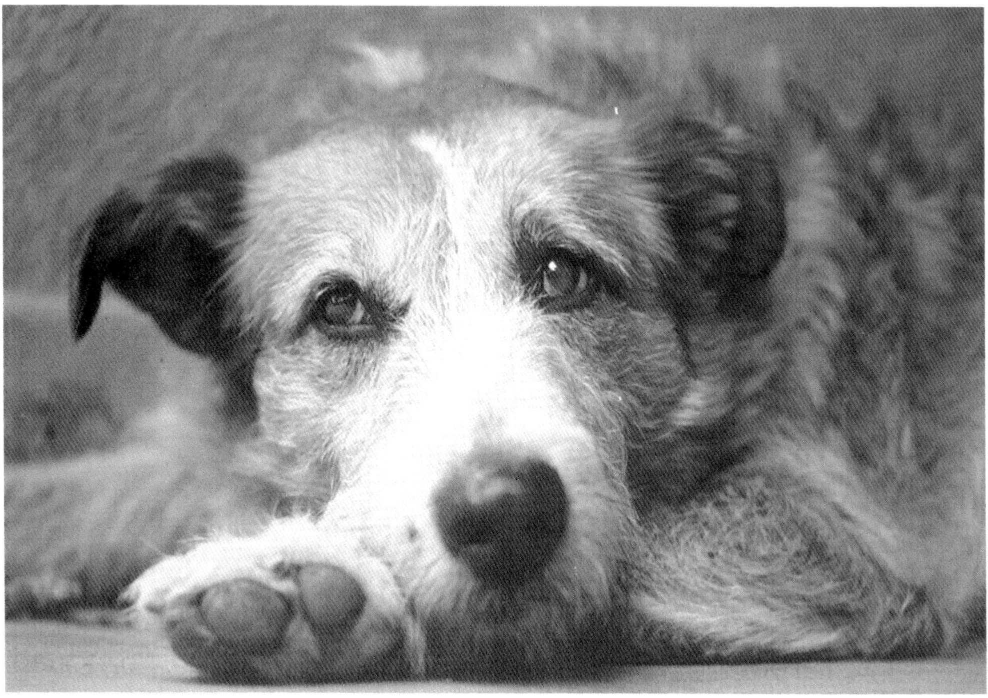

Chief

In the 1930s, a friendly fellow of unknown lineage made quite an impression on Los Gatos. Chief "attended classes" at Los Gatos Union Elementary School for 10 years and was appointed the official mascot. He snoozed in the aisles of the fourth-grade classroom but stood for the Pledge of Allegiance. Somehow, Chief knew when school was out and didn't show up on weekends or during vacations. On Saturdays, Chief sat next to the line of children buying tickets at the Art Deco Premier movie theater, and in the evenings, he was found on the porch of the Lyndon Hotel keeping an eye on the men patronizing the bar.

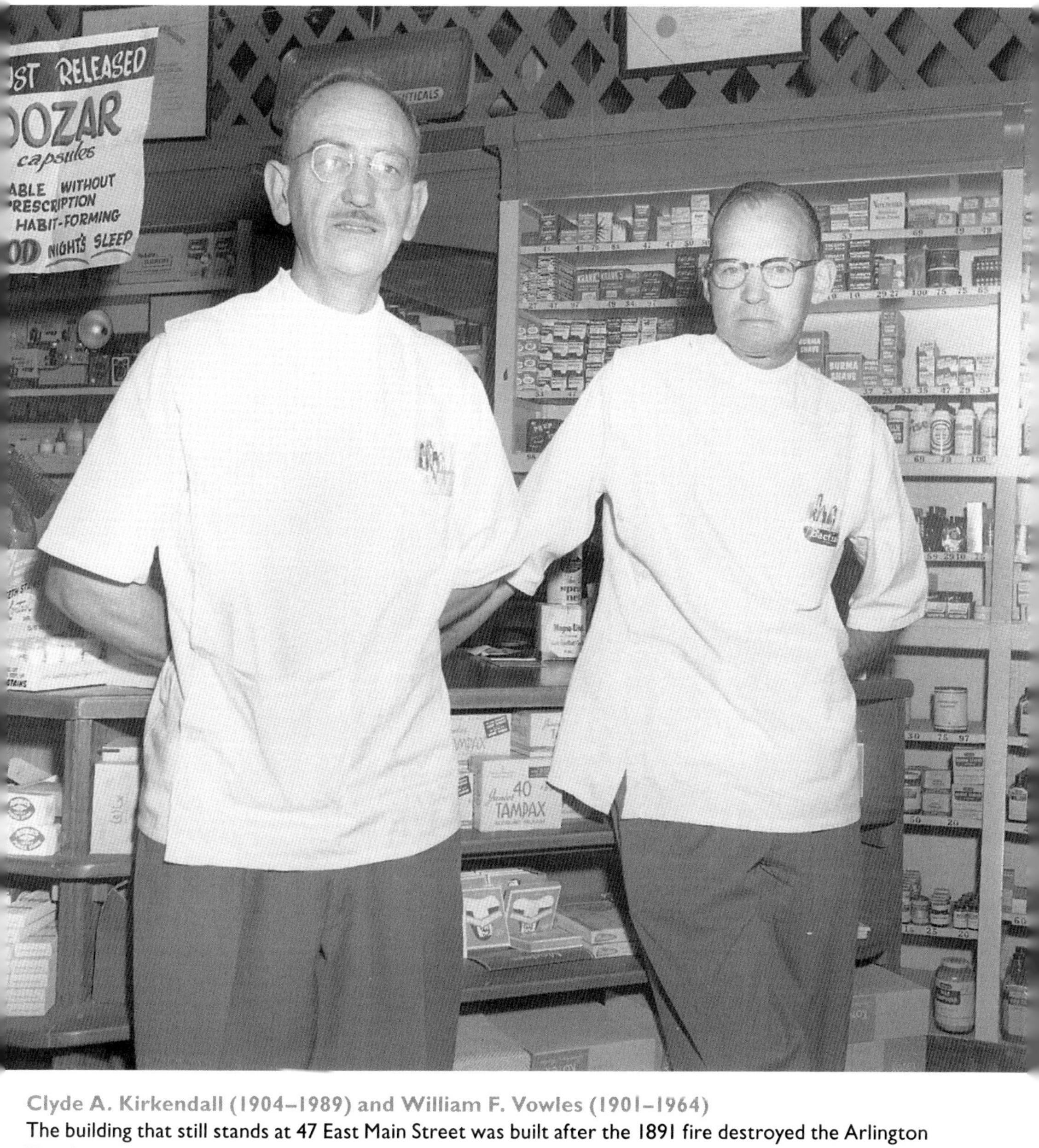

Clyde A. Kirkendall (1904–1989) and William F. Vowles (1901–1964)
The building that still stands at 47 East Main Street was built after the 1891 fire destroyed the Arlington Hotel, an ornate little hostelry with towers and turrets that had occupied that address. Entrepreneur W. John Whisenant bought the property in the mid-1920s in order to expand his grocery store and pharmacy. He sold out to pharmacists Clyde Kirkendall (left) and Bill Vowles. For more than 30 years, the Los Gatos Pharmacy, or "Kirk 'n' Bill's" as it was commonly known, was a town landmark. It was especially popular with teenagers from the nearby high school, who dropped in for root-beer floats or cherry Cokes at the soda fountain. According to Olivia de Havilland, Kirk and Bill were kind about extending credit to students but kept close accounts. When she returned to town in 1952 for a visit, they presented her with a bill dated 1934, and she happily paid the $1.81 she had left on the books. Kirkendall was active in town affairs and helped reduce the number of rats at the town's sewer farm in the 1940s, using his rifle. Vowles served in the US Navy overseas during World War I.

Ida L. Etzkorn (1912–2003)

A native of Los Gatos, Ida Etzkorn worked throughout her childhood at her father's store, the Los Gatos Market, and as an adult went on to own several businesses. Her last venture was as co-owner of Idamina's, a popular women's clothing store on North Santa Cruz Avenue in downtown Los Gatos. Women came from miles around to purchase the fashions and costume jewelry offered by Ida and her partner, Geraldine Fowler.

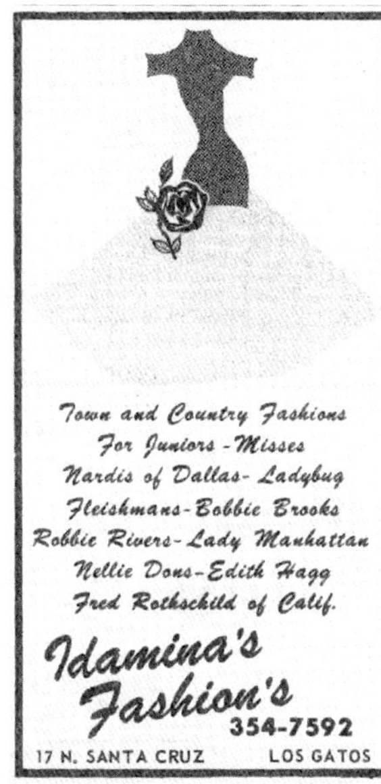

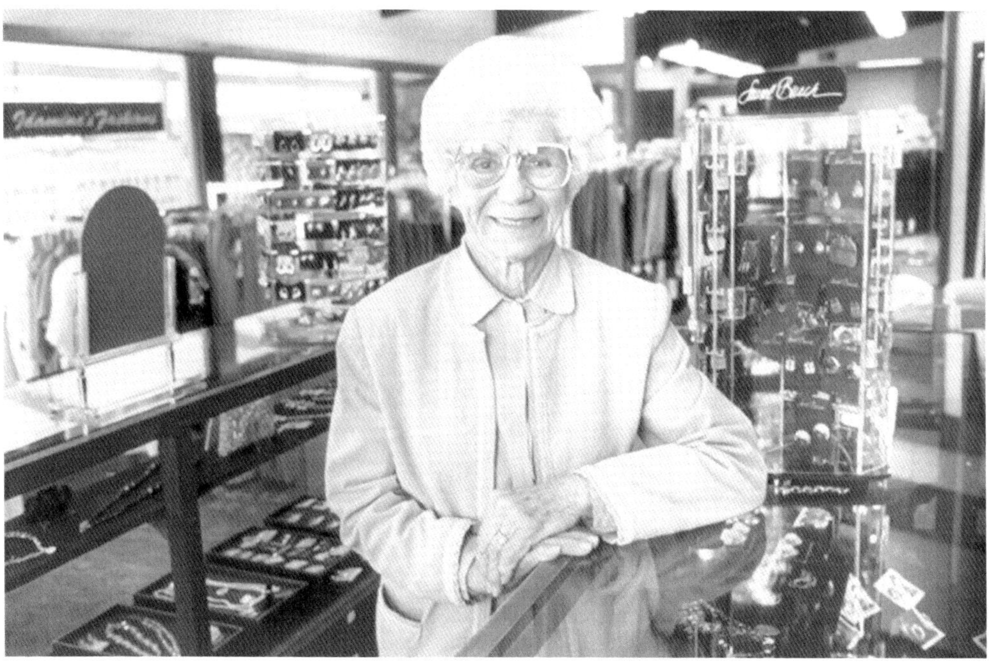

Geraldine Lepurin Fowler (1915–2002)

Los Gatos native Geraldine "Mina" Lepurin was born to Yugoslav immigrants who came to town in the 1880s. She graduated from Los Gatos High School in 1935. During World War II, she worked in San Francisco at a residence for servicewomen, sending her wages home to her widowed mother. After the war, she married Los Gatos native Robert Harold Fowler, and they built an adobe home in the Santa Cruz Mountains. In 1960, she and Ida Etzkorn opened Idamina's Fashions. Mina worked 363 days a year and treated every customer like a friend. On Thanksgiving Day, she took her family to the mountains to cut trees to decorate the store for Christmas. Idamina's Fashions closed in 1989 as a result of the Loma Preita earthquake.

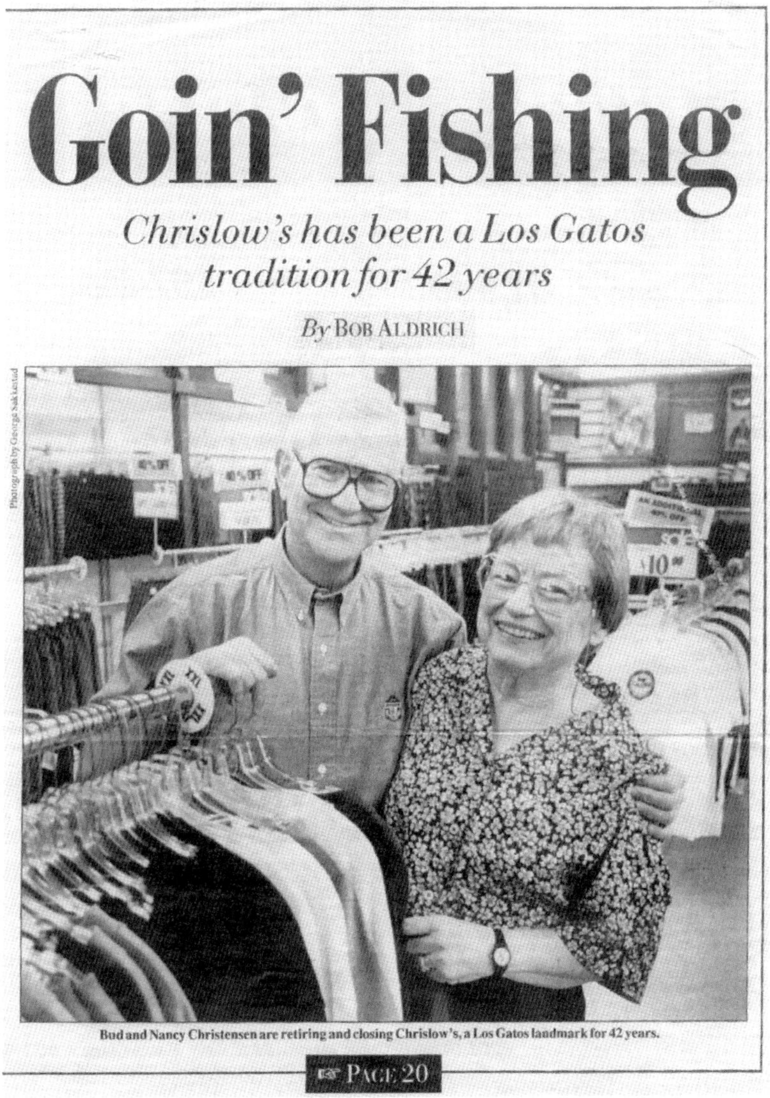

Goin' Fishing

Chrislow's has been a Los Gatos tradition for 42 years

By BOB ALDRICH

Bud and Nancy Christensen are retiring and closing Chrislow's, a Los Gatos landmark for 42 years.

☞ PAGE 20

Deal (1927–2013) and Nancy Christensen

Deal "Bud" Christensen Jr. and his wife, Nancy, owned and operated Chrislow's Department Store in Los Gatos for about 40 years. Chrislow's was founded in 1951 by Bud's father, Deal Christensen Sr., in partnership with Bob Whitlow and was located on North Santa Cruz Avenue in a small space next to Place Funeral Home. In 1957, the business moved to the corner of Nicholson and North Santa Cruz Avenue, where it remained until it closed in 1993.

Bud Christensen's retailing skills, his work with other town merchants and the chamber of commerce to encourage people to "shop Los Gatos," and the fact that he hired more than 2,000 local students and community members through the years all had a positive impact on the Los Gatos retail climate.

Because the store was his own business, Christensen was able to move quickly to bring new merchandise into the shop. Chrislow's was often the first store in the wider area to stock trendy clothes, such as the popular "surfer look." Despite the influx of large shopping malls, Chrislow's attracted people to town for its selection and service. Eventually, discount stores and outlets did impact the hometown department store, and the owners retired. (Courtesy George Sakkestad.)

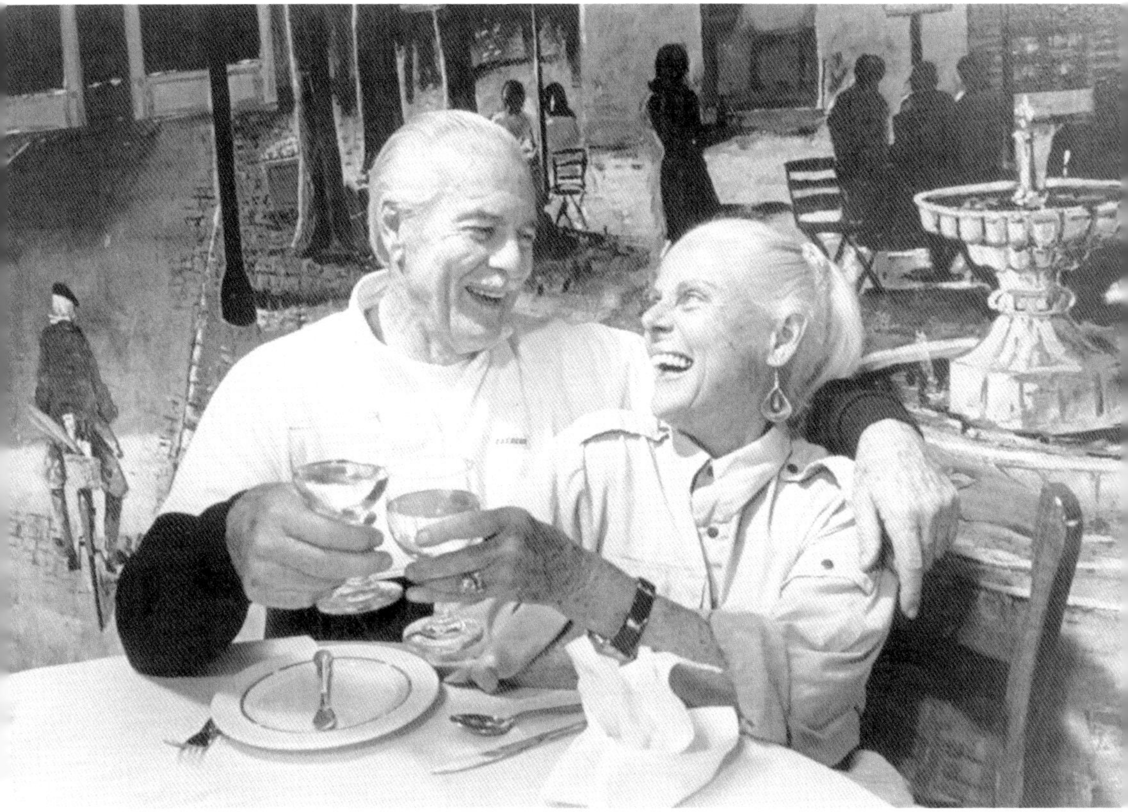

Bruce (1920–2003) and Diane Ogilvie (1919–2009)

The union of Bruce and Diane Ogilvie is described by their children as a love story that never ended. Diane, a high school dropout, was a risk-taker who became an accomplished businesswoman with numerous real estate holdings, including homes, commercial properties, and restaurants. Her crowning achievement was the 2002 opening of the elegant Hotel Los Gatos at 210 East Main Street, which she worked for years to accomplish.

Before arriving in Los Gatos, Diane had a successful career as a singer, performing all over Europe, in San Francisco, and in Las Vegas, where she opened for Wayne Newton at the Sands Hotel. She never completely abandoned her singing career and could sometimes be found of an evening singing at her restaurant, The Cats, on Highway 17 just south of Los Gatos. The Ogilvies purchased the Cats Estate in 1955.

Dr. Bruce Ogilvie, the grandfather of sports psychology, was a longtime professor at San Jose State University, where he developed such concepts as visualization and relaxation in relation to athletic success. He served as a consultant to US Olympic ice-skating contenders, individual professional athletes, and professional sports teams. He coauthored *Problem Athletes and How to Handle Them* with fellow professor Thomas Tutko in 1966. Although Bruce Ogilvie held a doctorate in psychology degree, he said the smartest person he knew was his wife, whom he affectionately nicknamed "Darling Diane."

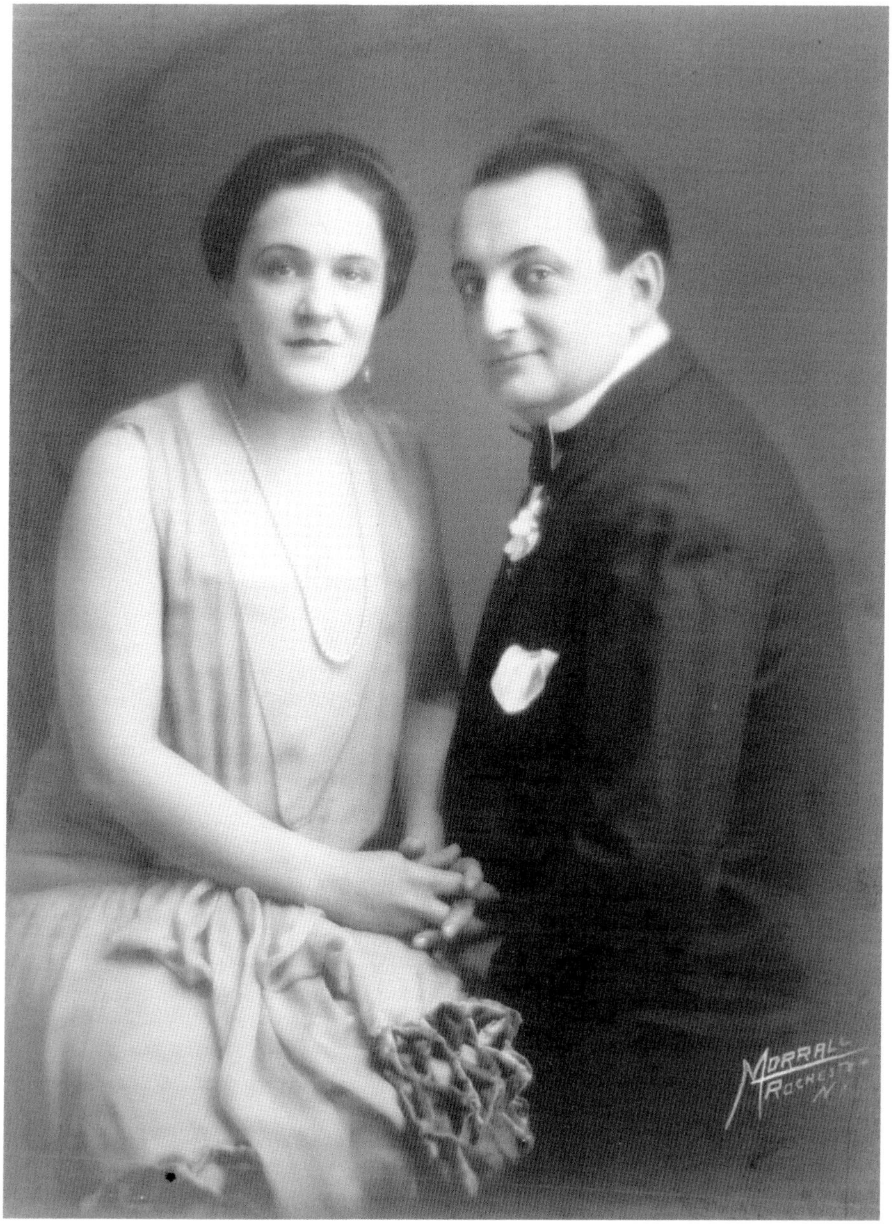

Morton (1886–1961) and Betty Baxter Harvey (1892–1980)
Morton and Betty Harvey were successful entertainers before they settled in Los Gatos in 1946 and opened a photography studio. Morton, a native of Nebraska, got his first job in vaudeville in 1907. In 1914, he became the first singer to record a blues song, "The Memphis Blues" by W.C. Handy. One year later, he recorded "I Didn't Raise My Son to Be a Soldier," a popular pre–World War I protest song that is still sometimes heard in documentary films. After the war, he toured the Orpheum and Pantages vaudeville circuits billed as the "Rolling Stone," a vagabond singer. Eventually, Morton teamed up with Betty, a stage and radio singer who hailed from Illinois. When vaudeville ended, the couple moved to Oklahoma and managed a radio station for 14 years. During their Los Gatos years, Betty worked as a vocal coach and piano teacher, while Morton photographed the changing Santa Clara Valley. (Courtesy Chuck Bergtold).

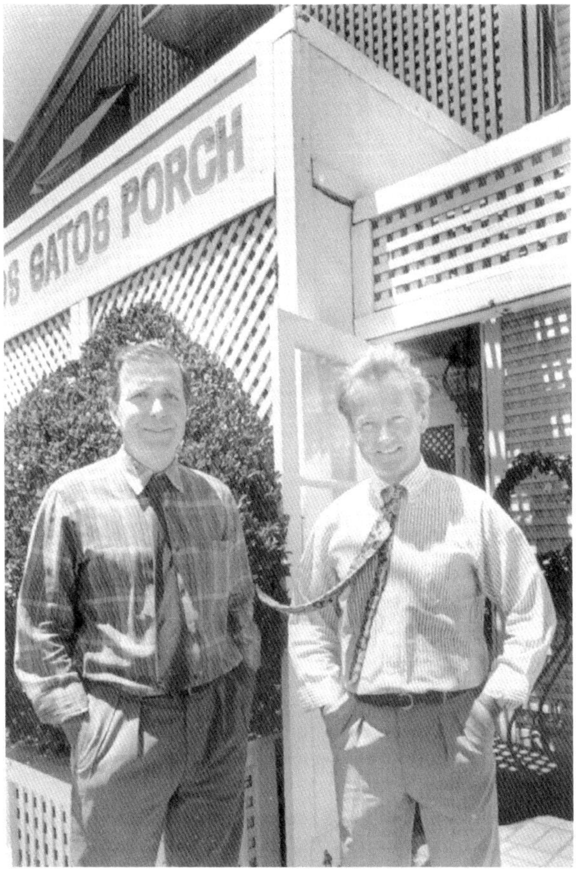

Larry Arzie and David Stonesifer

Larry Arzie (left) and David Stonesifer met in the art department at San Jose State University in 1962. They moved to Los Gatos while they were still in college for the same reasons they still love the town today. A beautiful natural setting, a small-town vibe, and generations of families who loved the location created a natural draw.

Stonesifer's first business venture was the Los Gatos National Porch, located behind the Opera House. Later, he and Arzie acquired the old Berryman Plumbing building on North Santa Cruz Avenue and opened the Los Gatos Porch, where they sold beautiful furniture and accessories for the home. Stonesifer's experience working in the display department at Gump's in San Francisco prepared him for his role as design director for the business.

The Porch was a town favorite for nearly 32 years. Displays were individual vignettes featuring unusual pieces in unique settings. Window displays often showcased one-of-a-kind treasures, and the traditional Christmas tree was a stunner. Their slogan was "good taste at great value," and the community agreed.

In 1981, Arzie and Stonesifer purchased La Estancia, their home on Overlook Road. The residence evolved from the original house designed by Willis Polk and built by Frank McCullagh in the early years of the 20th century. The house had fallen into disrepair, and extensive renovations began in earnest. Now, the elegant estate is often the scene of nonprofit fundraisers and other events.

After Arzie and Stonesifer sold their business in 2001, they pursued other interests. Stonesifer has become a recognized plein-air artist. His impressionist paintings were featured in a one-man show at the Triton Museum in 2012. Arzie works hard to preserve the attributes of the town that he has always valued. In recent years, this duo has generously underwritten the rent at 24 North Santa Cruz Avenue to secure space for the Los Gatos Museum Art Gallery.

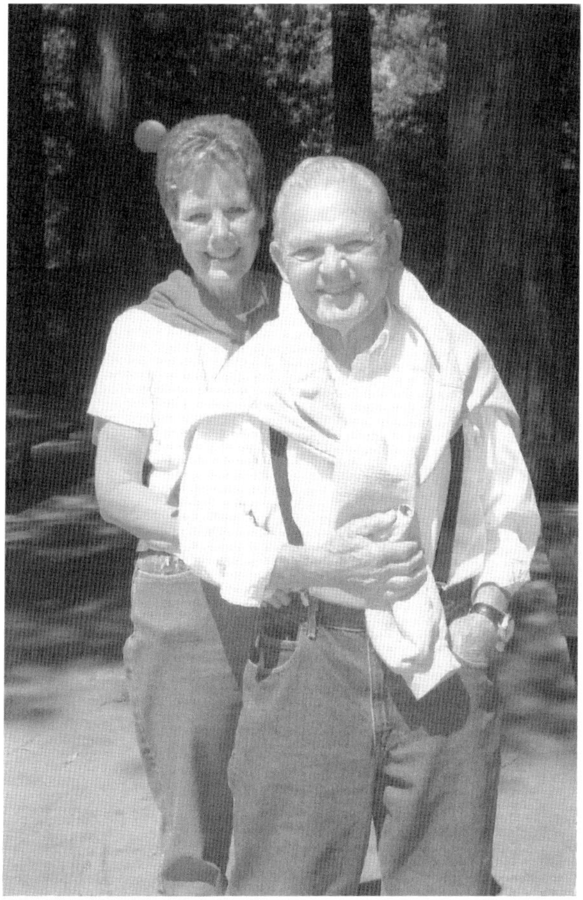

Ted Simonson (1925–2012) and Patti Hughes

Ted Simonson is a Los Gatos icon who grew up in Ojai. He developed a strong work ethic as a boy milking cows and packing lemons. The mechanical and construction skills he learned as a 17-year-old longshoreman served him all of his life. He was drafted when he was 18, and as a member of the 42nd "Rainbow" Infantry Division, participated in the monumental task of liberating prisoners from Germany's Dachau concentration camp.

Simonson married Donetta Jean Peyton in 1948, and he enrolled at San Jose State University. His career at Los Gatos High School began in 1951 when he drove the bus that transported mountain kids to and from school. During his 47-year tenure at the school, he served as a football and wrestling coach, a typing teacher, dean of boys, assistant principal, and finally, in 1979, principal. He was strict but empowering, and his leadership contributed to the strengths of a fine educational institution.

Simonson retired in 1998, a much-loved member of the community. He remained active in the Lions Club and the Los Gatos Community Foundation and attended reunions of his military unit, where a scholarship was established in his name. In 2010, he received the Los Gatos High School Lifetime Achievement Award.

New York native Patti Hughes arrived to teach English at Los Gatos High School in 1973. While attending her first faculty meeting, she noticed Simonson wearing a Masonic ring. Her father was a Mason and had told her that if she was ever in trouble she should find a Mason to help her out. She introduced herself, and that was the beginning of a life-long friendship. She retired from her job as assistant principal in 1998, and she and Simonson formed a landscaping business. When Simonson's health began to fail after the death of his wife, he often found refuge at the home of Patti and her husband in the Santa Cruz Mountains.

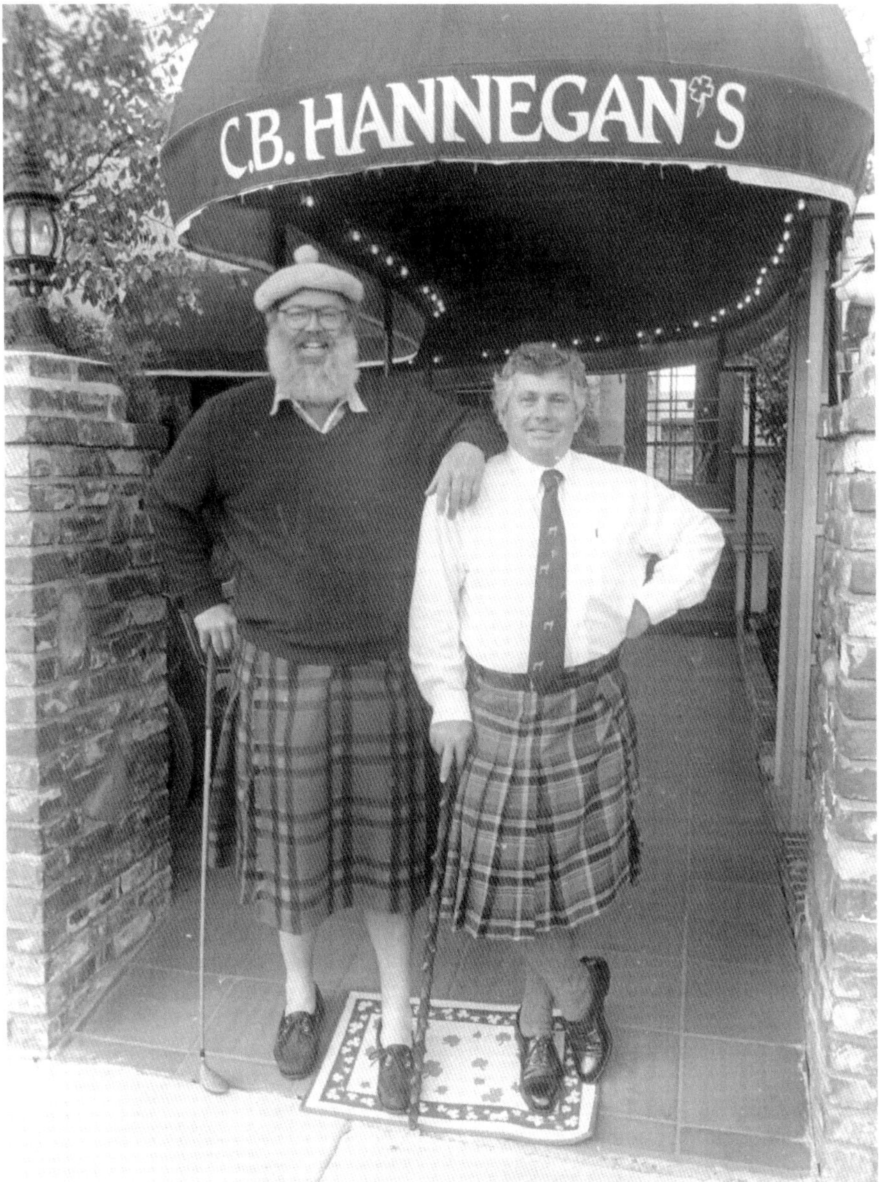

Chris Benson and Johnny Hannegan

Chris Benson (left) and Johnny Hannegan have operated their popular pub and restaurant on Bachman Avenue in Los Gatos for more than 30 years. Generations of locals, and thousands of others, have been welcomed into the warm, wood-lined setting where the feel of the Emerald Isle is always in evidence. Good food and a fine selection of single-malt whiskies add to the enjoyment.

With noteworthy generosity, Hannegan and Benson have consistently donated their time and services for charitable and community events, Benson often manning the barbecue. In times of crisis, they are always there, as they were after the 1989 earthquake, feeding emergency workers and people who need a hand.

St. Patrick's Day is celebrated in epic proportions at Hannegan's and is an all-day affair. Fostering the sister-city relationship between Los Gatos and Listowel, County Kerry, Ireland, also often falls under their purview, complete with regular visits from Irish dignitaries. C.B. Hannegan's is a legendary Los Gatos institution.

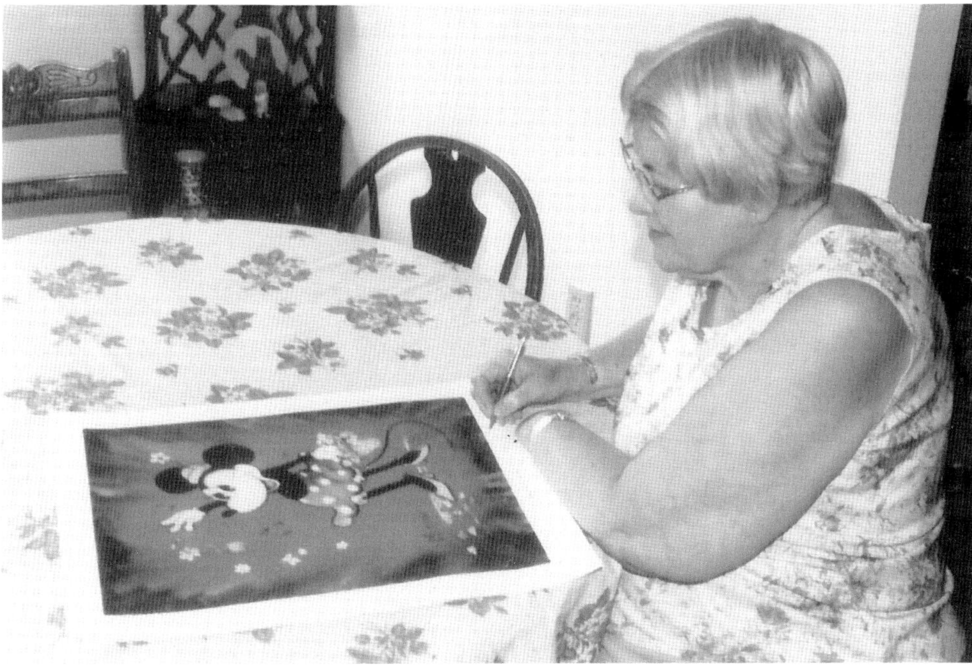

Marcellite Garner Wall (1910–1993)
From 1930 to 1941, Marcellite Garner was the voice of Minnie Mouse for Walt Disney Productions. Starting with "The Cactus Kid," Marcellite and Minnie were a twosome in more than 40 cartoons. She also worked for Disney as a cel painter and an inker. Marcellite married Richard B. Wall in the 1930s, and the couple had three sons. By 1945, the family was living at 208 Johnson Avenue in Los Gatos. Marcellite became a clerk at Green's Pharmacy and also created a cartoon character named Senor Gato for the *Los Gatos Times-Observer.* One of her sons, Richard B. Wall Jr., was appointed Los Gatos fire chief in 1957. Another son, Camden Wall, asked his mother to paint a "self portrait" of herself as Minnie Mouse. Marcellite is shown signing her painting in 1977. (Courtesy Camden Wall.)

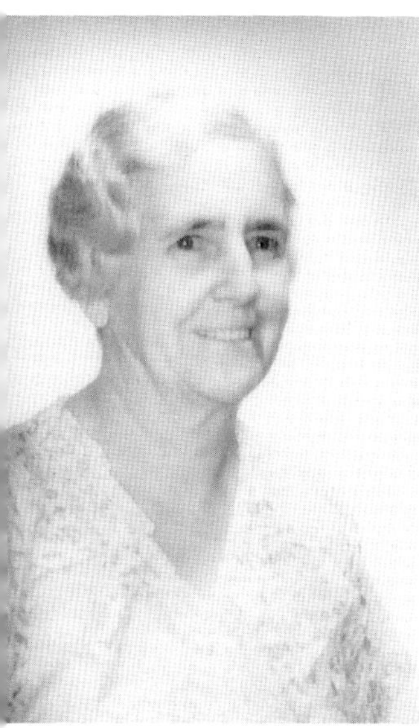

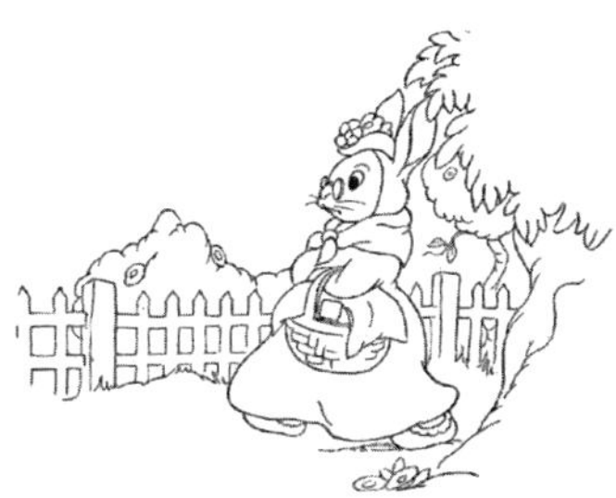

Minnie Rowe Crabb (1870–1940)
Born in Leicester, England, Minnie Rowe grew up in Nebraska. She worked as a teacher before marrying Charles Ellsworth Crabb in 1901. The couple had three children and moved often, but throughout her life, she wrote fiction and autobiographical stories. In 1925, the family moved to Los Gatos. Crabb was an avid supporter of temperance, and that passion is clearly evident in her *Mrs. Gray Bunny* books, which were written and published in Los Gatos from 1936 to 1938. Crabb served as director of child welfare for the Women's Christian Temperance Union of California. (Both, courtesy David Thayer.)

George Dennison (1873–1966) and Frank Ingerson (1880–1968)

This celebrated pair of artists established a studio home at Cathedral Oaks, above Alma, in 1911. A 1925 fire in the Santa Cruz Mountains destroyed their haven, but Frank Ingerson (left) and George Dennison rebuilt an oasis for themselves and the poets, musicians, and artists who found creative inspiration in the peace and tranquility of the property. Known affectionately as "the boys," the men were experts in many art forms: master painters, sculptors, goldsmiths, and silversmiths, they were also recognized for their ceramic, enamel, and leather work. Equally famed and widely traveled, they never sought publicity.

In the 1920s, the artists traveled to London to create a 3,000-pound bronze masterpiece titled *The Ark of the Covenant*, which was commissioned by the Temple Emanu-El in San Francisco. Locally, they were active in dramatic and musical productions, and in the early 1930s, they designed costumes for a play directed by Lillian Fontaine. Her daughters, Joan Fontaine and Olivia de Havilland, were the stars. In 1942, they helped to establish the Alma Trio and send it on its way to international success.

When the men's health began to decline, neighbor Yehudi Menuhin purchased their land and allowed them to live out their lives there, paying only property taxes. Menuhin eventually sold the estate to the Mid-Peninsula Open Space District, returning the land to nature. (Courtesy Sara Field Caldwell.)

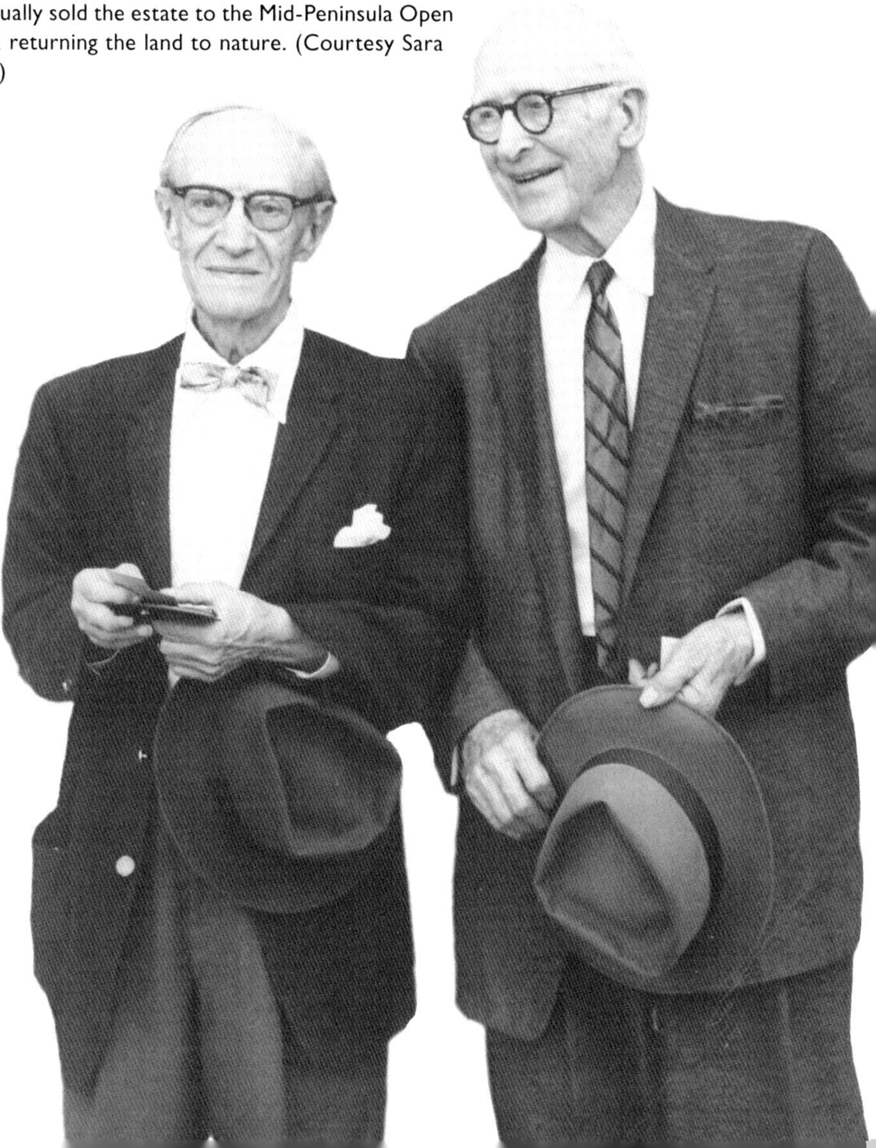

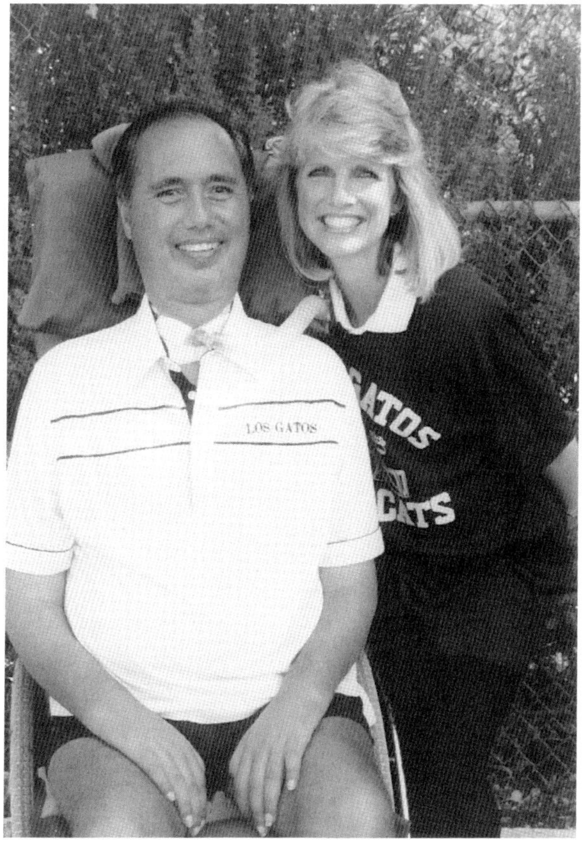

Charlie (1946–2010) and Lucy Wedemeyer

When Charlie Wedemeyer passed away in 2010, the governor of his home state of Hawaii, Linda Lingle, said that Hawaii had "lost one of its most inspirational and beloved sons." The same could be said of Los Gatos, where he taught and coached football for many years. Diagnosed with amyotrophic lateral sclerosis, also known as Lou Gehrig's disease, at the young age of 30, his life over the succeeding 34 years can only be described as heroic.

Wedemeyer grew up in an athletic family. He accepted a scholarship to attend the Punahou School in Honolulu, the same school from which Pres. Barack Obama graduated in 1979. He starred on the football team while there and also met Lucy Dangler, his future wife. When he was recruited with a full scholarship to Big Ten powerhouse Michigan State University, Lucy followed, and they were soon married.

After Wedemeyer completed his master's degree, the couple moved to Los Gatos, where Charlie taught math and later became head football coach at the high school. When he received his diagnosis of ALS, he was told he had about a year to live. At a time when most people would have given up all hope, the Wedemeyers decided they would persevere, and they did. By 1983, the disease had put Charlie in a wheelchair, but still they carried on. They worked out an arrangement with Los Gatos High School so that Wedemeyer could continue as coach. Lucy drove him up and down the sidelines in a golf cart and interpreted his whispered commands for the players and the rest of the coaching staff.

The media attention became enormous, and a documentary, *One More Season*, followed by a television movie, *Quiet Victory*, brought the Wedemeyers to national attention. When it finally all became too much, Charlie was asked to step down as coach. Remarkably, with the help of a strong religious faith and the acquisition of a portable respirator, the couple felt they had a second chance at life and even became motivational speakers for the disabled. This winning team refused to be defeated. Lucy Wedemeyer is now a successful realtor in Los Gatos. (Courtesy Wedemeyer family.)

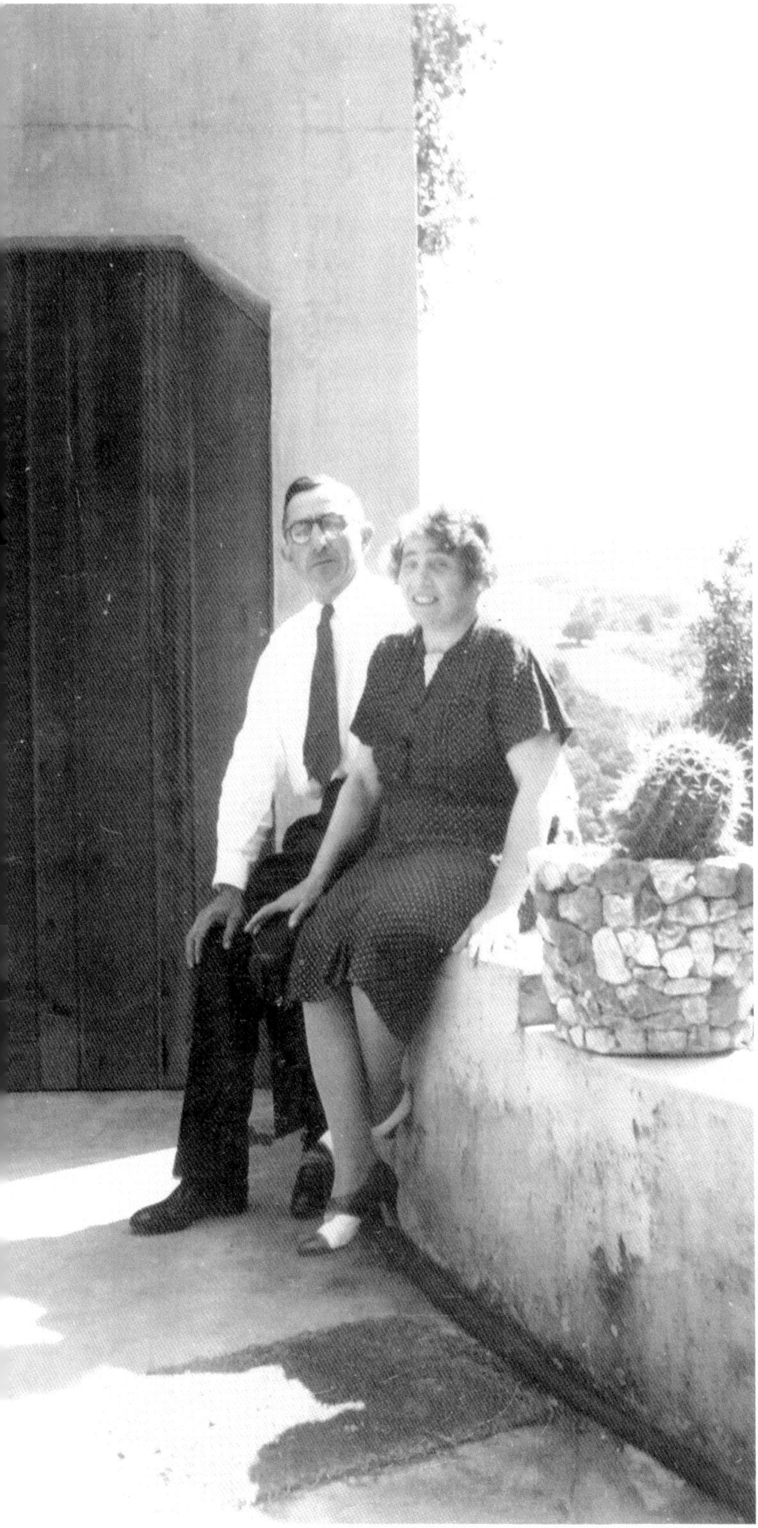

Vincent (1887–1965) and Mary Benevelli Gagliasso Marengo (1885–1974)
Vincent and Mary Marengo were Italian immigrants who worked at the Cats Estate as gardener-chauffeur and cook-housekeeper, respectively, from the 1920s until 1953. Vincent arrived in Los Gatos in about 1900 and was sent to work in the Jesuit vineyard south of town, where he learned to make wine. Mary arrived with her first husband, Pasqually Gagliasso, in 1902. Her marriage had been arranged in Italy and was not a happy union. She left her husband in 1923, causing a scandal in the Los Gatos Italian American community.

About that same time, Vincent went to work at the Cats Estate, and by 1926, Mary was working there too. They were married there in 1931, after Mary was able to obtain a divorce. They are pictured here in 1938 at the gatehouse to the estate, where they lived for many years. Sara Bard Field stated frankly that Mary and Vincent, who both labored long and hard, made life possible at the Cats Estate. When the Marengos retired in 1953 due to Vincent's severe asthma, Field purchased a home for them at 320 Bachman Avenue, where they lived out their lives. (Courtesy Marengo family.)

Gil and Sandy Decker

Civic involvement, pride in community, and benevolence are characteristics that describe Gil and Sandy Decker, who have made Los Gatos their home for 40 years. Sandy is recognized as an energetic and charismatic leader whose dedication to the town of Los Gatos and its residents is nearly unmatched. Her involvement in volunteer projects is legion, and she often serves as a catalyst for action. A few of her most notable accomplishments include service on the planning commission from 1994 to 2000, her election to the town council in November 2000, and her term as mayor in 2002. Recently Sandy chaired the Los Gatos Library Capital Campaign, which raised more than $2 million for the town's new library. Gil Decker is a private consultant for strategic planning and technology whose clients have included the Boeing Corporation, the US Navy, and Walt Disney Imagineering. During his career he has held a number of distinguished positions, often serving as president, chief executive officer, board member, or trustee of public and private organizations and corporations. Gil was appointed by Pres. Bill Clinton to serve from 1994 to 1997 as assistant secretary of the Army for research, development, and acquisition. (Courtesy Decker family.)

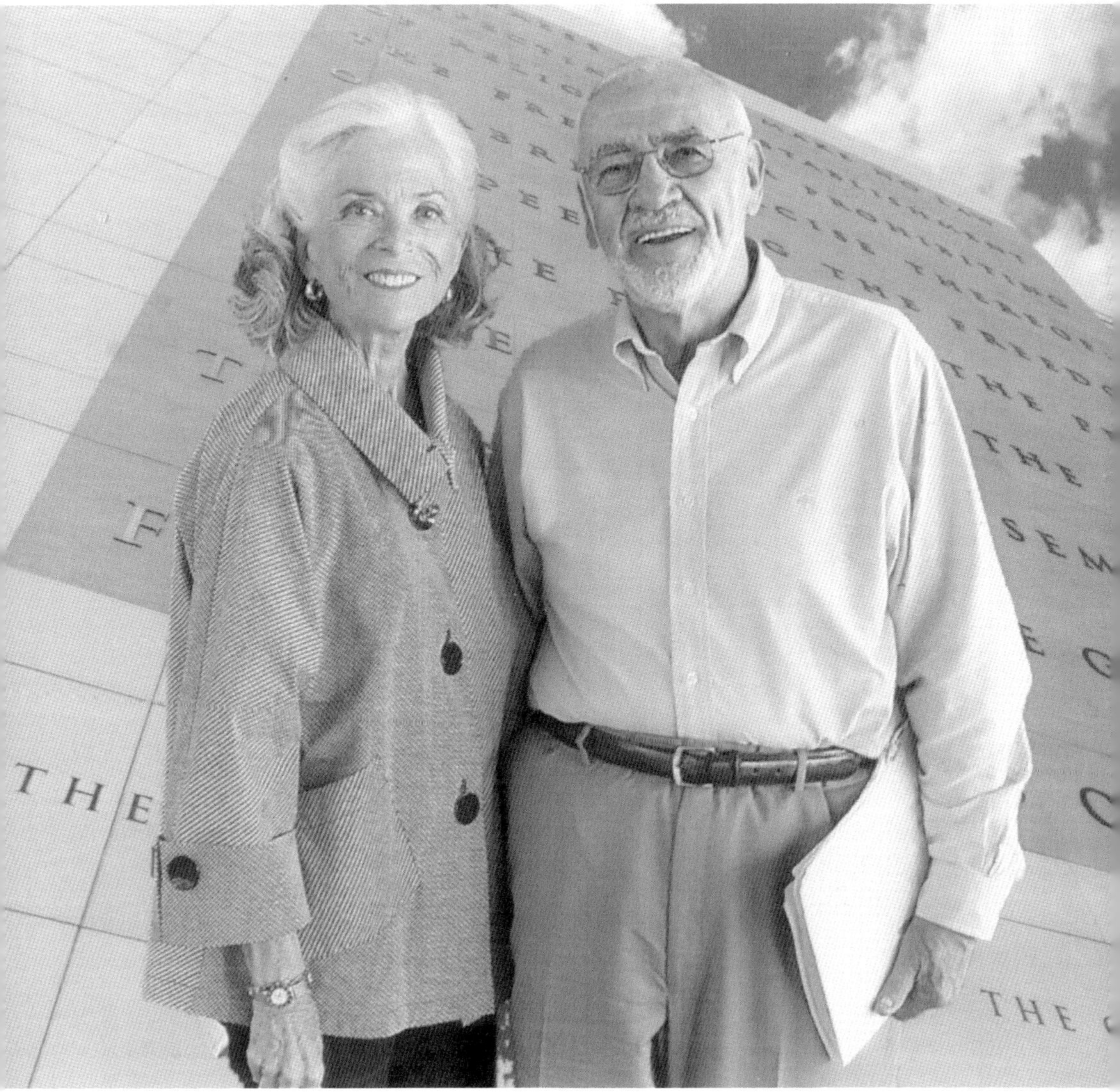

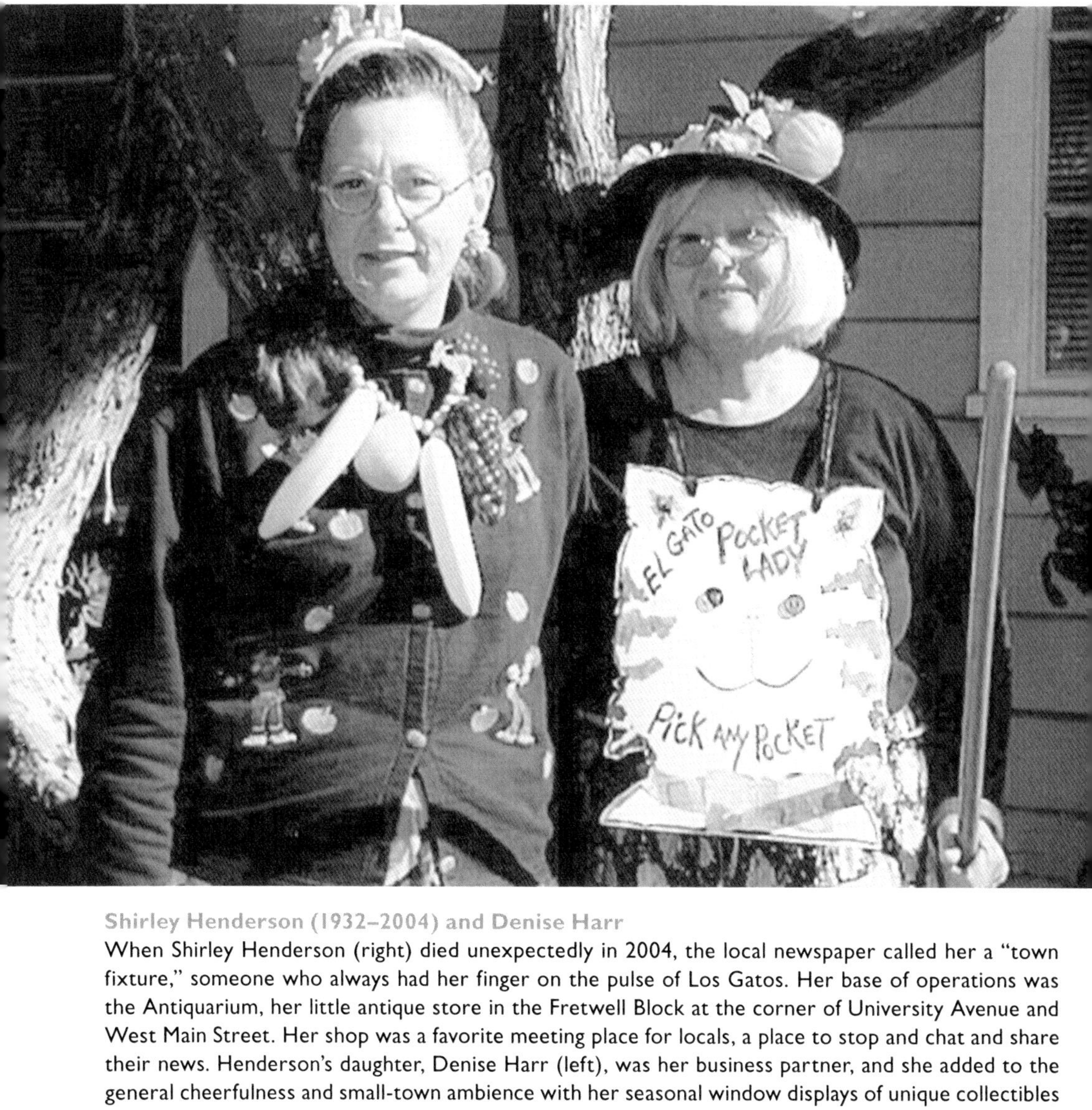

Shirley Henderson (1932–2004) and Denise Harr

When Shirley Henderson (right) died unexpectedly in 2004, the local newspaper called her a "town fixture," someone who always had her finger on the pulse of Los Gatos. Her base of operations was the Antiquarium, her little antique store in the Fretwell Block at the corner of University Avenue and West Main Street. Her shop was a favorite meeting place for locals, a place to stop and chat and share their news. Henderson's daughter, Denise Harr (left), was her business partner, and she added to the general cheerfulness and small-town ambience with her seasonal window displays of unique collectibles and antiques.

Henderson had an abiding love for Los Gatos and spearheaded efforts to preserve and enhance the downtown by serving as chair of the Los Gatos Chamber of Commerce Beautification Committee. The planters that line North Santa Cruz Avenue were part of her effort. But above all else, Henderson loved the people of Los Gatos. She knew most everyone, and called her customers by name. She is fondly remembered. (Courtesy Denise Harr.)

CHAPTER SIX

Heroes and Desperadoes

There are far more heroes than bad guys in the history of Los Gatos, but it may not have seemed that way in the late 1870s and the 1880s. The crime wave that hit the little country town during that period surprised and dismayed the population. Los Gatos was not a raw, crude settlement like those that had appeared 30 years earlier on the frontier, especially during the Gold Rush. There existed substantial homes, a number of churches, a railroad, a cannery, a school, several hotels, a news depot, a city band, and two doctors. Townspeople were beginning to realize the abundance that life in California seemed to promise. They practiced social responsibility and had begun to talk about incorporating the town.

Nevertheless, a series of shootouts and murders set the town on edge, and the people of Los Gatos began to wonder if their beautiful "Gem City of the Foothills" would become known only for its lawlessness. The son of pioneer Jonathan Parr was shot and killed in 1877. A young woman was stabbed 13 times and left to bleed to death on Main Street in 1882. Two innocent men were tortured and killed at their home above Lexington in March 1883—a grizzly crime that made national news. These incidents and many others set the course for mob violence that resulted in a lynching from the Main Street Bridge in June 1883.

The crime spree in Los Gatos lasted until 1890, but then as now, bravery, courage, and goodwill have always existed as a part of the culture of the town. Police officer Lyman Feathers took it upon himself to open Hotel Feathers for unemployed men during the Great Depression. Retired police captain Duino Giordano volunteers his experience and expertise managing natural disasters around the county. The service clubs in Los Gatos have been responsible for countless good deeds through the years. And on September 11, 2001, two young men, both graduates of the local high school and passengers on Flight 93, were instrumental in thwarting a probable terrorist attack on Washington, DC.

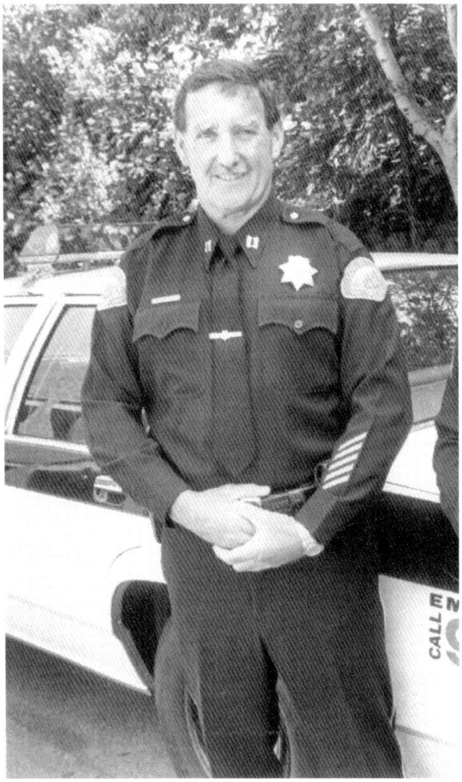

Duino Giordano

Born into the Italian community in north Los Gatos, Giordano served as a police officer in his hometown for more than 34 years. He retired from the Los Gatos–Monte Sereno Police Department with the rank of captain in 2004 and will be long remembered as an exemplary officer and a well-liked man who treated people fairly. He had a special interest in helping kids. Since his retirement, this veteran emergency responder has been deployed to 14 disasters around the country, most recently helping with Hurricane Sandy recovery.

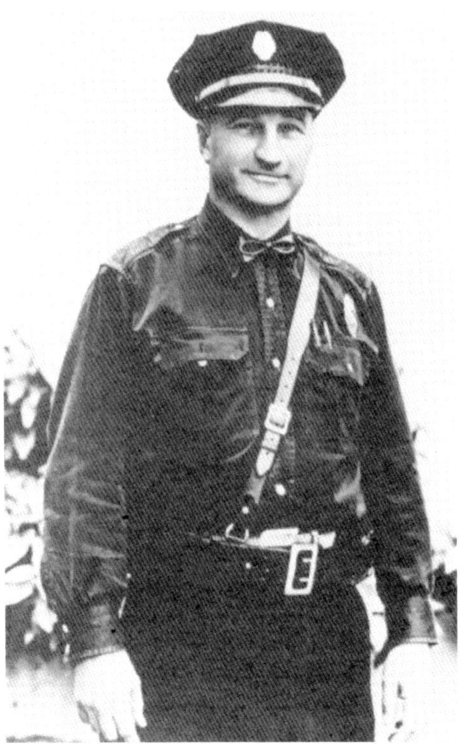

Lyman Feathers (1901–1954)

Lyman Feathers was serving as a Los Gatos police officer in the early years of the Great Depression when he founded Hotel Feathers. For two years, hundreds of unemployed men were provided supper, bed, and breakfast, courtesy of private donations and the Red Cross. In 1939, he was appointed chief of police with a salary of $175 a month. He served until 1943, when he resigned to go into the taxicab business.

Bruce Franks (1926–2013)

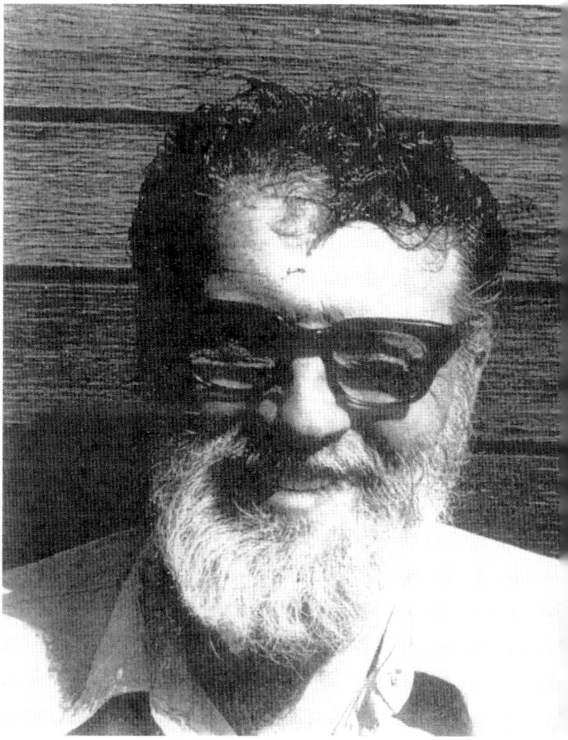

Bruce Franks was the grandson of Christian Frank, a sea captain from Germany who came to the Pacific coast on a lumber schooner in 1886 and purchased a 60-acre ranch in the current Chemeketa Park area. Franks was born in his family's home at 42 Broadway but spent his summers on his grandfather's land. He remembered walking up the hill to Holy City to get a "cornucopia" ice cream cone and marvel at the eccentricities of "Father" William Riker's town. For many years, Franks worked for the California Department of Forestry. His duties included the difficult task of fighting wildfires in the mountains. In more recent years, he had been the owner of Franks Water Service, servicing the mountain communities.

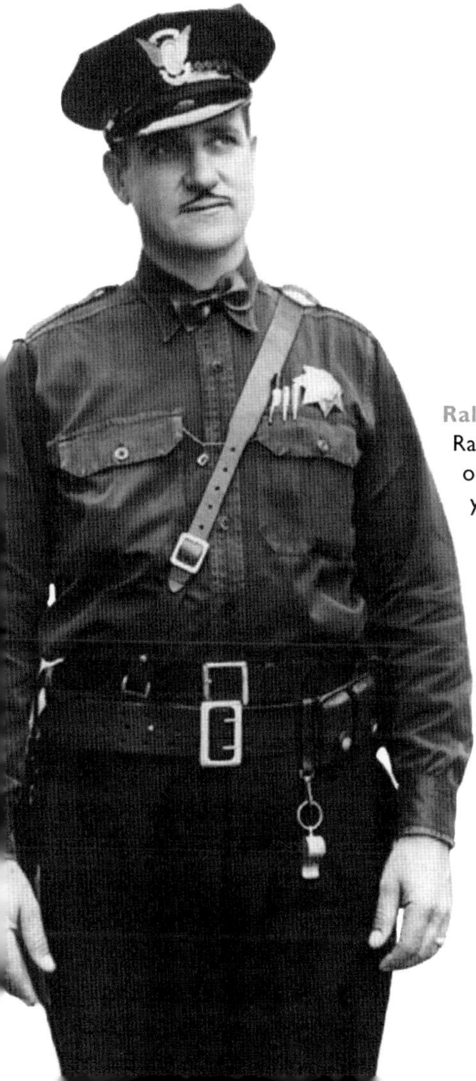

Ralph M. Phillips (1905–1981)

Ralph Phillips began his duties as a Los Gatos police officer on October 1, 1932. He stayed on the job for the next 38 years, serving as police chief from 1943 to 1970. With only three officers in his department when he became chief, he often dealt directly with any problems that arose in town. He is remembered as one of the founders of the Los Gatos Gymkhana Association, a group of enthusiastic horse owners. The Gymkhana Grounds, located in the area of the current town corporation yard, were dedicated in 1941. Rodeos and horse shows were held at that location until the freeway came through in the mid-1950s.

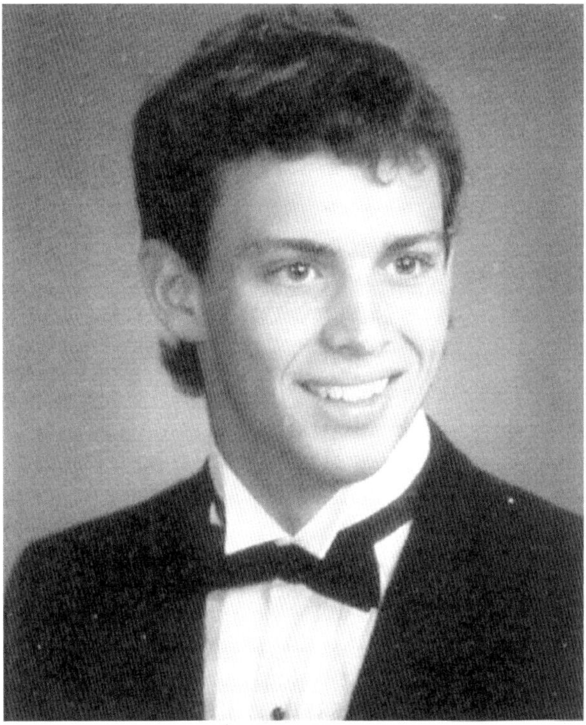

Todd Beamer (1968–2001)

Todd Beamer attended Los Gatos High School for his senior year, graduating in 1987. He was an all-league player for the basketball team and helped the baseball team win the West Valley League championship. On September 11, 2001, he was a passenger on United Airlines Flight 93 bound for San Francisco. When the plane was hijacked by terrorists, Todd used an onboard telephone to contact an operator. He calmly explained that he and other passengers were planning to take action against the hijackers. Thirteen minutes later, with the line still open, he was heard to say "Are you guys ready? Let's roll." The plane crashed in a rural area of Pennsylvania, and Beamer's heroic actions may have prevented the destruction of the Capitol in Washington, DC, a supposed target.

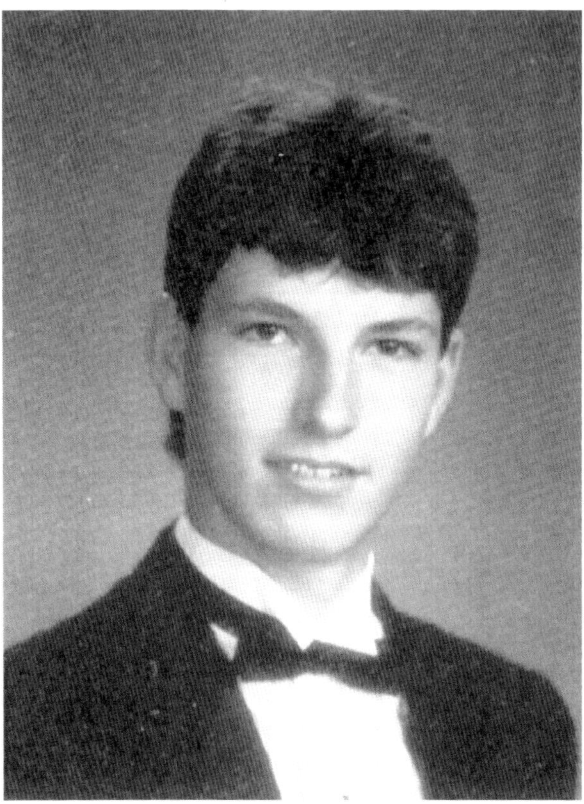

Mark Bingham (1970–2001)

Mark Bingham graduated from Los Gatos High School as a two-year captain of his rugby team in 1988 and was recruited to play for the University of California, Berkeley. On September 11, 2001, he was also a passenger on Flight 93. Shortly after taking off from Newark, New Jersey, he telephoned his mother and aunt and told them that three men had taken over the plane and that they had a bomb. Mark told his mother he loved her and then the line went dead. He is believed to have joined forces with Todd Beamer and other passengers in an attempt to overtake the plane's hijackers.

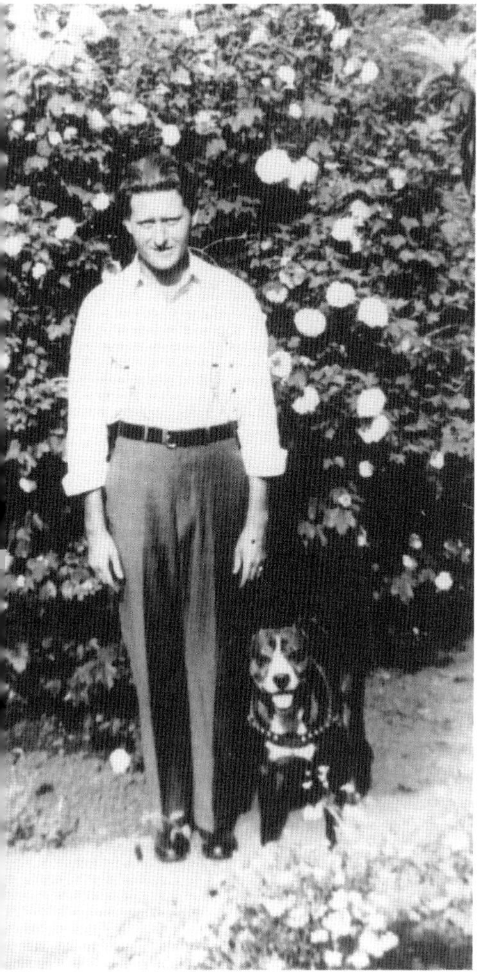

Victor Booher (1912–1991)

When Victor Booher died, a local newspaper headline read, "Town Will Miss Victor." Known as "Mr. Clean," he was a small, wiry man in a stocking cap who kept his eyes on the ground looking for bits of trash to pick up and put in his pocket. He lectured anyone who carelessly littered and saw himself as the caretaker of the town. Booher was a 1931 graduate of Los Gatos High School. He served in the Civilian Conservation Corps for three years and in the 1960s was the groundskeeper for Los Gatos Lodge. He is pictured here in Fairview Plaza, where a plaque was placed in his honor.

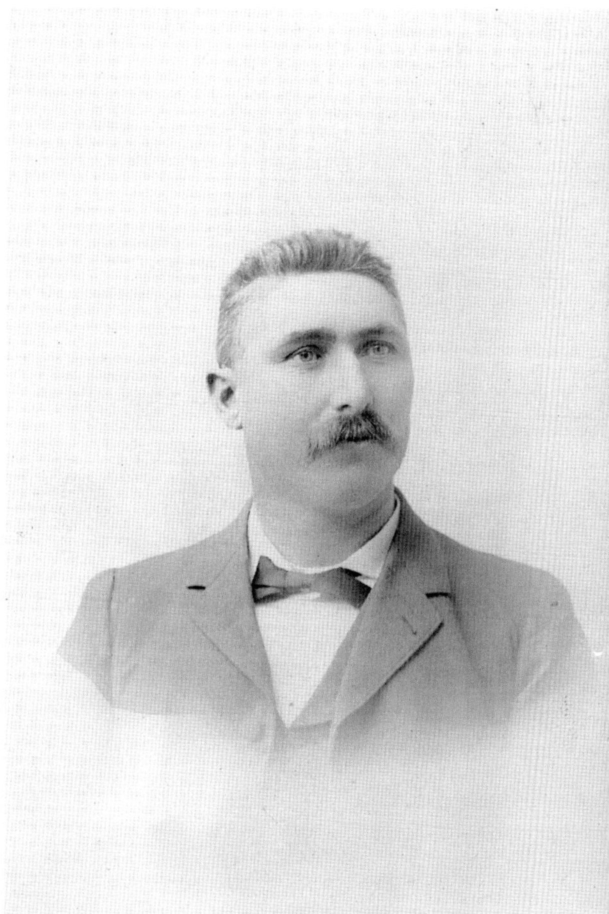

William Armstrong Pepper (1862–1905)

William Armstrong Pepper was a butcher by trade and the proprietor of the Union Meat Market on the south side of Main Street. When the great fire of October 13, 1901, obliterated the entire business district of town, and while the flames were enveloping his building, he stopped to help a disabled man escape from the burning building next door. He lost nearly everything in the fire but started up his business again on West Main Street, carrying on the legacy of his father, also named William Pepper, who founded Pepper's Meat Market in Los Gatos about 1881. The elder Pepper was born in New York in 1829, and when he decided to go west in 1867, he got on his horse and rode to Wisconsin.

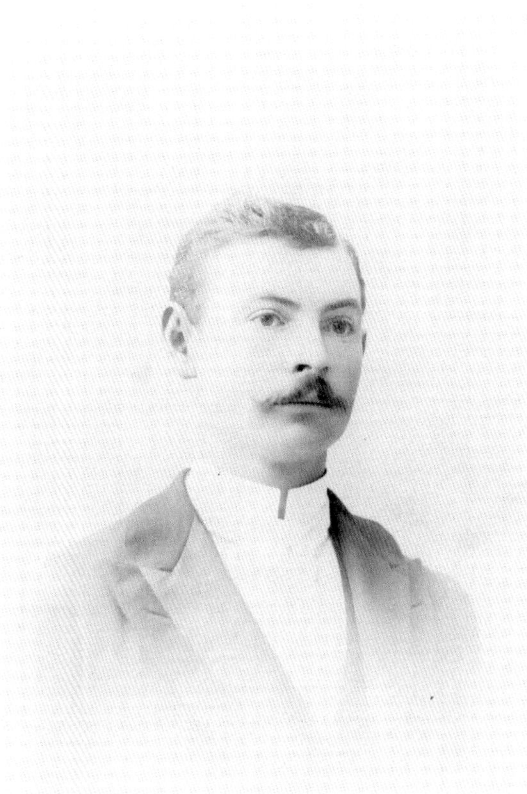

Junius Dalton Shore (1868–1934)

Junius (Dick) Shore was a civic-minded man whose long tenure as a firefighter stretched from the all-volunteer days until April 1, 1934, when he died from a heart attack a few days after fighting a forest fire. He rarely missed a fire in his 33 years of service. Shore served for a time as fire chief and was also elected to two terms as town marshal, from 1908 to 1912. He was a dedicated sportsman and often hunted deer in the hills south of town with other firemen. If the hunt was successful, the firefighters would hold a "venison feed" and invite the whole town. Shore married Nellie Taylor in 1897, and the couple had six children. (Courtesy Elayne Shore Shuman.)

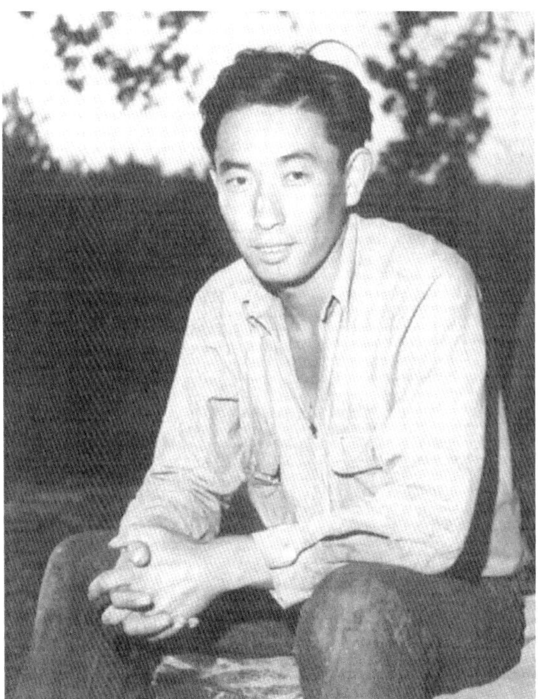

Isamu Oka (1918–2005)

Isamu Oka was the son of Japanese immigrants Tozaburo and Sumiko Oka. Tozaburo arrived in the United States in 1904, and Sumiko came in 1916 as his picture bride. Isamu enlisted in the US Army in 1942, was seriously wounded in combat near Siena, Italy, in 1944, and was discharged, the recipient of a Purple Heart. The Okas were well established on their orchard land in rural Los Gatos when they, along with other Japanese American families in town, were sent to internment camps in 1942. The Okas spent several years at Heart Mountain, Wyoming, before they were released and hurried back to their Los Gatos home. Oka Road is named for the family. (Courtesy Betsy Oka.)

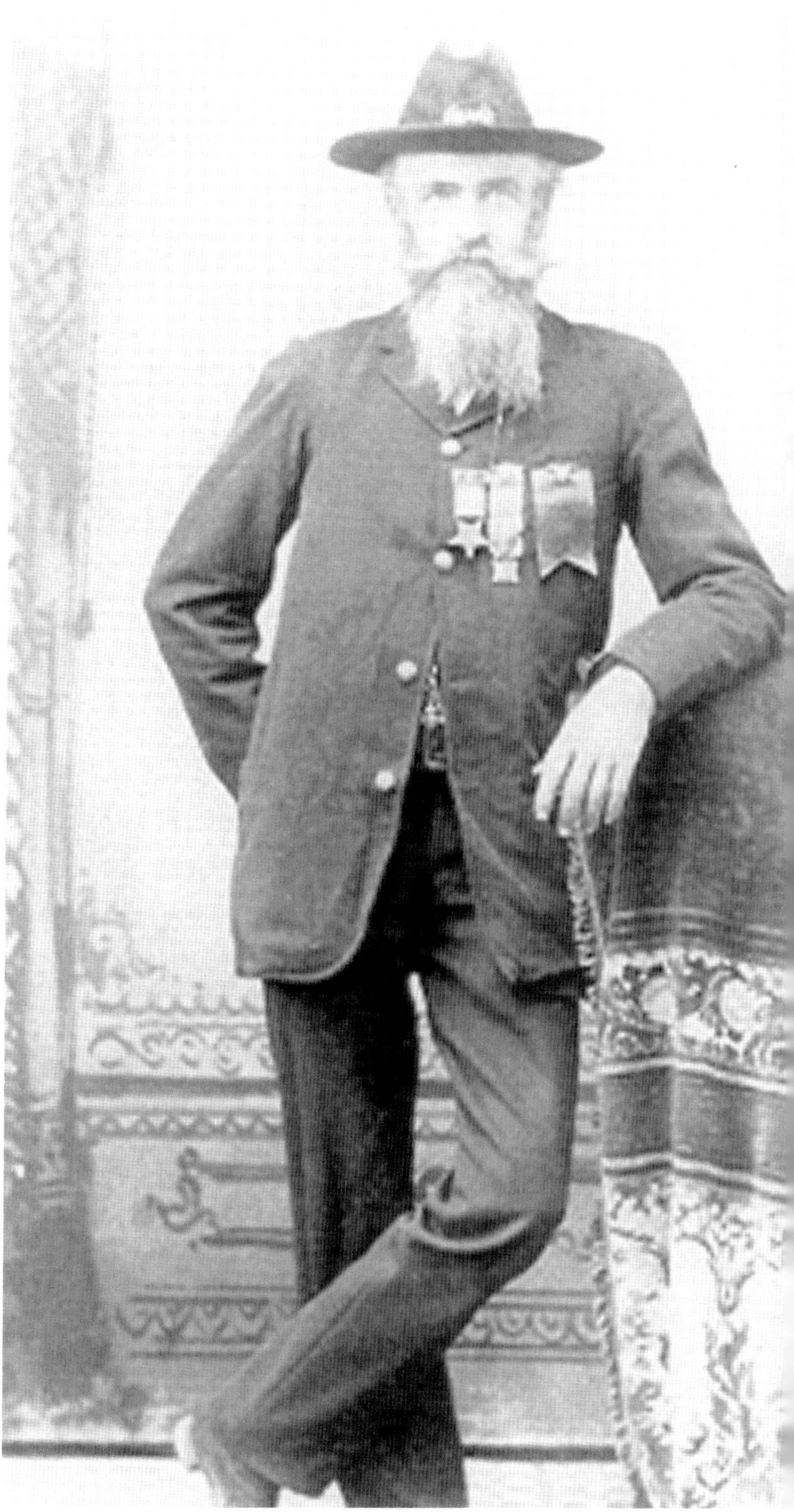

Magnus Tait (1837–1906)
Born in the Shetland Islands, Scotland's northernmost outpost, Magnus Tait was an infant when he arrived in America with his parents, Michael and Margaret Leisk Tait. He spent his youth in Illinois and married Antoinette Cooley in 1858. The couple eventually had four children. In August 1862, Tait enlisted as a sergeant in the 1st Light Artillery Regiment, Illinois. He took part in 22 Civil War battles and skirmishes, including Chickamauga and Missionary Ridge. He was captured on August 25, 1864, shortly before the fall of Atlanta, and spent the remainder of the war in Confederate prison camps, including the infamous Andersonville prison. He barely survived the experience and walked on crutches for some time after he returned home. The family farmed in Illinois and Kansas before migrating to California. By 1887, Tait was one of the city fathers who purchased and then developed the land that became the Almond Grove subdivision. The family home was at 231 Tait Avenue. (Courtesy Magnus Warren Tait family.)

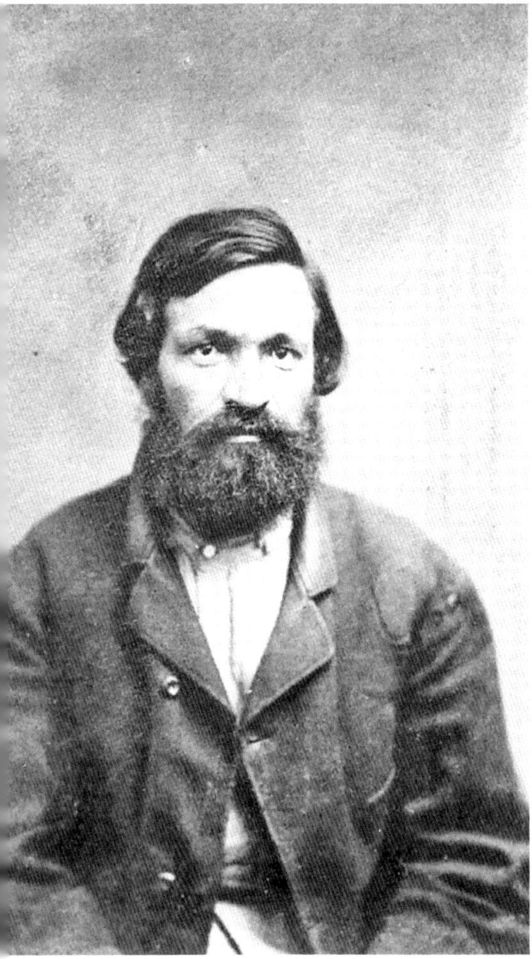

Rafael Mirabel (1833–1883)

Rafael Mirabel was a known desperado and cattle thief who had served two terms in San Quentin by the time he was present at the murder of Los Gatan Charles Parr in 1877. He sometimes rode with one of California's most infamous bandits, Tiburcio Vasquez. On June 17, 1883, Mirabel was murdered outside Lyndon Hall by Incarnation Garcia with a knife thrust to the heart. Mirabel had interfered with Garcia's love affair with Mirabel's sister-in-law, a married woman. Garcia, a cousin of Vasquez, was immediately captured by members of the Los Gatos Vigilance Committee and locked in the flimsy town calaboose. Within half an hour, Garcia was dragged to the center of the Main Street Bridge and lynched. For a time, Los Gatos was referred to in the press as "the town of big bridges and handy ropes." (Courtesy John Boessenecker.)

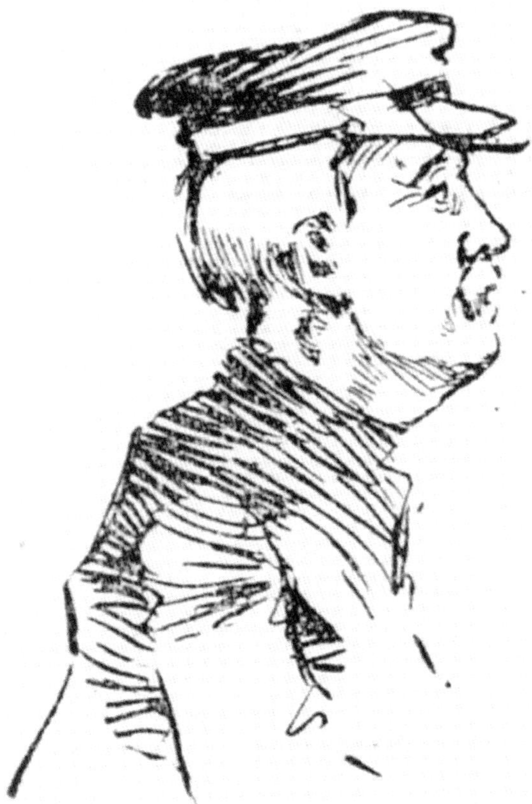

Ebenezer Frank Reynolds (1833–1908)

Frank Reynolds arrived in California in 1854 and was elected constable of Redwood Township in the early 1880s. During his tenure, he handled everything from an abandoned baby on a doorstep to ringing the Presbyterian church bell when the great 1891 fire broke out. Notably, a mob locked him in the town jail during the 1883 lynching. Reynolds was assisting Sheriff James H. Lyndon in the pursuit of the man who murdered the McGlincy family in Campbell when this sketch appeared in the *San Francisco Call* in 1896.

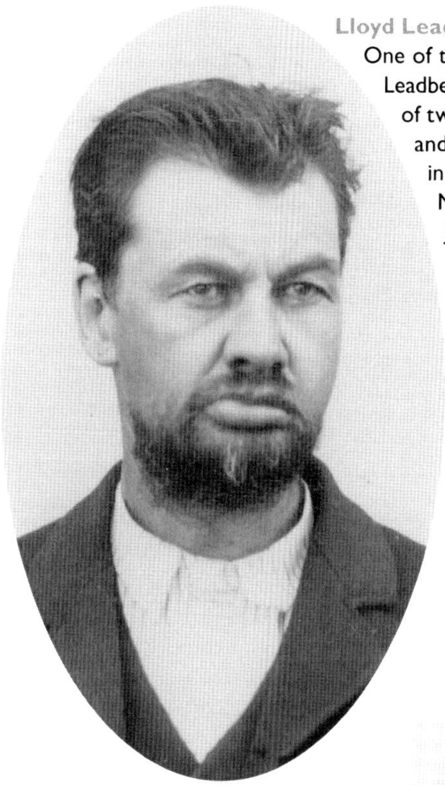

Lloyd Leadbetter Majors (1837–1884)
One of the all-time bad guys in Los Gatos history, in 1883 Lloyd Leadbetter Majors masterminded the grisly and infamous murders of two men in the hills above town. William Peter Renowden and Archibald McIntyre, peaceful men rumored to have gold in their cabin, were viciously tortured and killed by two of Major's accomplices, John Franklin Showers and Joseph Jewell. Press all over the country spilled gallons of ink writing about the crime. Majors was a Civil War veteran, a lawyer (University of Michigan Law School, class of 1870), a Methodist minister, a temperance advocate, owner of a Los Gatos saloon, and a serial arsonist. He was convicted of murder and hanged in Oakland. (Courtesy Santa Clara City Library.)

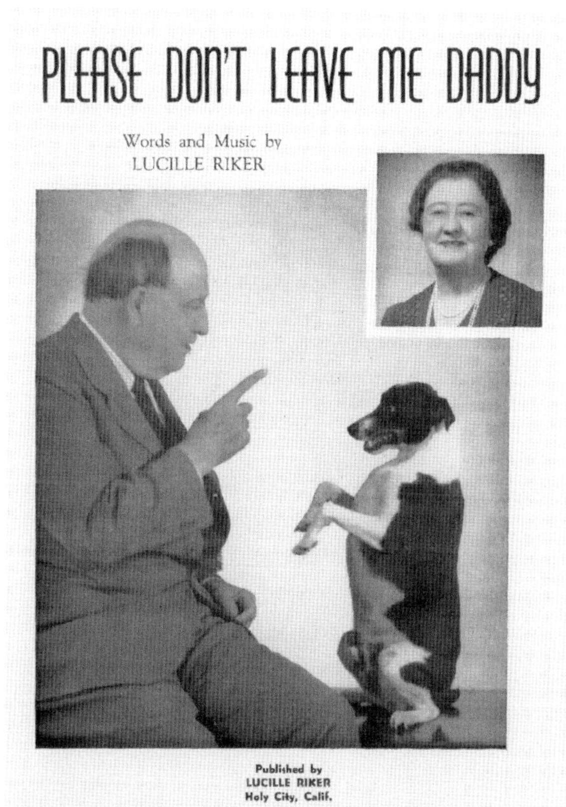

William E. (1873–1969) and Lucille Schutrum Riker (1874–1950)
In 1918, William E. Riker founded Holy City, a religious commune that also served as a garish roadside attraction for people traveling the old two-lane highway to Santa Cruz. He financed his utopia with the life savings of his followers. Tourists could use the restrooms, fill their gas tanks, buy ice cream cones, visit the dismal little zoo, and look at penny peepshows. "Father" Riker was a conman at best and a bigamist and white-supremacist at worst. He is shown here with his third wife, "Mother Lucille," who was an aspiring songwriter published by the homegrown *Holy City Press*.

INDEX